YEARS OF THE OX & TIGER

BOOK 2

Lunar New Years

Christian Adams

Disclaimer

This work is based on real events that occurred in real locations between real people. The author wishes the reader to know that certain names, dates, locations, and genders have been obscured or altered in a way that is not unrecognizable but, more accurately, not-accurate. Therefore, all characters in this work are technically fictitious; any resemblance to real persons, living or dead, is arguably coincidental. Some events in this work were referenced from the author's journals, diaries, and the best recollection, knowledge, and photographic evidence of said events, i.e., completely unreliable but not entirely the product of the narrator's imagination. Meanwhile, certain products, trade, and/or brand names appear in the narrative, mentioned without malice. Any statistical claims without a gratuitous reference can be considered subjective and a result of the author's speculation and/or bias toward (or against) statistics in general. Please do not encourage digital piracy and copyright infringement by copying or reproducing this work.

Dedication

For anybody who will never go home again.

For my father, who taught me to be myself without caring what other people think.

For everybody who was nice to me when it wasn't necessary.

Table Of Contents

In the Chinese zodiac, the Year of the Ox symbolizes strength, dependability, and stubbornness.

1

Paradise for Men, Hell for Women

Captain Felix had been talking about the 'secret island' for nearly a year. "One day, I will take you there," he'd say. "It's a paradise for men, hell for women." The concept and implications were tantalizing and offensive, respectively.

I'd reply, "Sounds like Thailand" (or some iteration thereof).

"Nah, Thailand is a filthy place. The women are diseased. This...is a *real fucking place*." Felix was exaggerating about Thailand, but when he said *fucking place*, he meant it like a bank or a smoking lounge. It was a place with a purpose. His descriptions of the island varied, but one thing remained constant: paradise for men, hell for women.

"What's the name of this island?" My right trigger finger poised on the mouse, the cursor hovering over the Google Maps search bar, left hand on the keyboard.

"It's an island not far from Zhuhai. We must take a boat to get there."

The southeast coast of China has *hundreds* of islands. I pressed Felix several times, but he had a way of changing the subject, a subtle mastery of conversation. *Whatever. Felix. I'll find it myself.*

After uncountable hours of concentrated internet searching, I was no closer to knowing the name of the island, let alone if such a place even existed. I did searches on everything from 'China sex island' to 'paradise for men, hell for women.' I asked some of my Taiwanese friends. Most said they'd never heard of such an island. One dude said his older brother might have mentioned it. "Let me ask him and get back to you." He didn't.

⋆✱⋆

Monday, April 6, 2009, around 10:10 a.m., Taipei was returning to work after a long weekend, but the Knowledge Press office was quiet. Only a few Beta-class robots were in their cubicles. Daisy was in Beijing for another week. Nobody was stressed about showing up on time today. Though the Captain was generally a stickler about punctuality, he never jammed people about coming back after a holiday. Meanwhile, I'd been sitting there since 8:30 a.m., stoned, jacked up on iced coffee, buzzed on nicotine from Swedish snus in my lower lip, just waiting, poised, ready to strike.

The front door slammed. *Felix.* He breezed into the executive office, sat down at his desk, and gave me the usual greeting. "Sir, how are you? Did you have a good weekend? Do you need anything?"

Twitching impatiently, I said, "So, when are you gonna take me to that secret island?"

He smiled, eyes narrowed, peering above his aviator glasses. "When do you want to leave?"

"Whenever you're ready."

He looked down at his desk. "I have so many monkeys on my back."

"I know, Felix. *I'm* one of those monkeys."

Felix scowled. "No, Charlie. You're not a problem to me. You don't ask for anything."

"But I just did."

The Captain waved me off. "I will take you there. Someday. But right now...is not a good time." He shuffled through the papers on his desk.

Undeterred, I pressed on. "That's alright. Just tell me the name of the place, and I'll figure out how to get there."

"It's not safe for you to go alone."

"Ah," I scoffed, "you say that about everywhere in China."

He laughed gently and said, "*Mei guangxi.*" (No problem.)

Gretchen entered the control center with paperwork for Felix to sign. That was the end of it.

Felix returned to the office at 5:00 p.m. "Charlie, do you have any plans this weekend?"

"Nope."

"I will take you to Xiachuandao."

* ✳ *

Xiachuan Island. *A real fucking place.* Fourteen kilometers off the coast of Guangdong Province. The island stretches 23 km north-south, 12 km on the east-west axis. With an area of 98 sq km in the subtropical zone, Xiachuan is covered with dense forest and lush farmland and enjoys year-round heavy rain and warm, humid weather. Wang Fu Zhou is the provincial holiday resort. Much of the development has been funded by Taiwanese investors. The beach extends to 1.6 km on the south side of the island, lined by a promenade of coconut trees. The resort area has accommodation for 3,000 travelers at the beach, its back against the mountains, and the reputation as "Bright Pearl of the South China Sea." Xiachuan and its neighbor Shuangchuan Island have been established as Tourism Open Integrated Experimental Zones.

* ✳ *

On Thursday night, we flew from Taoyuan International Airport (IATA code: TPE) to Macau (IATA code: MFM), took a taxi straight to the Gongbei border crossing, and found a hotel in Zhuhai—the Banghui Hotel, just steps from *jiuba jie* (bar street), at 200 yuan per night (US$28). The water pressure in room 404 was impressive. We had dinner at a nondescript restaurant, and afterward, Felix declined to join me on a tour of Lihua Bar Street.

"Go and do some reconnaissance but be careful," he said. "Don't bring any women to your room. They'll rob you blind."

* ✳ *

For the record, Zhuhai is a busy, opportunistic metropolis of 3 million people in Guangdong Province, 60 km southwest of Hong Kong, across the fence from the Macau Peninsula. Entering Zhuhai from Macau, immigration and customs is more like a Walmart checkout counter on Black Friday than an international border crossing—a seething mass of humanity funneled through an enormous labyrinth of lanes, 20–30 meters long. Unlike other destinations in Asia, it's a breeze once you get to a Chinese immigration officer. Despite the unending crush of human flesh, the immigration folks are polite, efficient, and chronically uninterested in you or what you're doing.

At this time, during the Hu Jintao era, Zhuhai was on the cutting edge of the New China. Open borders were one of the hallmarks of New China. They assumed you're crossing the border to spend money, and nothing got in the way of business in China. *Nothing.*

All Asian bar streets are unique, but the premise is routinely the same. It's a street (or pedestrian area) with a bunch of bars in proximity; each bar has a different name or theme, but most follow the same template and, more importantly, attract a similar demographic—mostly men looking for trouble and the women who have it.

The bar street in Zhuhai was a pedestrian area on Lihua Street with roughly 20 nearly identical little outdoor bars, each about the size of a small, pop-up camper, maybe 10-by-10 feet square or rectangular. The bartenders were mostly female, and many joints also employed freelancer bar girls who sat and drank with the customers while plying their services. Sometimes, you paid a "bar fine" to take the girl back to your hotel, but not always. Retail shops comprised the boundaries of the plaza. The bars were usually open from mid-afternoon, but the real action didn't start until after 10:00 p.m. and ended around 3:00 a.m.

Bar girls are women who either work "for" the bar and (sometimes) get a cut of the alcohol sales, or women who have a freelancer-pimp relationship with the bar, and they're allowed and/or encouraged to interact with the male clientele. Depending upon the bar in question, bar girls can be considered social companions ("hostesses") with or without predetermined sexual contact on the table, or they can be straight-up hookers who will gladly go back to your hotel room and have sex for money.

More prostitution lingo. A "bar fine" is a fee paid by the customer to "take the girl out of the bar." It's a standard cost of doing business, like taxation or a finder's fee. The average bar fine in Zhuhai at this time was US$15.

I sampled a couple of bars, having one beer at each stop before walking past a joint where the bartender called out to me in English.

"Hello! Come drink with me!"

None of the previous bartenders said anything other than, "*Xuyao shenme?*" (What do you want?) so I posted up to the bar and settled in.

The bartender's name was Tianyi, but she told me to call her Tiffany. She was cute, fresh-faced, maybe 25 years old, with a fun yet mature personality. I liked her straight away. It was early in the evening, maybe 9:30 p.m., so I was her only customer. We talked and drank. I told her my story, and she told me a little about herself. Other patrons arrived, so Tiffany couldn't give me her undivided attention. I was more than content to sit there, soak up the atmosphere, and get a good buzz.

Around midnight, I paid the tab and started to leave. Tiffany reached across the bar and grabbed my arm. "When you be back?"

"*Wo bu zhidao.* (I don't know.) "We're leaving in the morning."

"If you come back, promise you come see me."

"I promise."

Tiffany was not convinced. "Really? You promise?"

"Yes."

She held up her pinky and waggled it in my face. "Pinky swear," she said.

I wrapped my pinky with hers and shook on it.

The next morning, Felix hired a driver for the 65-kilometer trip to Shanzai Port. We stopped for breakfast but caught the 10:00 a.m. ferry boat to Xiachuan. The sea churned to a medium roil. Many people on the boat were seasick. A nauseating 50 minutes later we were on the island. A minibus drove us to the resort area.

We hadn't been in the lobby of the Guiyang Hotel for a minute when a tall brown guy with a glass eye and missing a few teeth showed up. He stood at the far end of the reception desk with an elbow propped on the counter, grinning at me. I *had* to give him a nickname: Shifty Jim.

Felix went to check the rooms with the manager. Shifty Jim offered me a cigarette.

"You want girl?" he asked in English. "I get for you."

"No, thanks. Maybe later."

"You want?" pretending to smoke a joint. "I get for you."

"*Buyao, xie xie. Wo shi hen gaoxing.*" (I'm good, thanks.) Shifty Jim smiled and nodded. We smoked in silence for a while. Then he said again, "You want girl?"

A middle-aged woman entered from the back of the lobby. She took one look at me, spun around, and disappeared. I mean, *I saw it happen in real-time.* She said, "Fuck! A foreigner! Gotta go get my girls."

The colloquial Mandarin term for "woman who runs a brothel" is the Japanese loan word, *mamasan.* Captain Felix would say, "Oh look, the *mamasan* is arguing with that old man" or "Those girls look way too young to be here, but they're safe with the *mamasan.*" There were other terms for a *mamasan* in Chinese, e.g., *baomu* (babysitter) and *laobao* (female brothel keeper), but Felix didn't want to be rude and say *laobao* in a conversation with a foreigner. *Mamasans* are women past their marketable prime but savvy enough to run a crew of girls, like the manager of a baseball team. Not all *mamasans* were veterans of the game, i.e., previously worked as prostitutes. Many are just shrewd businesswomen, but all seemed to be very tough characters.

The Guiyang Hotel *mamasan* returned with a couple of women in flimsy sundresses and painfully high-heeled shoes. I didn't get a good look at the women initially. Shifty Jim wandered off. The *mamasan* started talking, but I was busy digging out my passport from the backpack.

A bell rang. The elevator door opened, and Felix walked out. "Charlie! I got you the room with the best view!"

The Captain jawboned with the *mamasan.* I stood and watched. The shorter of the two women approached with a wide smile.

"Don't say yes to anything yet," Felix said, placing himself between me and the girl. "See what they have to offer. Don't settle for second-best. Only take the most beautiful girl." The second girl made a pick-and-roll around Felix to get a look-see at yours truly. The pressure was intense and *somewhat unnecessary*, I thought.

After check-in formalities, all five of us jammed into the elevator. Felix did the talking. The *mamasan* kept pushing me into the smiling girl.

"You take her," Mamasan said. "She is good for you."

I looked warily over my shoulder at Felix, and I'm not exactly sure what he said, but it made the *mamasan* very unhappy. Thankfully, it was a short ride. The *mamasan* and the girls got off on the second floor with Felix. My room was on the fourth floor. The room numbers weren't exactly sequential, so I stumbled around for a minute. I hadn't shut the door when the *mamasan* came around the corner with the same two girls in tow. She was yammering in Chinese, but I knew exactly what she was saying.

I said, "*Deng yixia!*" (Hold on a minute!) and closed the door. I walked to the window and took in the view. Lots of coconut trees, a sandy beach, and an expanse of blue-gray-green water. The garish glow of low-rent Daytona Beach seemed a bit softer from the fourth floor.

"Hey, hello!" Mamasan called. She knocked a few times. "*Ni hao, xianshang?*" (Hello, sir?)

The in-room landline rang before I even got my backpack off. I walked over to the nightstand and sat down on the bed. I sighed and waited a few rings before answering.

"Charlie! What's going on? What's happening? Did you pick a girl?"

"No, Felix. The *mamasan* is standing at my door with those two right now."

"Did you pick one yet?"

"No, not yet."

"Don't be in a rush. Pick the best one. Don't settle for anything less."

"I'm not ready to decide. We just got here."

"Tell the *mamasan* to go away."

"Can I do that?"

"Of course!" Felix laughed. "No problem. Tell her to go away."

I went back to the door. The *mamasan* was on her cell phone. The shorter of the two girls was leaning against the door frame with a wide, toothy smile. She was a cute little thing with big, bright eyes, lots of black hair piled on top of her head, and no more than five-foot-three in heels. There was something there. I felt a certain swelling just being around her. The second girl couldn't make up her mind about the situation and kept a slight distance.

The *mamasan* was aggressive and persistent, but I wasn't ready to decide. I said, "*Wo bu zhidao. Zhihou huilai ma.*" (Come back later.) Mamasan was understandably nonplussed by my response. Either that or my Chinese was so terrible that she thought I said, "I'm a park bench for the duration not long horse."

"What time?" Mamasan pressed.

"*Zhihou. Xianzai bie guan wo le ma.*" (Later. Leave me alone now.) And in English, "Jesus, Mary, and Joseph, give me a fucking break!"

"What time?" Mamasan insisted.

"Three o'clock. I'll come see you at three."

"You come downstairs and see me at three o'clock," Mamasan said severely.

"Yes, yes. I will." They left, thankfully.

High season in Xiachuan is roughly May to October. Mid-April is considered the early high season. The ferry boat was loaded with Chinese dudes and a couple of hookers in street clothes, but once we arrived at Wang Fu Zhou resort area, we were among the few paying customers in the hotel and/or on the island. I loved being one of the few guests in a Chinese hotel, mostly for a mundane bit of comfort: there's always hot water. *Friday afternoon in a Xiachuan three-star?* Volcanic lava—you could boil an egg in it. Towels, water pressure, linen thread counts, and internet access. I cared about that stuff because I traveled uncomfortably in the past. If I wanted to "rough it," I'd go camping. As a former Boy Scout, I got all that pup tent and sleeping bag bullshit out of my system as a teen. As a former indie musician, I slept on too many floors, futons, and couches to revisit the experience. As a full-grown adult expat, I never skimped on creature comforts when they were available. I made a big deal about it because I was already 7,000 miles away from home, didn't speak the language, and stood out like a festering sore in public, so I was already uncomfortable, you know?

Currently, it was 32°C/90°F with 80% humidity and I was drenched in sweat. The only thing I wanted from Xiachuan Island at this point was a nice, warm shower, and a fresh set of clothes.

After the shower, I put on my surf shorts and headed to the beach. The seawater was gross—a warm, turbid, foamy brown slosh. I left the beach disappointed and returned to my room to grab some money. Then I went down to the lobby and walked around the rear of the building to a little shop selling beachwear and touristy shit. I was looking for a beach towel so I could lie on the sand and get some sun. The shop owner asked what I wanted, and as I answered "towel" in Mandarin, the smiley girl with the hair piled on top of her head came out of the hair salon.

I bought a paper-thin Mickey Mouse towel for 15 yuan. As I turned to leave, the smiley girl moved in close.

"Do you want me to come to your room now?"

"Um," I said, stalling. "Maybe. I don't know."

"Don't you want me?"

What I wanted to say was, "I've only been on this fucking island an hour, and I haven't seen the rest of what it has to offer." However, my penis was not invited to that conversation and started to swell within seconds as she pressed her tits into me, made eye contact, and said, "I want *you*."

What a fucking professional! With a flush of embarrassment, I tried to shield my growing erection with the towel, but it was obvious something was going on down there. I was shirtless and wearing surf shorts. The girl looked down and up at me and winked.

"Wait a moment," she said, ducking back into the hair salon. She returned less than a minute later—not enough time for the half-erection to fade—with a hand purse and that bright smile. It was 1:15 p.m. when we passed through the lobby and took the elevator to my room.

Felix gave me a brief tutorial on how things worked in Xiachuan during the flight from Taipei to Macau. First, the girls are available in one of two ways: short-time (200 yuan for up to three hours) or long-time (600 yuan/USD$82 for up to 24 hours). There's no tipping. ***You are not, under any circumstances, to give them extra money no matter how good they fuck.*** Felix said, "Tipping ruins the whole system. Pretty soon every girl will be expecting a tip even if she did a lousy job." The 200-yuan deal is the way to go, he said. Fuck her and send her away. Find another girl you want. Rinse and repeat. "Never get laid with the same girl twice."

I was more inclined toward the 600-yuan deal. If I found someone I liked, it would be nice to have her around for a day. Get a couple of good fucks in, have fun, get to know each other a little bit. Felix's argument stemmed from the fact that if you kept the girl for 24 hours, that also meant you were on the hook for feeding and entertaining her, which can get costly.

It was around 3:00 p.m. when my girl got up from the bed and parted the curtains, flooding the room with afternoon sunlight. We showered together, shared a cigarette, and began to dress. I put 200 yuan in crisp bills on the nightstand and said, "Thank you. I had fun." She came over to the bed, sat in my lap, and kissed me.

"Let me stay with you," she said.

I shook my head. "No." She kissed me again.

"Don't you like me?"

"Yes, I like you but..."

"I really like you. We can have fun together. I will take good care of you."

We kissed again. She got up and closed the curtains.

Judging from our first two hours together, I guessed Fang to be around 19–23 years old; she had a high school education and came from the northern province of Ningxia; the shitty new butterfly-slash-angel tattoo on her right shoulder meant she belonged to a syndicate or a pimp; her interests included dancing, surfing the internet, and drinking. She didn't have stretch marks, but I knew upon seeing her breasts and telltale stomach scar that she had a child—recently—especially when she lactated a few drops of breast milk during sex, and I wondered just how long it had been since the baby.

We went for dinner at the restaurant in front of the Guiyang Hotel. It was now around 5:30 p.m. Upon sitting down, I was approached by a young guy who introduced himself as Mr. Chen. He spoke decent English and gave me his business card. Chen said if there was anything I needed during my stay, he was the man to call.

"Can you get us some *longxia?*" I honestly don't know why I asked for lobster. I couldn't tell you the last time I'd eaten lobster. Maybe I knew the Mandarin word for lobster and wanted to use it in a tropical seaside location.

"No problem," Mr. Chen said. He got on his cell phone and 20 minutes later, an old man rolled up on a Kymco 150cc with two live lobsters in the saddlepack. Mr. Chen weighed them and said, "Two hundred yuan." *Good enough for me. Cook 'em.*

Another 20 minutes later, Felix emerged from the hotel and approached the table, now covered with the dishes Fang ordered. There was enough food to feed 10 people, easy. A bland soup with baby clams. Several types of braised greens including spicy *bok choi.* Half a rice wine chicken (rooster, complete with beak and vane). Bean curd in a Sichuan sauce. A plate full of shrimps. Steamed rice and a mound of chicken liver stir-fried noodles. Several bottles of beer. Oh, and the lobster. I was digging into my second lobster tail and wearing a napkin as a bib when Felix showed up.

"Wow!" Felix cried. "You really know how to enjoy yourself!" He turned to Fang. "*Ni hao, xiaojie.*" (Hello, miss.)

"Felix," I said, rising from my chair. "Please join us for dinner."

"No, thank you. I've already eaten. Enjoy yourself! I'm going for a massage." He bumped my arm. "You must *really* like this girl."

"She's great!" I gazed at Fang. Felix shook his head and walked away.

After dinner, Fang and I returned to the seaside bar, drank beer under the coconut trees, and watched people sing karaoke in Cantonese. We held hands and kissed gently. Fang caressed my neck and said, "I love you." Her eyes glowed with affection. Bought and paid for or not, it's a look that can't be faked: genuine affection, though temporary.

Aside from the fact that the only thing worse than Mandarin karaoke is Cantonese karaoke, it was a gorgeous evening. A few of Fang's "co-workers" stopped by the table to congratulate her foreign catch. Some Cantonese guys came over and tried to speak English. It was all very nice and lighthearted, and honeymoon in Hawaii. The worst part was it could have been one of the best nights of my life if Fang wasn't a hooker and I wasn't an irredeemable loser.

We took a long walk along the beach, holding hands. Locals set off fireworks. We went back to the hotel and made love again. It feels odd saying "made love." In every other reference, I say fuck or have sex or some colloquial variant. If you can fall in love with someone after knowing them for fewer than 12 hours, I was falling toward *something*.

Based on previous experience, I always took the landline off the hook when settling into a Chinese hotel room. Otherwise, the *mamasan* or the hookers in the "hair salon" would be calling non-stop. In this case, leaving it off the hook was unnecessary.

At 7:03 a.m., the in-room landline rang. I *knew* Felix would be calling, so I rolled over and picked it up on the third ring.

"Foshan, that's the happening place," Captain Felix said. "Meet me in the lobby in twenty minutes."

Fang wiped the sleep from her eyes.

I said, "My boss wants to leave now."

She held tight to my torso as we rode the elevator to the lobby. Felix was in the restaurant, slurping congee, and smiling as usual. He sized up the situation in a heartbeat.

"Sit down, Charlie. Eat something nutritious. You like her, I can tell. This is *not good*. You can stay if you want, but I think you should leave with me."

I lit a cigarette and sat across from Felix. "I'm not hungry. I just want some coffee." A server came and took my order. Fang stood to my right, hesitant to move.

As I motioned for Fang to sit beside me, the Captain turned sour. He said to Fang, "He paid you already, right?" She nodded and looked at me. "You can go now. Leave him alone. We're not staying here." He waved her off.

Fang spun around and walked out. I sat facing Felix, speechless.

"If you really want to stay with her, *just stay*." His eyes were cold, unsmiling. "You can meet me in Macau when it's time to go home."

"I...think it's better to go with you."

Felix relaxed and softened his tone. "Charlie, *I know*. You like her. I can see it in your face. But it's for your own good that we leave. *Now*."

When Felix finished breakfast, we stood outside the hair salon and waited for a minibus to the ferry terminal. Inside the hair salon, Fang was getting scolded by the *mamasan*. I deplaned my backpack and found my business card and a pen. I quickly scrawled my personal email and Taiwan cell phone number on the card and walked into the hair salon. I heard Felix shout behind me, "***No, Charlie, don't go in there!***" I approached Fang and handed her the card. She looked confused. The *mamasan* leered at me.

Fang said, "*Shenme shihou ni huilai kan wo ma?*" (When will you come back to see me?)

"*Hen kuai. Wo bu zhidao. Dan wo hui huilai de.*" (Soon. I don't know when. But I'll be back.)

"Charlie!" Felix cried out. "Let's go. They're waiting for us."

Who is waiting for us, Felix? Tell me. Who the fuck is waiting for me? No one, except this girl right here.

Half a dozen dudes were waiting in the minibus at the tourist gate. And they were even more pissed off by the fact that they were waiting for *me*— a foreigner. It was 7:45 a.m. and sticky hot; easily 30°C/86°F with 80% humidity.

As the minibus pulled away from the resort area, I was overcome with sadness. Not the usual "isn't that tragic" ephemeral sort of sadness or sympathy for a homeless guy sleeping under a pile of cardboard. This was deep, aching psychological or emotional distress. Ringing like a giant bell. A low, resonant, warm vibration. Silent tears were coming. I fought the tears, but I knew it was too late. My eyes glazed over with a thick film of salty wetness.

The minibus descended from the hills into the flat-as-a-pancake alluvial rice fields. I stared at the back of the driver's head for a while. Then I gazed out the window at the villagers bent over in the fields and the longhorn steers wandering across the road ahead. *A blur of green, rust, and gray.* I leaned my upper body forward so the tears—when they fell—would fall onto my shirt and not run down my cheeks.

Fortunately, I regained composure before we arrived at the ferry terminal. We stood on the pier waiting to board the boat, but I was shaken, and Felix did his best to talk me out of it.

"I know you're a sensitive guy but forget about that girl. She's a dime-a-dozen. Don't let yourself get attached. We have bigger, better things to see."

He was right, so I did my best to put on a front and shrug it off. "I'm fine. It was nothing. Don't worry about me."

⋆ ✱ ⋆

The three-hour bus ride from the Shanzai Port to Foshan shook and scared me out of the sadness. People were puking five minutes before the bus left the station. *Jesus.* For whatever reason, Felix decided we should take the "local" bus instead of the express. Instead of gliding down the highway at 100 km per hour (60 mph) in relative comfort, we snaked our way through the back roads of Guangdong in a reeking, clattering death shuttle.

The bus driver had no reservations about swerving, merging, laying on the horn, and slamming on the brakes without notice. I stopped counting the number of times he veered into oncoming traffic. Half an hour into the trip, I watched helplessly as the driver forced a guy on a motorcycle to ditch his bike and dive for the safety of the brown grass lining the side of the road.

Not all buses are equal, but I *hated* riding the bus. A huge part of the expat lifestyle is learning how to live uncomfortably for extended periods.

Halfway to Taishan, the midpoint of the trip, I looked across the aisle and saw Felix's head tilted to the side, eyes closed, a gob of spittle drooling from his mouth. *How the fuck could anyone sleep through this bullshit?* I craned my head around to survey the passengers. Every single one was either passed out cold or bent over in the universal posture for puking. The bus smelled like a frat house, minus the beer.

At least I'm seeing the Real China, I reminded myself.

Leaving the countryside, we were gnarled in provincial traffic for an hour. I started seeing signs for Guangzhou and Foshan, so I knew we were close. All Chinese cities with a population over 500,000 looked alike to me. There was no way to tell where Zhongshan ended and Humen began.

Anyway, we were on the big highway headed toward Foshan, going maybe 80 km per hour (48 mph), when Felix got up and started talking to the back of the driver's head. Words were exchanged. The back of the driver's head did not seem pleased. Felix returned to our seats and said, "Grab your bag. We're getting out here."

The bus began to slow as we approached the next interchange, crawling on the off-ramp and stopping about halfway up the incline. The door swung open.

We jumped off the bus and onto the "shoulder" of the road. Many Chinese roads don't really have shoulders. There's a road, and then there's not-road. We hit the not-road part. Either way, it was not where we wanted to be. The bus rolled in reverse down the off-ramp, paused, and merged into highway traffic like nothing happened.

We walked to the top of the incline when a blue minivan pulled up, driven by a shirtless and very brown-skinned Chinese guy with a cigarette hanging out of his mouth. Felix negotiated in Chinese. Took maybe 10 seconds.

Felix opened the passenger side door and said, "You get in first. I want to sit on the right side and keep an eye on this guy. I think he might be trying to cheat us."

No shit, really? Where is this cynicism coming from, Felix?

Captain Felix was right; the guy tried to cheat us. He drove us about 2 km toward the city center of Foshan and then said (even *I* understood what he was saying) that the price just went up from 15 to 30 yuan, which is not that much money, a couple of dollars, but it was the principle. Felix snapped and cursed the driver, who slammed on the brakes and told us to get out—in the middle of a busy intersection. We got out and proceeded to catch a "legitimate" taxi the rest of the way to downtown Foshan.

The Crown Point Plaza Hotel in Foshan was swanky. None of that mid-level Chinese hotel cheap façade. Unfortunately, we weren't there to book rooms; we were there for the lunch buffet. "You need something nutritious to eat," Felix said. Nutritious was one of his favorite words. He spent the better part of a year mastering its precise pronunciation.

The buffet was awesome. I filled five or six plates with all the good proteins: shrimp, crab, prime rib, etc.

"You've had enough?" Felix asked.

"And how," I replied.

He summoned one of the service staff, I thought, for the check. She returned to the table with two heaping platters of raw oysters.

"Eat this," Felix said. "It's good for the fucking. It's an *aph-ro-de-si-ac*. You'll need it. We're going to the best sauna house in Foshan."

"I'm pretty fucked out, boss."

"Really? How many times did get laid with that girl?"

"I dunno. Several."

"How many times a day can you fuck?"

"As many as she'll let me."

Felix let out a deep belly laugh. "You live for today because tomorrow may never come."

"That's the idea."

I managed to get about half of the oysters down before giving up. I sat there shaking my head in mock disgust. "I can't do it," I said. "I'm stuffed." Felix summoned the waitress. This time it was for the check. He paid, and we left. Next stop, the "best sauna house in Foshan" according to the taxi driver who brought us there.

2

Is This Going to Be a Problem?

We will go where the wind takes us," said Captain Felix. We arrived in a city like Foshan at noon and got on a bus to Zhongshan before sundown. Or even better—in a hired car. Felix didn't like to stay in one place for too long and he frequently rode in style.

After the preliminary procedures of disrobing and showering (separately, of course), Felix and I stood side by side, wearing matching white terrycloth bathrobes emblazoned with a red and gold Chinese crest, in a hushed room richly decorated in plush fabrics. We were waiting.

"Take your time," said Felix, touching my forearm. "Choose the best one. Don't settle for second-best."

A young male attendant entered and spoke to Felix. I couldn't decipher what he was saying. Felix would translate if necessary. All the blood in my body converged upon my digestive tract. I was dizzy, floating, and fixated on a red velvet curtain in the far-left corner of the room. The curtain rustled every few moments, signals of activity from behind. They were lining up. There was just enough space between the floor and the bottom of the curtain to see feet in high-heel fuck-me pumps. In a minute, the room would glow with a dozen women in glassy satin bikinis, standing single file, in order of height, with number tags pinned somewhere in clear sight. Maybe a third of them would be good at pretending to enjoy this part of the day.

"They will come out soon," said Felix. "Be careful not to point. When you see the one you like, just remember the number. Pick two, just to be safe."

At that moment, inexplicably struck with a conflicted sense of gratitude, I said, "Felix, I need to talk to you about something serious."

He didn't look up from admiring his toes and said, "OK, no problem." He remained perfectly still.

"I just wanted to say thank you—for everything," I started earnestly. "I appreciate you more than I can express."

"No problem, Charlie. You deserve it. You deserve more."

"I hope I'm useful to the company."

"You're a very important person in our company. You're the person we can't do without. You're the straw that stirs the drink."

It was pointless, even counter-productive to push the subject any further.

We spent the next three days/three nights making an epic loop around cities in the Pearl River Delta. We stayed overnight in Dongguan and Humen before returning to Zhuhai for the final night. We got separated twice: once in Dongguan and once in Shenzen. Felix tracked me down with local help both times. There were several sauna houses involved. Though my "want-to" waned, I participated wholeheartedly.

Everything was on the Captain's dime, including my night-time forays into the bars and clubs. Felix didn't join me until the final night in Zhuhai to visit the woman I met named Tiffany on Bar Street during the first night of the trip. Unfortunately, Tiffany wasn't there.

We stayed at the Zhuhai Holiday Hotel, which is a little more upscale than what Felix usually prefers, but I didn't complain or make note of it. He went to the sauna house for a massage. I drank at a random place with a bar girl from Thailand who didn't even speak Chinese, let alone English, so I got my fill of beer quickly. I staggered back to my room and passed out.

We crossed into Macau and took a taxi to the airport on Tuesday morning. During the ride, Felix asked, "How many times did you get laid on the trip?"

"I'm not sure. Do you want me to count?"

Felix chuckled and shook his head. "What was that girl's name? The one you met in Xiachuandao?"

"Fang."

"Ah! You remember!" He grimaced and leaned toward me. "Forget about her. Did you give her your number?"

"Uh-huh. And email address."

"Don't try to contact her. And don't pick up the phone if she tries to call you. Don't talk to her again. Girls like that are a dime-a-dozen."

We arrived in Taipei around 3:30 p.m., and Felix said, "Sir, do you have any plans right now? Let's go straight to the office and see what's happening."

It was a full house at Knowledge Press HQ. Daisy was waiting for us in the executive office. Within minutes, Susie (the accountant) came rolling in with a stack of chits and forms that required Felix's signature. Lloyd popped in and out, relaying messages from a cram school manager on the phone. Gretchen came to take dictation for a message from Felix to the local media. Nobody acknowledged me or said a word in my direction. *Just the way I liked it.*

I browsed the internet, kept my mouth shut, and watched the clock. Come five o'clock, Felix would say, "*Zou le*" (Let's go) and they'd leave.

There was a brief lull in activity at 4:43 p.m. when I caught Felix eyeballing me for a quick minute. *Something* was on his mind.

He said to Daisy (in Mandarin), "I think Charlie fell in love with a hooker from Xiachuan."

Daisy coughed. "Is this going to be a problem?"

"I don't know. But keep your eye on him."

3

I'm a Writer!

Knowledge Press Ltd. was the publishing division of the Zhang Yi English Academy system, owned and operated by Captain (Zhang Yi) Felix. Most of KP's books were sold in the Zhang Yi cram schools. The materials were almost exclusively educational, specifically engineered for Taiwanese kids. For example, if students enrolled in a TOEIC (Test of English for International Communication) class, they had to buy the Knowledge Press TOEIC model test book. However, more than a few of our books were available in bookstores across Southeast Asia, including airports. I was credited with writing or editing dozens of books, even though exactly how much writing or editing I did was a slippery slope. Ultimately, Zhang Yi took full authorship credit on 98% of published work. The highlight of my "Knowledge Press career" was browsing a bookstore at Hong Kong International Airport (IATA code: HKG) and spotting a book I *wrote*—with my name on it.

I got the job at Knowledge Press through my friend, Stephan, a Canadian expat teacher at the ZYEA main cram school in Taipei. We met on my third day in town and stayed in touch. About a month later, I was teaching English at a miserable cram school, when Captain Felix told Stephan he was looking for a writer (exclusively from the U.S.). Stephan said he knew a guy. Felix hired me without seeing a resume, let alone samples of my written work. Felix and his assistant Daisy asked me two questions:

1. Are you a writer?
2. Do you want to write for us?

The truth is I was a writer by some marginal definition. Creative writing has always been my "secondary" aspiration. Who's to say what's good writing, but some people said I could write. I wrote for my high school newspaper, *The Reporter*, and briefly served as a teen columnist in the local *Darien (IL) Progress*. In 1986, I attended the University of Wisconsin-Whitewater's Creative Writing Festival, where I received an Honorable Mention in Poetry.

Throughout the 1990s I wrote for a series of Chicago-based music magazines (aka fanzines), doing record reviews, opinion columns, and a few feature articles. During this time, concurrent with my music career, I also attempted to write two books: *How to Kill Your Parents and Get Away With It*, and *That's Why They Call It Death Metal*. Both books were a hodgepodge of personal essays and drug-addled storytelling, neither of which had anything to do with killing your parents or death metal.

When I returned to college in the late 1990s to get a degree, I majored in creative writing because it was the easiest degree to get, and aside from music (and traveling), writing was the only thing I really knew how to do. At age 34 in 2002, I received my bachelor's degree from San Francisco State University and briefly considered a teaching career. Two months of substitute teaching English in a high school summer program put the kibosh on that idea.

I continued to write after college and started a blog in 2003-ish, publishing stories, essays, and wine reviews that nobody read. Overall, it was not an impressive track record, and I could hardly call myself a writer. I wanted *to be* a writer but lacked the gumption to make it happen.

Fortunately, Captain Felix and Daisy took almost everything at face value, sometimes to a fault. If you *say* you're a writer, *you're a writer*. How good of a writer? *We'll find out*. Once I got the hang of the gig, it was simple work that required a quirky type of creative thinking, i.e., "figuring it out." I learned what Felix wanted by trial and error. They didn't need a writer as much as they needed somebody who could **figure things out** and knew what good writing *looked like*.

Everybody who worked for Felix was a machine of sorts, including me. As a foreigner by default, Felix treated me differently than everybody else. But I referred to myself and my co-workers as "robots." We were programmed to produce specific results without concern for outcomes. We knew how to obey a discreet set of directives. But most robots malfunctioned if you gave us a command prompt that went beyond our algorithm. In that way, I was a "quasi-robot," or a robot with human characteristics because I *figured things out.* And I was gaming the system from the get-go.

* ✱ *

During my first year with the company, I almost always had some project in the works—sometimes several at once—whether it was compiling model test prep books for English as a Second Language (ESL) programs or writing and editing tests, reading passages, speeches, and essays for the cram school kids. Now in my second year at KPHQ, there was very little they could throw at me that couldn't be managed.

Sometime after the new year, book development and output at Knowledge Press seemed to reach a standstill. I completed a run of model test prep books and various other reference books, and there wasn't much for me to do except wait for Deborah or one of Sherry's minions to ask me a question about English grammar. Paranoid without cause or reason, I started to worry that my utility had run its course. Mainly because some Taiwanese companies got rid of people by not giving them anything to do. A month after returning from Xiachuan, I was sitting on my hands most of the time.

As the Captain's assistant-slash-lover, Daisy was my main go-between the other robots and Felix, too. Whenever I had a problem, I went to Daisy first, and she straightened things out.

So, one day, I approached Daisy as delicately as possible. "Listen, darlin', I'm running out of things to do. Is there anything on the horizon? I feel like I'm getting squeezed out."

"You're not getting squeezed out," Daisy scoffed. "I'll talk to him."

Later that day, Captain Felix breezed into the office and said, "Charlie, *you think too much!* Don't worry about anything! You are a very important person in this company. Give me a couple of days. I'll find something for you to do." Maybe a week later, I rolled into the office to find a stack of vaguely familiar children's books on my desk.

Mr. Men and *Little Miss* is a series of illustrated children's books by British author Roger Hargreaves. Each book in the series introduced a title character with a singular personality trait. The stories were basic moral and ethical dilemmas. So I was thumbing through titles like *Mr. Tickle* and *Little Miss Bossy* when Felix came through the door and said, "Ah! There you are! Do you know what I want you to do?"

"You want me to write a series of children's books based on these?"

"Exactly!"

The original plan was for me to write 12 books in total: six male and six female-themed titles. However, Felix added the obligatory twisted degree of difficulty: each title had to contain a certain vocabulary word from the high school English proficiency test and include some sort of alliteration.

I quickly put together some titles and came up with a list of characters like Buddy Bright, Marty Marginal, Angela Almost, and Glenda Glutton. Once Felix signed off on the list, he told me to coordinate the graphics with the story, so they 'made sense.' He thought I should have some input on the artwork, which *seemed* like a good idea—at first. But I was paired with an illustrator from the graphic design department, Emily, and that's where the problems began.

Emily barely spoke English, which probably led to her extreme social anxiety that only seemed to kick in when I was around. She flinched every time I walked into the graphic design office. She couldn't or wouldn't make eye contact and never responded to anything I said to her—even if I spoke Mandarin—and it got so off-putting that I stopped checking on her progress. Eventually, Meredith, the head of graphic design, offered to act as our mediator.

It only took a week to flesh out the characters and the stories, but Captain Felix was getting anxious. I wasn't moving fast enough for him. But he agreed to start with three books and see how things played out, i.e., if the kids liked them. Above all, each book had to contain a positive message and encourage the students to learn English.

It took two days to bang out a draft of the first book, *Buddy Bright*, which was about a kid who was so smart ("bright") that he glowed, and he couldn't sleep at night because his "brightness" illuminated the room. Buddy's dilemma was figuring out how to turn off his brain and stop thinking so much—something of a personal allegory. Buddy realized the solution was to keep oneself so busy that you didn't fall asleep as much as you passed out from exhaustion. Emily's illustrations were nice. I kinda liked it.

Felix and Daisy **hated it**. Daisy didn't use foul language very often, but she got about three pages into the book and cried, "What the fuck kind of a children's story is this?" Felix shook his head and said, "The story is inappropriate for children. It's too dark."

Buddy Bright version 1.0 was passed around the office, and everybody came back with the same sentiment: "I don't get it."

I pitched several new storylines that were summarily rejected. Felix decided to assume creative control. Every morning for a week, he convened a committee of Gretchen, Deborah, and Daisy, and they hammered out the storylines for the books. My input was requested only at the end of each session. Felix gave me his blessing to "change things" here and there. The books weren't *horrible*. I just wanted the whole thing to be over.

Eventually, the first three books, *Buddy Bright*, *Conrad Careless*, and *Glenda Glutton*, were published. The day before the books were released, Felix took me out to dinner and said, "Sir, you're going to be a famous writer!" KP and ZYEA launched a joint promotional campaign, and the books were distributed for free at the cram schools. Captain Felix was *beyond* excited about the books, but I didn't know *why*.

On the surface, I was unmoved, stoic, as usual, and I didn't bitch about having to appear in public at the book release party and give a few speeches at bookstore readings. Fortunately, they had Deborah do the in-store readings because she was more "aesthetically pleasing." The promotional blitz only lasted a few days, and they left me alone.

Internally, I cursed myself for getting involved. None of this would have happened if I'd just kept my mouth shut instead of asking Daisy for something to do.

The following Tuesday, Captain Felix came bouncing into the office just before noon and lunchtime on the eighth floor. He was wearing a suit, a departure from his typical "golf casual" outfits.

"Charlie! I have good news! Your books are a huge success! They're the top-selling children's books in Taiwan!"

My head nodded to the left, and I stared at the floor, "You've *got* to be kidding me."

"Congratulations! You did a great job!" He reached into his suit jacket pocket and pulled out a familiar red envelope, which contained 15,000 Taiwan dollars (roughly US$500).

I was relieved that the books were successful, and Felix was happy. But I said, "Please tell me we're *not* going to write the rest of them?"

"No. This was an experiment. We got lucky. Those books are too costly to produce." Felix left the control center, and we never spoke of the children's books again.

Daisy showed up in the office later that afternoon and immediately started in on me. "What do you think of those children's books?" she whispered.

"They're okay, I guess. I sent a few copies to my friends back home to see what they think."

Daisy grunted softly and shifted position in her chair. "It was a bad idea from the start. You have no business writing children's stories."

"*No shit.* I'm just glad that Felix isn't losing money on them."

"Oh, we're losing money, that's for sure."

"But Felix said they were best sellers."

"Do you know who bought most of those copies?"

A series of bells and whistles went off in my head, "Ohhhhhhhh..."

Daisy started typing on her keyboard. "Don't tell him I told you, but that's how it works in Taiwan."

Felix arrived at 4:30 p.m. and said, "Charlie, when was the last time you saw your parents?"

"That's a good question," I replied. "I think it was 2007, maybe? I honestly don't remember."

"In Chinese culture, the family is very important. I think you should go visit them. I want them to see that I am taking good care of you." Fact:

25

my parents were not pleased that I flew back to San Francisco last September and didn't visit them in Phoenix, Arizona.

"Yeah!" Daisy interjected. "And this time, we know you're coming back!" I appreciated Daisy's participation in the matter, and I loved her like a sister, but sometimes I wanted to pinch her on the arm as hard as I could and say, "Shut the fuck up, Daisy."

"We'll be here when you get back," Felix said. "This is your home now. You're a part of our family."

★✱★

A little more than a year since I decided to leave San Francisco for this open-ended adventure in Taiwan, I still didn't want to give up my apartment in the Sunset District, affectionately dubbed The Cave. Though it was a cold, somewhat cavernous ground-floor "in-law" or "garden" apartment near 46th and Judah, I *loved* that place. I lived there for five years, the longest I'd ever lived in any one spot. Coincidentally, my best friend Tom Taylor was ready to make a change in his life and agreed to sublet the apartment on a short-term basis (and take care of my cat, Mao-mao). My landlord, Wilson, who was indirectly responsible for the entire Taiwan gambit, supported the arrangement. There was no problem with leaving some of my stuff in the storage area and garage. Tom didn't have a ton of furniture, and he was initially happy with keeping most of the fixtures in place. That way, if things didn't work out, I could always come back, and all "my stuff" would be right where I left it.

Two months turned to six months, which turned into a year. Wilson remained supportive, but he didn't care because Tommy was paying the rent. Tom grew to like The Cave, but he was "tired of living with all [my] shit." If he was going to stay there, he wanted to move his shit *in* and my shit *out*. So, I relented to Felix and agreed to go home for two weeks. He bought the round-trip ticket and gave me some spending money.

The S.F. trip was full of complex feelings, emotions, and psychedelic experiences. Tommy and I resolved our issues at The Cave. I visited my parents in Phoenix for five days: five days of my mom asking, "What *exactly* are you doing in Taiwan?"

4

A Series of Unforced Errors

Life in Taipei returned to normal because it's the kind of place where things change but nothing really changes. I worked at Knowledge Press during the day and drank at night.

Two months after the trip to Xiachuan, Fang kept popping in and out of my mind. Her contact information was in my phone, but I couldn't remember when or how it got there. The details were in Mandarin, using a single character for her name: 芳 = Fang. *I didn't know how to do that.* I wondered if she might reach out to me (she didn't), but there was plenty to keep me occupied at KPHQ and elsewhere.

One day in late June, Felix asked, "What are you doing this weekend?"

"No plans."

"Where would you like to go?"

"I dunno. Somewhere in China."

"You want to go back to the fucking place. To see that girl." He wasn't asking.

"No, not necessarily to see that girl but...why would you even suggest it?"

"Don't go back there," Felix warned, "and *do not* see that girl."

"Nah, I wouldn't do that," I said, clearly full of shit.

"I'll buy you a ticket. Hong Kong or Macau? From there, you can take a train or a bus anywhere you want to go."

"Hong Kong."

"Done!" He picked up the phone and called Susie. "Book the foreigner a ticket to Hong Kong for Friday afternoon."

I immediately regretted choosing Hong Kong because Macau would have been the better choice. But I called Fang that evening. She was surprised and excited to hear from me. We arranged to meet that Friday night in Zhuhai. I assumed that we would leave for Xiachuan on Saturday morning. Felix once told me that it was common for hookers to meet their customers in Zhuhai and accompany them back to the island. I tried not to think about Fang as a sex worker, but either way, it didn't bother me enough to lose any sleep.

I landed at HKG around 6:00 p.m. After a 20-minute crawl through checkpoints and corridors, up an escalator, down an elevator, and a 15-minute wait followed by a 5-minute express bus ride to the ferry terminal itself, I just barely made the 7:00 p.m. Turbojet (high-speed boat) to Macau. Around 8:20 p.m., I zipped through the Macau/Zhuhai border crossing and walked out of Gongbei at the northeast exit. Fang was already waiting. She greeted me with a soft hug and a peck on the cheek. "Where's your hotel?"

Fang's appearance was a brilliant wake-up call, humbling in a good way. *She looked like a regular woman.* Jeans, Britney Spears T-shirt, and a pair of black Chuck Taylors. No make-up. Jet-black hair flowing down her back. I'd only seen her in hooker mode, so this was a revelation.

Earlier in the morning, I booked a room online at the Holiday Inn Zhuhai in the Jida Residential District, far from Gongbei and the bar street. It was a last-minute panic reaction to a temporary weed-influenced paranoia. There was *no reason* to book a Chinese hotel room in advance unless you were traveling during the peak holiday season. Booking this hotel was the first in a series of unforced errors.

At this time, the Holiday Inn Zhuhai was one of the nicer hotels in town—and a legitimate Holiday Inn property. It was good for people with money to burn. I reserved the room for 700 yuan (US$118), which was both pricey and cheap for the location, but I thought Fang would appreciate the effort and luxury.

The taxi driver was a fucking moron, so it took 45 minutes to find the joint. And then, Fang hesitated to enter the lobby of the hotel. It took a few seconds to convince her that everything was fine. *They're familiar with foreigners.* (They were certainly used to seeing foreigners with hookers.)

At the front desk, Fang stayed two feet behind me and wouldn't help with my piss-poor Chinese. I handed over my passport, paid the deposit in cash, and signed the hotel receipt. *Fang is my girlfriend. I'm a normal guy checking in. I'm not a sex tourist.*

The clerk, a snotty, bookish fellow in his mid 20s, said, "Check-out is at noon, Mr. Birch. But *she*," referring to Fang, "must leave by midnight tonight." Some high-end hotels have a policy about hookers: they aren't allowed after a certain time (usually 11:30 p.m. or midnight); otherwise, you need to pay extra. Lower-end places don't always enforce this rule, but the rule exists.

"She's my girlfriend," I protested.

"I can give you a double room," the clerk deadpanned. "It's twice the rate you paid."

I sighed. *I'm not gonna win this one.* "She'll be gone by midnight."

We went up to the room and I remembered what I liked about Fang in the first place: the sex was genuine. The union may have resulted from a client-server relationship, but it didn't *feel* that way. She could have said, "OK, we're done. Hand over the money." But she didn't. Unlike our time at Xiachuan, I didn't use a condom, and she didn't request that I wear one.

At 11:30 p.m., we left the hotel and took a taxi to Bar Street, stopping at a bar where Fang knew the girls. Something told me that Fang had worked there before.

"Do you want to meet one of my friends?" Fang asked.

"Sure. Why not?"

She made a call, and maybe 30 minutes later, a skinny young woman showed up at the bar. She was 20–22 years old, at most. Her name was Peichi, which sounded like "Peachy" to me. After the introduction, she sat on the opposite side of Fang. Every so often, Peachy would lean forward on the bar and take a sideways look at me. Otherwise, she and Fang were engrossed in playing a Chinese drinking game with dice.

We stayed until 3:00 a.m. Fang was buzzed and happy. The bar was closing, so they gave me the bill. As I pulled out my money, Fang said,

"I'll take care of it," and took the wad of cash from my hand. She peeled off 300 yuan for the bar and another 200 yuan that she furtively stuffed into Peachy's palm. She returned the remaining cash to my hand, kissed me on the cheek, and said, "Good boyfriend."

We took a taxi back to the hotel, where we had unprotected sex once again. I don't remember if I came that time. *How many unforced errors are we at now? I count at least three.*

In the morning, before we left the room, Fang said, "*Wo bu xiang gen dianyuan shouhua.*" (I'm not talking to anybody at the front desk.)

"*Mei guangxi. Ni bu xuyao.*" (No problem, you don't need to.)

At the front desk, I paid with a credit card, and they returned my cash deposit. Fang stood near the revolving door. As I put my passport away, the snotty night clerk appeared from the back office.

He said, "Sir, just so you know, you'll be charged for a double."

"You can charge it to my card."

"May I see your credit card?"

"No, you may not." I spun around, walked to the entrance, took Fang by the hand, and walked out.

"Let's go to the bus station," I said.

Fang was perplexed and irritated. "*Why the bus station?*"

"Aren't we going to Xiachuan Island?"

"*No. I don't want to go back there now.*"

I didn't ask any more questions. I couldn't imagine that any woman would want to go back to Xiachuan if she didn't have to. We got in a taxi headed for Gongbei and Lihua Street.

They remembered me at the Banghui Hotel. "Oh, hello, Mr. Charlie. So nice to see you." They even gave me my favorite room, 404—the one with the good water pressure. We checked into the room and had sex. After showering we lay on the bed watching TV. Fang got up and fished the Mandarin pocket dictionary out of my backpack. After a few minutes of thumbing through the pages, she returned to the bed and pointed at "birthday" in the book.

"It's your birthday? *Today?*"

"Today."

"Why didn't you tell me before?"

"My birthday is today." She flipped through the pages of the phrase book for another minute before pointing at the word "*liwu*" (gift).

"You want a gift?"

"Will you buy me a gift?"

"Sure. What do you want?"

I assumed the 600 yuan (US$80) per day for her long-time services. Three days: 1,800 yuan. I continued to add expenses in my head. *Five hundred yuan for the hotel, another 500–1,000 a day for general expenses.* I had a total of 5,000 yuan (US$675) on me. And *now* she wanted a birthday gift? So, we went shopping, of course. Our first stop was a jewelry store on Lihua Street. She selected a gold necklace. The price: 6,000 yuan. I walked out of the store and lit a cigarette. Fang came out a minute later.

"*Cha-lee*," she said and wrapped her arms around my waist. "I'll find something else." We walked around the massive underground mall for several hours. I gave her a wad of bills without counting them. She wound up buying 1,500 yuan (US$210) worth of shoes and lingerie. *Work clothing.* Fang gave me a little fashion show back at the hotel. It was cute how she looked at herself in the bathroom mirror before saying, "What do you think? Do you like it?"

We were at dinner when I asked, "How old are you now?"

"I'm twenty-five."

"Oh, twenty-five." Two years older than what she told me in Xiachuan. Other bits of her original story changed. Instead of being divorced, she had never been married. She was not an only child, and her father was not dead. She mentioned her son, who was nine months old. Her parents took care of the boy while she worked. Little things, sure, are to be expected from a hooker, but the little things add up. The only thing I believed was she hated working in Xiachuan and owed money to the *mamasan* at the Guiyang Hotel.

It rained on Sunday, so we had nothing to do but stay in the hotel room, eat, sleep, and have sex. The rain stopped at dusk, so we went down to Bar Street for dinner and drinks. We met a Taiwanese couple who spoke a bit of English. It was a nice, relaxed atmosphere. Peachy (the skinny friend) showed up later in the evening. She was much more friendly toward me this time.

31

"Do you want her?" Fang asked.

"*What?*"

"Do you want Peachy? She likes you."

I honestly couldn't tell if she was joking. "I think she's very cute," I said.

Fang slapped me gently across the face and laughed. Peachy flashed a coy smile. *Are they suggesting what I think they're suggesting...?* Fang gave me a deep kiss while Peachy pawed at my crotch for a few seconds and said to Fang, "*Hen hao!*" (Very good.)

Peachy's phone rang. She said something to Fang, who tapped me on the shoulder and said, "Money." I reached into my pocket and handed her everything I had on me. She gave another 200 yuan to Peachy, who ran off into the night.

"What was that for?" I asked.

"For her time," Fang said.

"*What?* Why?"

"I asked if you wanted to meet my friend. You said yes."

It was pointless to argue. Peachy and the money weren't coming back.

About an hour later, I heard a female voice calling my Chinese courtesy name, *Bisheng* (sounds like "bee-*shung*"). How I wound up with the courtesy name is too long and complicated to explain. *Bisheng* means 'I will win. I must persevere' or something like that. Captain Felix gave me the courtesy name. It was on my business card. Anyway, I kept hearing a woman yelling out, "*Bisheng!*" and I kept looking up and down the row of bars, my head on a swivel. *Who the fuck?*

And then I saw Tiffany waving at me from a good 20 yards down the row. *Dammit. I forgot about her.* I excused myself from Fang and walked down to see Tiffany. She was smiling and giving me a dirty look at the same time.

"What happened to promise, *Bisheng?*"

"I'm sorry. I'm here with my girlfriend." I pointed toward Fang, who had by now gotten up to see what I was doing.

"You said you no have girlfriend, *Bisheng.*"

"I don't. Well, I do. I mean, she is my girlfriend—*for this weekend.*"

Tiffany was scornful. "What about me?"

"I came back to see you last time, but you weren't here."

"When?"

"Last time I was in Zhuhai. I think it was a Monday night."

"I don't work on Monday."

Fang was bearing down hard on us, and I started backing away. "I can't talk now. I'll come back and see you."

Fang rattled off a vicious stream of Mandarin at Tiffany and dragged me back to the other bar, bitching the whole time. I tried to explain that Tiffany was just a friend and nothing more, but Fang wasn't having it. She was alternately sullen and defiant for the rest of the night. Even the sex had an element of anger I hadn't seen before.

Monday morning, I woke up at 8:00 a.m. and quickly packed. Traveling taught me so much, but if nothing else, the telemetry of personal effects. If every item in my backpack was strewn across the room, I could still be packed up and ready to go in under two minutes. Toothbrush, toothpaste, passport, money, credit cards, headphones, power supplies, USB flash drives, passport, itineraries, earplugs, money...*everything.*

I stood at the foot of the bed and watched Fang sleep for a minute before waking her.

"*Qin ai de. Women xianzai bixu zuo le.*" (Darling, we have to go now.)

It took her a while to get her things together. I sat by the open window and chain-smoked. After check-out, we went to breakfast. When the server cleared the dishes from our table, I slid 1,800 yuan from my pocket across the table. Fang pushed it back.

"No money. We're not at Xiachuan."

"But...for your time? Three days?"

"Not necessary. I love you."

"I love you, too, but I want you to have it."

Fang looked me in the eye and then down at the money. She peeled off 500 yuan and gave the rest back to me. "That's enough."

We parted at the entrance to Gongbei. She gave me a very quick kiss, turned, and walked away. I stood there, stupid, watching her leave. I called her name, but she didn't turn back. She got to the corner and realized I was still watching her. She waved and crossed the street.

33

5

You're the Father (and a Fool)

After the long weekend in Zhuhai, Fang and I stayed in touch with text messages and occasional phone calls, usually very late at night. She was, after all, a working girl. Fang said she would stay in Zhuhai as long as possible before returning to Xiachuan. A month later, she was back on the island. When she didn't call or text at night, I knew she was "busy."

All communication took place in Mandarin. Fang had grown quite fond of saying "I love you" in English, which, along with no, yes, money, and OK, comprised the entirety of her English vocabulary. Translating and understanding her text messages was an elaborate game of verbal Sudoku. She would text in Hanyu Pinyin without the tonal diacritical. So, her messages looked like this:

Qin.ai.de.wo.xiang.nian.ni.
Ni.chi.fan.le.me?
Ji.dian.zhong.ni.gong.zuo.ban.ma?

The message you see above is quite simple. *Dear, I am thinking about you. Have you eaten yet? What time do you get off work?* But some messages turned into spreadsheets. If I had immediate internet access, I could type the message one word at a time into the MDBG translator and diagram the possible meanings.

Six weeks passed. Fang sent me a message saying she was pregnant. *Of course, you are.* I called her immediately.

"You're pregnant?"

"Yes."

"And I'm the father?"

"Yes."

Goddammit.

* ✳ *

Nobody except for Felix had any idea that I'd even met Fang, let alone got her "pregnant." And I couldn't go to Felix. It was out of the fuckin' question. Above all, of course, any rational human being would think it was bullshit. *This girl is just trying to get money.* But I didn't know *for sure.* That *bothered me.*

With few Mandarin-speaking friends I could trust (and, more importantly, who didn't have direct ties to Felix), I made a mental list of people and crossed them off one by one. There were only two names left on the list. My friend Martin was the first choice, but he was swamped with a toddler and a newborn.

The second choice, Barney, was a super cool bartender at Roxy Rocker and a decent friend, but I was never inclined to burden him with my problems...until I asked him to make this phone call. Once I explained the situation, Barney was irritated.

"Aw, man," he whined. "How did a mainland hooker get your cell phone number?"

"I gave it to her."

"You should change your number and forget about that bitch. It's a scam."

"Dude, I just want to do the right thing."

"Fuck that, man. She's a hooker. *A fucking hooker.* Do you think she's going to tell you the truth? Come on, man! She sucks dick for a living."

"Just help me out, Barney. Talk to her, that's all I'm asking. What can it hurt?"

I asked Barney to find out:

1. Was she really pregnant?
2. Was I really the father?

3. And if so, what did she want to do about it?

Questions 1-2 were/are completely stupid. *Yes and yes.* I was hoping Barney would have enough savvy to grill her about it. Ask her questions I hadn't thought of and vice versa.

Barney reluctantly agreed. "Alright, you owe me for this."

I dialed Fang and handed the phone to Barney.

"Hello? Yeah, this is Charlie's friend. You say there is some trouble?" [Pause.]

"OK, sure. I understand that. What do you want from him?"

[Even longer pause.]

Barney put the phone to his side and said, "She says she wants to keep it."

"What!?"

"She wants to keep the baby. Something about chemistry. You guys have chemistry. I dunno. She said that's life, basically. You know she has a kid already?"

"I know. And you're sure she's telling the truth?"

Barney rolled his eyes and spoke into the phone. "He wants to know if you're telling the truth."

[Another long pause.] "She said she loves you," Barney said, "and wants to know your opinion. Or she will respect your decision, I guess."

"Ask her why she didn't tell me she wasn't on the pill."

Barney put the phone on his shoulder. "You want me to ask her *that?*"

"Just do it."

[Pause.]

"She says she thought you knew or didn't care. She seemed really confused by the question. All she wants is to know your opinion. Do you want the kid or not?"

"Tell her I need to think about it. I'll call her tomorrow."

The next afternoon, I called Martin—a desperate decision because, again, I didn't want to saddle him with my problem. But Martin was a very good voice of reason. And he'd been through a few similar situations.

Martin heard the story and said, "The most important thing you have to consider is it's not about *you*. It's about the kid. *Is it fair to the kid? Is it going to have a good life?*"

"That's really all I've thought about. I'm not capable of raising a kid right now."

"I grew up in a fucked-up family where my mom left my dad," Martin continued, "and my brother and I had to choose sides. That wasn't cool. It might appear on the surface that my wife and I have a perfect marriage, but we don't. It's fucking bad sometimes, man, *really bad*. I worry about my daughters all the time. Are they going to be fucked up because my wife and I can't stand each other? What if we get divorced? So, you gotta ask yourself: do you love this girl? Can you see yourself marrying her, maybe moving to China to raise the kid?"

"I don't know. I can't answer those questions."

"Are you in love with her?"

Did I love Fang? Deeply conflicted, I *thought* I loved her. Nothing about this situation felt right—except for the physical element, the sex.

"Come on, man," I said, "don't ask me shit like that."

"Right, so, if I were you, I'd tell her you don't want to keep it. Then I'd get a new cell phone number and forget about her."

"And then there's the possibility that I'm not the father or she's not even pregnant."

Martin cleared his throat. "Fuck, man. You're not the first Western guy to knock up some random mainland girl! This shit happens *all the time*."

"I just want to do the right thing. I don't care if it's a scam. I can't live with the idea of a kid running around China, not knowing its father."

"That's a problem." I could hear him nodding, like *yeah, dude*. "Is there any way you can send her money in China? How much is an abortion in China?" He chuckled. "*I* don't even know."

"I didn't get the specifics."

"OK, here's what we're going to do," Martin said, and I was so relieved to hear that he had a game plan. "We can get her on a conference call tomorrow. I'll tell her what you told me. Which is...that it isn't fair to the kid, and you're willing to pay for the abortion."

"Fine."

"What bothers me," Martin said slowly and carefully, "is that you might have to go back there to take care of this. I'm worried that you might show up and a couple of guys take everything you have or beat you up, or fuck, man, even worse. Who knows?"

"No. She's not like that. She's dishonest but not a true villain. Plus, I think she really does care for me."

Martin laughed again. "Yeah, man, *we'll see about that.*"

The next evening, we got Fang on a conference call. Thanks to Martin's mediation, we agreed that I would return to Xiachuan to solve the problem. It wasn't just the money, Fang said. She wanted to see me and know that we made this decision together. From Xiachuan, she would go to Taishan, where she had friends, and have an abortion there.

⋆✳⋆

Captain Felix didn't bat an eye when I told him I was going to Macau for the weekend. He only wanted to know how much I paid for the ticket. Twenty minutes later, Susie came in from the accounting office with a red envelope full of cash.

"Have a good time," Felix said.

Daisy, on the other hand, was skeptical. "What are you going to do in Macau, Charlie? You don't gamble, so I know you're not going to the casinos."

"Cross over into Zhuhai, I guess. Hang out on Bar Street. You know, have fun?"

Daisy wasn't buying it. "*Who* do you know in Zhuhai?"

"Nobody, just a few bartenders and bar girls."

She shook her head. "You better be careful," she warned. "Those people will rob you blind if you let them."

⋆✳⋆

Getting to Xiachuan was easier than I imagined, except for a minor panic attack in the taxi to TPE. My heart was seizing every other beat until I arrived at the airport. I bought two bottles of water and a Haruki Murakami novel, *Kafka on the Shore*, in the bookstore by the gate. TPE to MFM is a 90-minute flight. Even though I had everything in place—a business visa, SIM card, bus and boat schedules in Chinese—the panic attacks kept sneaking up on me. I threw myself into the novel during the flight, skipping food and beverage service. I breezed through immigration in Macau and Zhuhai. The bus to Shanzai was running late. It was supposed to leave at 1:35 p.m. but it was 1:55 before it pulled out of the station. Traffic was bad. I was panicked about missing the last boat to the island and getting stuck at the Shanzai ferry terminal. There was a nice hotel above the terminal, but there wasn't shit to do within 30 kilometers. The bus driver was blaring awful pop music, but he kept things moving. The aroma of vomit. A pleasant three-hour trip by Chinese bus standards.

The anxiety subsided when I was the last person to board the last ferry boat to Xiachuan of the day. The boat was crowded with Chinese families dressed in Aloha shirts and kids clutching inflatable toys. Halfway through the hour-long trip, I called Mr. Chen, the young guy from the Guiyang Hotel, and he said he'd meet me at the tourist gate. Then I called Fang.

"Where are you?"

"I'm on the boat."

"Where should I meet you?"

"Guiyang Hotel."

"Why there?"

"Why not? I want to stay there."

"OK," she said and hung up. I *did* want to stay at the Guiyang; they had a stable internet connection and nice bathrooms.

The minibus dumped everyone at the entrance gate to the tourist area. I waited 20 minutes for Mr. Chen. Fang called at least three times, testing my patience. Chen wasn't picking up my calls. I took a motorcycle taxi to the hotel, where the front desk lady immediately recognized me.

Shifty Jim was bearing down from the far side of the lobby. We met at the counter.

"Sup, Jimbo?" I said. "Fuckin' dirtbag."

"American," Shifty Jim said and smiled.

"You need to see a dentist, man," I said in English, brushing him off. "And *soon.*"

"You want girl?"

I asked for Mr. Chen, but the desk clerk said, "I don't know him."

We got down to business. The clerk quoted me 700 yuan for tonight, 800 for Saturday night, 300 for Sunday night, and 250 any night after that. Those prices were *outrageous*, even for high season.

"Can you give me something cheaper?" I asked, reading directly out of the phrasebook. The clerk punched a few numbers in a calculator and turned it towards me. The figure 1,500 flashed in green LED lights—plus a deposit of 2,500 yuan. Total out-of-pocket: 4,000 yuan (US$550), way more than I wanted to spend. On the positive side, they accepted Visa. Honestly, I was sweating through my clothes and just wanted to take a shower. I didn't give a fuck about the money.

Fang walked in as I was looking through the backpack to retrieve my passport. She kissed me and exchanged words with the desk clerk. "We already have a copy of his passport," the clerk said. I produced my Visa card and the *mamasan* came out from the hair salon. She got a look-see at Fang and they went at it, man. The ensuing argument worried me enough to stop what I was doing, close my backpack, and put it on my shoulders. I snatched the Visa card from the clerk's fingertips.

"We aren't staying here," Fang said, taking me by the arm.

"No kidding."

Fang led me across the main drag to the Honghai Hotel, which looked nice from the outside. The hotel only wanted 1,200 (US$165) yuan for three nights. No deposit. I couldn't refuse. Except, they didn't take Visa.

It took less than a minute to realize that Fang *used to* work at the Guiyang but *now* she worked at the Honghai. Her job was sitting in the "hair salon" lounge area, smoking, watching TV, or polishing her nails, until some greaseball like me came along and said, "You, hooker. Let's go." She gave 50% to the *mamasan* if the john was staying in the hotel. If you wanted to bang a Honghai hooker in the Guiyang, there was a problem. The hair salon girls were discouraged from freelancing, although with a small kickback to either party, you could ostensibly get away with it. There was a complicated system in which a girl could snag a john out on the beach promenade and bring him to her hotel, clear it with the *mamasan,* and then go to the john's hotel. Captain Felix told me to avoid this type of arrangement at all costs.

The Honghai clerk handed over the room keys. As we approached the elevator, Fang insisted we make a detour so she could show me off to the new *mamasan* and some of her friends in the hooker lounge, I mean "hair salon." She introduced me as *nan pengyou* (boyfriend). They all knew the score.

The first room they gave us was the worst hotel room I ever stayed in China. It was everything I feared and hated about budget hotel rooms. Threadbare carpets, the smell of stale cigarettes and condoms, and a concrete slab of a twin bed. Towels like sheets of sandpaper. A squat toilet in a black mold bathroom. A garden hose for a bidet. A single bar of soap that doesn't create any suds. Ten-year-old television set. Peeling wallpaper. Chipped laminate of cheap furnishings. At that point, I was desperate to get out of my sweat-soaked clothes and into the shower.

The water was cold. The shower was short but effective. Fang went in next. I dried myself, dressed in fresh clothing, and sat on the edge of the bed. Fang came out of the shower wrapped in a towel. She was surprised to see me dressed.

"*What...is this?*"

Fang closed the curtains while I undressed.

When it was over and Fang got up to open the curtains, I noticed a reddish, blood-brown wet stain where we'd been. "Fang, what happened?"

Fang looked at the stain. "I don't feel well."

"Are you OK?" I rubbed her stomach.

"Yes, I'm fine."

She rousted me out of bed and removed the white bedcover. "I don't know what that is." She went into the shower and stayed for a while. Her handbag was sitting next to the TV, so I went over and opened it. There was one unused tampon inside. I gathered up the white bedcover and examined the stain again. It looked remarkably like what you might see

41

after you have sex with a woman on the last day of her period. I'd seen that stain before. I brought my nose to the bedsheet. *I know that smell.*

Fang came out of the shower and wrapped her arms around me. "I'm fine now."

After dinner, we stopped in a mom-and-pop to buy beer for me and ice cream for her. Typical Chinese storefront. Shit piled everywhere, a 12-year-old girl behind the counter.

Back on the street, I cracked the beer while Fang sized up the competition on their way to the island's only disco, which we could hear bumping from 500 yards away.

"*Wo men qu tiaowu, Cha-lee!*" (Let's go dancing, Charlie!)

"*Bu yao. Wo bu xihuan tiaoyu.*" (No. I don't like it.)

Fang squeezed my hand. "*Mei guangxi.*" (No problem.)

Walking back to the hotel, Fang suddenly pulled my arm and dragged me toward a medicinal-pharmacy-looking place. We went inside and she bought a pregnancy test for 5 yuan. I kept thinking back to what Felix told me, "Never fuck the same hooker twice."

The next morning, we got up around 11:00 a.m., and Fang immediately went to the bathroom. After a minute, she called for me.

"See? Blue. Positive."

"Are you sure?"

She didn't look happy. "Yes, *I'm sure.*"

I inspected the box and instructions in Chinese. *Couldn't make heads or tails of it.* Fang kissed me and went back to the bathroom.

We had lunch at a place with the worst English menu I had seen in China so far. Some Chinese "tourist" menus seemed like more of an insult than an attempt. I ordered a **"sandwiches f americn club"** and got a fried egg between two pieces of dry toast. *That was it.* The price: 24 yuan (US$3), about four times what I would have paid if I had ordered it in Chinese. Fang laughed and said, "Is that what Americans usually eat for lunch?"

You can't complain about that shit. *You can't.* I was mad at myself for not speaking better Mandarin. So, I ate the sandwich and watched Fang scarf down a three-course meal of watery clam soup, fried noodles, and rice wine chicken.

⋆✳⋆

Back at the hotel, every inch of the third floor was wet from a recent mopping. A thin breeze of bleach in the air. We walked gingerly back to our room. The Honghai claimed to have internet access, but it didn't work in our room. Fang begrudgingly got on the phone after I badgered her for several minutes. ***I must have internet access. It's not negotiable.*** The manager came up and moved us down the hall to a room that was wired for DSL. Or, *it would be* by early afternoon, which is what I could glean from the conversation. Five minutes later, a maid came by and mopped the polished stone floors of the new room. *Something really fucking bad happened on the third floor of this hotel last night.*

The smell of bleach was overwhelming. We laughed because our eyes were burning, so Fang opened the window for fresh air. We were lying on the bed (clothed) when a guy came in unannounced through the open window with the frayed end of a gray cable clenched in his teeth. He wore nice pants, a pressed shirt, new shoes, and a tie, like he just walked out of an office building in a major city. I started laughing, not even slightly alarmed. "The fuck is this guy doing?"

After exchanging words with Fang, the intruder dropped the cable next to the desk and climbed back out.

The Honghai was L-shaped and our room was at the inside corner. The guy simply stepped across to the kiddie-corner window and disappeared into the adjoining room. Fang got up and closed the curtains.

"What about the internet?"

"He will take his lunch now," Fang said. "Return in one hour." An hour later, she threw open the curtains and turned on the TV. I went to the beach.

Three months earlier, I looked at the water and said, "Nope. Not going in there." But it wasn't as bad as I expected. The fishy sewage smell was gone, and it looked fairly clean. Not clear by any measure, but it was good enough to swim around with my head above the surface. I was out there for 45 minutes. When I came back up the beach, Fang was waiting for me under a coconut palm tree. "You should come inside now," she said. "Too much sun. You will burn." We went back to the hotel room.

The DSL guy returned while I was in the shower, and he was gone when I emerged from the bathroom with a white towel around my waist. Fang sat on one side of the bed, holding the DSL cable. "Here," she said in a mocking tone. "Now you have internet."

I didn't appreciate the snark, but I ignored her attitude, snatched the cable from her hand, plugged it into my laptop, and felt a warm wash of relief when the connection kicked in, and I could open an email.

✱

Fang didn't understand why internet access was so important to me. She was irritated that I made a big deal out of it. This was 2009, mind you. We, as a global society, hadn't reached critical mass in the clouds. Today, one can't imagine the travel industry without internet access. But Fang never considered the vulnerability of an expat traveling in a foreign country with a dodgy local SIM card. So many times, I thought to myself, *Goddamn, if something happens to me out here, I'm absolutely fucked.* Internet access, even confined to a hotel room, allowed me to breathe. And, of course, book flights, buy train tickets, and reserve hotel rooms.

✱

Most people, knowing even *half* of what I knew, would have bailed out by now. Fang was probably scamming me, but *I couldn't be sure.* There was no way I could know if she was pregnant, at least with my child, unless I trusted her. And that was impossible. *Why did she have a tampon in her bag?* The fact that I went back for her says more about me than I can articulate.

The next two days were spent in bed when the sun was up, and out at the beachside bar at night. I wrote a few hours each day. Fang occasionally pretended to be sick and conjured dubious vomiting sounds from the bathroom. Otherwise, it was the same old routine. Eat, fuck, sleep.

On Sunday afternoon after sex, Fang was lying on the bed, propped up on pillows, watching TV. I was laid out on my belly, reading the Murakami novel, facing away from the TV.

Fang said very quietly, "*Cha-lee, women you wenti.*" (Charlie, we have a problem.)

"*Shenme le? Xuyao shenme?*" (What is it?)

"Money."

"*Duoshao?*" (How much?)

"*Bu zhidao.*" (I don't know.)

I was gonna give her whatever she wanted for the abortion, plus the cost of her services for the weekend, which, of course, the Honghai *mamasan* wasn't about to forgive. And Fang owed 500 yuan to the Guiyang *mamasan*. But the language barrier made it next to impossible for either of us to express ourselves in a way that the other would understand.

"No problem." I pulled some cash from my pocket—about 2,500 yuan in 100 notes. I handed it to her. "OK?"

Fang took the money and threw it on the floor. "You don't understand!"

No, I don't understand. "How much do you need?" I asked repeatedly. **"Just write down a number!"** Fang kept giving me long answers in Chinese. All I could say was, "I don't know, gimme a number" and desperately scrolled through the phrasebook. Then she started crying. The phrasebook was tossed aside.

Fang got on the phone and made a few calls. I opened my laptop and tried to get a DSL connection. *Nothing. It was dead.* This instance was a perfect example of why I insisted on staying in hotels with a decent internet connection. Fang and I usually had no problem communicating with the online translator. Thumbing through pages and pointing at a phrasebook was futile. She was driving me insane by talking non-stop in Chinese when she knew I didn't understand a tenth of it. And when I begged her to speak slowly, *please*, she would talk so slowly that I, again, had no idea what she was saying.

I called Martin.

"Haha, man! I was expecting this call. *Haha.* What kind of shit are you in now?"

"Dude, find out what she wants from me."

"Is she giving you a hard time about money?"

"She is."

"Put her on."

Their conversation went on forever. I had nothing to do but sit there and stare out the window. Finally, Fang handed the phone to me and went into the bathroom. I took the phone out into the hall.

"Well?"

"Basically, she's saying that she won't know how much it will cost until she goes through with it. She says she'll go to stay with a friend in Taishan and have the abortion there. For now, she'll need at least enough money to live on for two weeks."

"She's not pregnant."

"Probably not, but it's too late now. What do you want to do?"

"What would *you* do?"

Martin sighed heavily. "Charlie, it's hard to say, man. You're not getting out of there alive without paying her *something*. Did you actually see the pregnancy test?"

"Kind of. It's in Chinese. I can't read it. Does 'blue' mean positive or negative?"

"It depends on the test. What was the other color option?"

"Either green or black. I don't remember."

"If it was made in China, who knows?"

"*Fuuuuuuuck*, I forgot to tell you about the tampon in her handbag."

Martin cackled. "How much cash do you have with you?"

"Ten to twelve thousand Chinese yuan. Most of it in Taiwan dollars. Maybe a grand of back-up cash in U.S. dollars. Twenty-five hundred bucks in total."

"Can you change it there?"

"Yes. For sure."

"How much do you need to get back to Taiwan?"

"A thousand yuan, tops."

"Give her the rest and get the fuck out of there."

Fang had been in the bathroom for a long time. When she finally emerged, I was standing by the door. "I need to change money," I said.

"Go to the place next to the fruit stand."

Once Fang had the money (roughly 15,000 yuan/US$2,000) in her hands, she started talking about marriage. *Do you want to get married? Do you want me as a wife?* It went on and on. After dinner, we strolled hand in hand along the waterfront.

Fang was uncommonly happy throughout the night, hardly complaining about a thing. We watched a basketball game between China and Iran. Fang sat on the edge of the bed and shouted, "*Jia-you!*" (Let's go!) as the Chinese national team got crushed by the Iranians. Later that night, the power went out. We left the hotel and went to one of the beach bars with a generator. We drank beer, held each other, and kissed softly while watching the karaoke tragedy.

★✱★

Waking early Monday morning, I went over my printed flight itinerary. The paperwork showed that I booked a flight to Taipei for *tomorrow*, Tuesday. I called the airline. *Yes, that's correct.*

"What's wrong?" Fang asked.

I said, "Nothing, let's go."

We took the minibus to the ferry terminal and the boat to Shanzai. From there, we had to get on different buses since I was taking the express to Zhuhai, which didn't stop at Taishan along the way. I offered to ride with her to Taishan, but Fang said it wasn't necessary. She wouldn't go to the hospital until next week at the earliest. We said goodbye with a long embrace. She said, "Call me when you get back to Taiwan."

I boarded the bus and watched her from the window as she stared off to a place somewhere beyond space. As the bus departed, I wept silently on the final pages of *Kafka on the Shore*.

6

Lessons Learned the Hard Way

Fang and I were in a gray area of the hooker-john relationship. She told me she loved me at least two dozen times, in and out of bed. When someone in China says, "I love you," it's a lot like when someone in L.A. says, "I'll call you." It makes you feel good to hear it, but whether they mean it is another story. Fang might have meant something akin to "I love you" but closer to "Get me out of here."

For a while, I told Fang I loved her, too, and I was certainly *in something* with Fang, but what? Long-term lust, maybe? Extended infatuation, perhaps? Ambiguous feelings of "love" in that I cared about her well-being and wanted her to enjoy my company; however, parsed to the bare minimum of pretext, the lust, infatuation, and chemistry were ephemeral? *Another doomed relationship.* I knew it couldn't and wouldn't work. First, the language barrier. I spoke and understood basic street-level Mandarin, largely due to total immersion. Fang had zero interest in learning English.

The second reason: geography. If we got married or had a serious relationship, one of us would have to move. And I wasn't moving to China. Considering the sweet deal I had with Felix, why would I want to fuck that up? Fang would have to move to Taipei, which raised as many problems as fast as I could think of them. Every single logistic involved Felix and, ostensibly, Daisy. And I knew they wouldn't like this timeline one bit, *no sir.*

It didn't matter if Felix recognized Fang from 'Paradise for Men, Hell for Women' because he really didn't *look at people*, just like he never listened to them. Daisy told me that behind those Peter Fonda glasses, Felix was rocking 20/70 vision at best, and that's why he had the office robots read everything out loud for him.

I couldn't ask my Taiwan Godfather to be an angel investor in a "save-a-hooker" marriage to a woman I'd known for a total of six days (meaning the actual amount of time we'd spent together).

It was bad enough that I lived from payday to payday in Taiwan. Add a kid and wife to mix, and that sounded like a disaster. I wasn't fooling myself. Felix paid me well by Taiwan standards, but it was shit money compared to Western salaries. I had to work significant overtime to make $4,000 a month. But the main reason I couldn't or wouldn't marry Fang was I didn't *want* to get married. At least up until *that* moment, I never wanted to get married—or divorced. That's not to say I wouldn't at some time in the future.

✶

After parting with Fang, I arrived back in Zhuhai early in the afternoon and checked into the Yong Tong Hotel, which was literally on top of the bus station and across from the border crossing. You could see Macau from the second floor. After the preliminaries, I took a long nap. I didn't sleep very well in Xiachuan, go figure.

Somewhere around 9:00 p.m., I went down to Bar Street, looking for Tiffany, who wasn't thrilled to see me until I told her that my "girlfriend" was in Taishan. *And yes, you can drink with me.* Zhuhai Bar Street bartenders had a habit of "sharing" your beer, helping themselves by pouring a serving into a small glass on their side of the bar. Tiffany would routinely drink a third of every beer I ordered.

Now, I liked Tiffany and her moxie. She had a pleasing way about her. She wasn't smoking hot; in fact, she had these adorably chubby cheeks. But she never considered selling her body. I liked that. And she was fun. At least she could speak a little bit of English. The other bar girls looked up to her for it.

Tiffany got yelled at by a couple of locals for paying too much attention to me and not to them, so she kissed her index finger and put it to my lips. *Good enough for me.* Finally, I got to drink an entire beer on my own.

Around midnight, I felt a pair of female hands touch both sides of my torso, which became a full-on embrace from behind. I twisted around to see Fang's skinny little friend, Peachy, and she was on me like spiderwebs. She was so lightweight that I stood up from the barstool without effort, her feet dangling a foot above the ground. As I wrestled my way around to face her, she planted her mouth on mine.

"*Wah!*" Tiffany called out.

I was fucking *shocked,* man. I didn't know what to do except what I was doing. Peachy finally relented and I gently put her back on her feet. She was smiling at me like a maniac.

Tiffany and Peachy had words. Not sure exactly what was said, but I think Peachy explained to Tiffany how she knew me. Peachy's hands were everywhere. Tiffany gave me a startled look and leaned her body back, like, "Am I really seeing this person the way I thought I was seeing this person?" Peachy now had me by both hands, trying to lead me away from the bar. I looked at Tiffany and said, "I'm sorry," before pulling free of Peachy, fishing out 200 yuan from my pocket, and leaving it on the bar. I didn't look back.

At 1:47 a.m., I escorted Peachy to the hotel lobby and casually waved goodbye as she walked away. There was no money exchanged. I made a beeline for Bar Street. Tiffany had her arms folded across her chest when she saw me. She stomped her heel and spun away when I sat down on a barstool.

"Ooooh, she's mad at you, buddy," said the Chinese guy sitting to my right in plain-as-day English. I turned and stared at him for at least five seconds.

"James," he said, extending a paw in my direction.

"Charlie."

James and I were the same age. He was born in Hong Kong, went to high school in Singapore, attended Julliard on scholarship, played violin in the Philadelphia Symphony for 12 years before relocating back to H.K. He was also a concert-level pianist who earned a sizable living as a tutor to prodigal children of mega-wealthy H.K. elite. Even though James was married, he kept a weekend retreat in Zhuhai simply because he could, and his wife didn't ask too many questions. All of which I learned in the space of ten minutes. I pelted him with questions about Leonard Bernstein and Glenn Gould. James was effusive in his answers.

Tiffany slowly started asking James questions about me, which he was hesitant to translate until he learned that we knew each other—tangentially. James was intrigued by the whole situation and moderated a discussion. I was forced to show part of my hand and explain that Fang was a hooker I met in Xiachuan (he knew all about Xiachuan), and I was here to make things right.

"So, buckle up," James began. "Girls like [Fang] have at least three or four guys on the line at any given time. Again, I don't know her, but I guarantee you're not the only guy she's banging."

I shrugged and nodded in acknowledgment. For some reason, it didn't bother me what Fang was doing in Xiachuan or any other place. *She was a hooker. So what?*

"Maybe," James continued, "*maybe* you're the father? She already knows you're a stupid foreigner who thinks with his dick. She's got you pegged. *She wants a ticket out of here.* That's what most of these girls are looking for. [Pausing to take a shot and light a smoke.] Charlie, I don't have to explain prostitution but *think*, if it were you, as a hooker, what would you prefer? A steady stream of local customers, most of whom are uncivilized and uneducated and treat you like shit, or a sugar daddy foreigner who can magically transport you from the hell that is mainland China to the amber waves of grain? If you're a woman, that is. Now, consider your position. Would you rather spend time and money trying to 'save a hooker,' or would you rather have a girl like Tiffany here, who isn't interested in a White Knight? She isn't a hooker. She doesn't want to leave China. She likes you because you make her laugh, am I right? [I nodded and looked down at the bartop.] She said you guys had a good time together when the girlfriend or whatever she is isn't around. That's what makes a real relationship. Let me ask you, does this Fang person speak English?"

"No."

"How's your Chinese?"

"Marginal."

"Well, there you go. She's preying upon your ignorance. She knows you don't understand what's going on, am I right?"

"Yes."

"Like I said, I don't know the girl, but judging from what you've told me, it's a no-win situation. Cut her off. If she has an abortion in Taishan, then she does. Either way, I believe you paid for it, am I right? [I nodded vigorously.] Tiffany is the kind of Chinese girl you want to get involved with. She works. She doesn't ask for much. She's a barrel of monkeys. And most of all, she doesn't see you as some sort of savior cash cow who is too stupid to know when he's getting scammed. If it were me, and I'm just saying this as a dispassionate observer, you're far better off with a girl like Tiffany than whatever-her-name-is from Xiachuan."

"What was all that about?" Tiffany asked James.

"I told him that if he likes Chinese girls, you are the one he's been looking for."

Tiffany backed away from us. "No, I don't believe it."

James said, "Yes, it's true."

Tiffany looked at me and smiled. Then she turned to James. "Can I trust this guy? He just took that skinny little hooker back to his room."

James said, "You can trust this guy. He might fuck a few hookers here and there, but he isn't going to leave you when times get tough. He's legitimate. He has a conscience."

James turned to me. "I just told her that you..."

"I know what you just told her."

No, Tiffany. James is wrong. You can't trust me. I can't trust me.

Those three days on Xiachuan Island may have taken a few years off my life, but what happened next might have shortened it by a decade. I went back to see Fang three weeks later in Zhuhai. If I was stupid enough to come back to her after everything we'd been through, I deserved a cosmic beatdown. Ironically, it was Captain Felix's idea.

"I want you to do some reconnaissance for me," Felix said. "Look for business opportunities."

"The only businesses I know about are the hotels and bars on bar street."

"Find out if any of the bars are for sale. We can invest in them."

It was a ludicrous proposition, but Felix had the hair-brained idea that I could manage a couple of bars in Zhuhai and use that as a springboard into opening a language school. I couldn't talk him out of the idea, so I took the ticket. Daisy was busy with family visiting from out of town.

It was only for the weekend. Fang was still with her friends in Taishan when I called. She met me at the border crossing again. We stayed at the Yong Tong Hotel above the bus station. When I asked about the abortion, she said, "No problem. It's done." During the day, we went shopping or stayed in bed. At night, we went to Bar Street, consciously avoiding Tiffany's spot. Fang refused to go any further than the first stall where her friends worked. Fang said Peachy went back to Wuhan or wherever she was from—they weren't friends as much as co-workers. I was relieved that Peachy didn't mention our little get-together.

In private, Fang talked about her desire to get married, and she asked many questions about my life. Many more than ever before. At the end of the day, I truly believed she loved me. We lived as if the abortion had never taken place and maybe it didn't. I will never know for sure.

During lunch on Saturday afternoon, Fang asked, "How old are you?"

"I'm forty-one. How old are you?"

"I have to tell you something."

"What?"

"I'm twenty-seven. No, twenty-eight. Soon."

"When?"

Fang produced her Chinese citizen ID. Her birthday was October 21. It was early September. I remembered her asking for a birthday gift a few months ago, and I turned salty.

"Hmm, that's interesting."

"Will you visit me on my birthday?" she asked.

"I don't know."

I've always had trouble saying "no" to women I care about. I'd say, "I don't know" or "maybe" but I frequently struggled with the emphatic "no." It's not fair to the women I've been involved with, but really, I'm the loser. So many times, in the spirit of compromise, which is essential for all relationships, I've said "yes" to things I didn't want to do and sorely regretted it.

Fang couldn't believe I hadn't been married already and pressed me on it. "Tell me the truth."

"Never married."

"No children?"

"No children."

Fang looked suspicious. "Why?"

"I don't know."

She shook her head in disbelief. "Not possible." She didn't say anything for a while and started browsing through my Mandarin phrasebook. She was in the "green" section—the area of relationships—and as her finger scrolled down the page, I got nervous. Fang pointed to a phrase and said, "Here. This."

"Do I want to get married?"

"Yes."

"We have only known each other for three months." I didn't say it nearly so eloquently, but she knew exactly what I meant.

"How long?" She meant, what was the acceptable amount of time we knew each other before I would marry her?

"One year."

"When?"

"We met in April."

Fang counted the months on her fingers and said, "Seven more months. You will marry me?"

"Let's talk about it next year."

A few minutes later, Fang said, "Charlie, I have to tell you something. Please don't get mad."

"Go ahead. I won't get mad."

"There's another man, a professor from Taiwan. He wants to marry me."

At first, I thought, *Captain Felix!* But he'd *never* marry a hooker.

"I understand."

"If you don't marry me, I'll marry that other guy."

"OK."

"Are you sure you understand what I'm saying?"

"Yes, I'm sure."

She called her parents in Ningxia.

"My father says he has to meet you before you can marry me," she said.

"Sounds reasonable," I replied in English. Then she thrust the phone in my ear as her father rattled off a string of Chinese. I heard her infant son squealing in the background like someone was tickling him.

* ✱ *

Later that afternoon, Fang said she wanted to go shopping. It was insanely hot and humid, and I begged her to wait until the sun went down, but she got dressed anyway and stood by the door. "Let's go. The underground mall has air conditioning."

First stop: a jewelry store. Fang was already looking for an engagement ring. I almost choked on the price of the first one: 60,000 yuan (US$10,000). Fang asked the shop owner to pull out the entire rack of gold bands. "The diamond," he said, "is not included in the price." I turned and walked away, stopping at the store's threshold, and lit a cigarette. I said out loud, "I don't have ten grand, Fang-fang."

The internal monologue began. *What the fuck am I doing? I need to get the fuck out of here.*

A few minutes later, Fang came up behind me and put her arms around my neck. "Let's go," she said. "This guy wants to cheat us."

Before the afternoon was over, Fang settled for about 2,000 yuan (US$280) worth of clothing.

* ✱ *

In the evening we hit Bar Street, both of us drinking *hard*. Like most Chinese women I met on the bar circuit, Fang could handle her booze. At roughly the mid-point of the evening, we hit a lull in conversation and played a weird, buzzed-up game of staring at each other—like we were looking for something *in there*. Like a telepathic connection.

Breaking the stare, Fang asked, "What are you thinking?"

55

It was the one and only time I asked Fang about her business. "Why are you working in Xiachuan?" meaning why did you decide to be a prostitute?

"What else am I going to do?" she scoffed. "Work in a shoe store? Be a secretary?"

I couldn't argue with that.

★✱★

Monday morning, we said goodbye at Gongbei; this time, Fang teared up. She said she loved me and wanted to be a good wife and a good mother for our children. Maybe she was feeling those things.

A month later, Fang's last message to me was, "I'm sorry, I didn't understand what you said." This came in response to my earlier message that read, "This is my new cell phone number."

And surprisingly, I stopped hearing from her, which was a relief. And I started reviewing all the events in my head, adding up all the time and money. *I'm lucky. It could have been a lot worse.*

★✱★

In those days, I lay in bed at night, hoping I wasn't the only person who knew that my life meant absolutely *nothing*. Alone in that nothingness is a cynical place to be. Loneliness and solitude are interchangeable when nobody and nothing matters.

We're all a bunch of liars, but we mostly tell white lies. They're meaningless and/or pointless. A small but significant number of lies wind up hurting others. Without a sense of regret, I thought about *honesty*, mostly because I couldn't make it through a day without being dishonest (in some small, insignificant way). *But am I being honest with myself?* The resounding answer: "I'm trying."

7

An Important Move

The rooftop apartment in the Wenshan District had a few benefits but mostly drawbacks. As an illegal fifth-floor addition to a four-story building, like a poorly constructed tiki hut on a larger pavilion, it was just asking for trouble. Its main benefit was size, with 400 square feet of living space and 200 square feet of patio. Plenty of room for a bachelor. The kitchen and dining/office areas were separate from the living and bedroom areas, giving the space a "two-room feel." The patio had some aged bamboo furniture for lounging. It was a great place for hanging out at night, smoking and drinking, weather permitting. There was an OK Mart convenience store on the corner, open 24/7/365, keeping my beers cold for me.

The drawbacks of the rooftop were myriad. First, the bathroom and utility room were under the same roof but separate from the main house. A door near the bedroom led to a small outdoor washing area with a sink, two steps away from the tiled bathroom. Whenever somebody needed to use the facilities, they were vaguely "exposed" to the elements—and the neighbors. It wasn't a big deal at night when the lights were off, but I sleep naked, and, like most people, the first thing I do in the morning is take a pee. I never bothered to put on a pair of boxers or wear a robe, even during the cold winter months.

Two adjoining buildings of approximately the same height formed a vaguely L-shaped cluster. Another four-story building (with a fifth-story addition) stood just a few yards from my front entrance. One vista of my rooftop looked directly onto the outdoor area of that apartment. Now, the neighbors and I weren't staring out our windows at each other, but we were familiar. Maybe three months into my residency, I popped up one morning at seven o'clock, went to the bathroom (door closed, of course), stepped back into the washing area, and paused momentarily. An older woman was hanging wash on her patio in full view of me and my bathroom, staring at my nude body while pinning undergarments to the clothesline. I waved at her with a weak smile and ducked back into the house.

Meanwhile, the rooftop's location was awful. The neighborhood was eerily sedate, not much more than automotive shops and residential properties. It was tucked away on the south side of the city, close to the Wanlong MRT station, but isolated from "the real action" found in Daan, Tianmu, Xinyi, and Ximendeng. I got choosy about special occasions because it was so expensive to get home late at night. Those taxi fares started to pile up, and I hated wasting the money.

The last place you want to be during a typhoon is some half-baked cement adobe with a terracotta roof. And with every inclement weather forecast, I had to drag all the plants and patio furniture into the house. The patio's drainage system was generally efficient, but during Typhoon Morakat, the rain fell so hard and fast that the patio flooded. The water threatened to encroach on the apartment itself, just a centimeter from breaching the threshold of the front door. If the water kept rising, the whole apartment would flood in minutes. The winds were howling at 90 miles per hour, pushing me around the patio. Desperate to avoid total disaster, I tied a 30-foot extension cord around my waist and anchored it to the building, while using a bucket to bail out the water like a sinking ship.

We continue with the drawbacks. The building didn't have an elevator, so it was five-down, five-up, every time I needed to hit the grocery store. Good for calf muscles and cardio fitness. Bad for coming home blind drunk, or worse, with a tipsy date.

The rooftop directly next door on the south side of the patio—not the apartment where the woman saw me naked—was occupied by three or four children from pre-teen to young adult. These children belonged to the family who owned that building, and their parents lived on the lower floors. My landlord said he was good friends with the father. One of the kids was in his early teens and something of a troublemaker.

During my first weekend in the apartment, I was taking advantage of the abundant late spring sunshine, basking on a lounge chair in the corner of the patio, to my knowledge, out of sight from any neighbor's view.

Suddenly, I felt something small and round, like an acorn or a walnut, land on my chest and fall to the ground. I leaned up, looked around—there were no trees except a couple of potted palms on the patio—said, "Huh," and lay back down. A minute later, I felt another small round object hit my forehead. It was, in fact, an acorn of the tropical variety and identical to the previous object. *That's odd. Those trees on the hill over there are too far away, and there's no breeze today...* Popping up, I went around the corner but didn't see anybody over at the neighbor's joint. Laying down again, I spotted the teenage neighbor kid crouching on top of the roof that vaguely connected our apartments. He had a cache of acorns in one hand while giving me the middle finger with the other.

"Hey!" I shouted. "The fuck are you doing?"

The kid spat, "*Gan!*" a Chinese variant of "fuck you" and nimbly scampered off the roof and out of my sight.

Over the next few months, I'd catch the kid up on the roof, leering at me, tossing those little acorns onto my patio. He could have easily accessed the patio and apartment from the roof, but he seemed relatively harmless. The apartment had decent locks on everything, so I didn't fear any kind of true mischief. I ignored him whenever I saw him creeping around up there. However, one day I came home from work and noticed my BBQ grill had been moved from one end of the patio to the other. I moved it back and didn't give it a second thought. I could have done it the night before. Being constantly high or drunk gives you some leeway for interior and exterior decorating. Sometimes, I'd wake up in the morning and ask, "When did I move the TV into the bathroom?"

This went on for a year. I swept the acorns from the patio every Saturday afternoon.

★✱★

On my return from the first trip to Zhuhai, the patio had been completely rearranged—and not for the better. Tables were akimbo to chairs, plants were moved into the shade of the roof eaves, and the BBQ was in the utility washing area off the bedroom. Clearly, somebody had been playing games with me—probably that damn kid. *Oh well. What can you do?* I stayed vigilant about keeping things locked up tight, and there was never any sign of an attempted break-in.

My elderly landlord insisted that the rent be paid in person and cash on the fifth of the month, with no exceptions—unless I paid a month in advance, which I did on several occasions. A pair of Australian-born Taiwanese dudes lived on the floor below, so the three of us would truck out to the suburbs of Yonghe and meet the old guy at a hot pot joint for dinner, where we'd hand our envelopes of cash over to the old guy's daughter, who didn't speak English and treated us with open contempt. *Whatever, honey. Fuck you too.*

Eventually, I told the landlord about the neighbor kid on the roof, and he said, "Oh yeah, watch out for that kid. He's trouble."

"Can you do something about it? Can you tell his family? Make him knock it off?"

The old man smiled weakly. "I have tried talking to them. It's no use. To call the police would create far too much bother and ruin my relationship with the father."

One of the Aussie guys, Mitchell, said, "Ay mate, the next time the little rugger is up on your paddy, let me know and I'll shake him out—give him a hard scare—maybe break a few bones!"

Entering the rooftop required a two-step process. First, you had to get through the door leading from the stairs *to* the rooftop. There was a second door leading into the crib itself.

When I returned from the final trip to Zhuhai, I came through the heavy steel door from the stairway, stepped out onto the patio, and found the other door into the apartment was wide open, creaking in the breeze. Within seconds, I realized the patio and its contents had all but been destroyed. The BBQ grill lay on its side, coals everywhere. A couple of bamboo chairs were smashed. Inside the house, the joint had been ransacked. I'd been robbed. Well, *maybe* I'd been robbed. I might have left the front door unlocked because there was no sign of forced entry.

After further investigation, it appeared that nothing was missing, but stuff had been smashed or thrown across the room. If I didn't know any better, it looked like someone—a junkie or a violent transient—spent some time on it. The dining room table and chairs were knocked over. A kitchen knife was wedged into a door frame. Empty food and drink containers were piled up on the coffee table in the TV lounge area. They didn't bust up the TV, but the standalone bookcase was knocked over, books strewn around the room, ripped pages everywhere. And the kitchen—*aw Christ, they destroyed the microwave*—even pulled the sink off the outflow pipes. Pools of water everywhere. The worst was reserved for the bathroom—I had blood in my eyes. There was no way—*no way in hell*—I was going to clean that shit up.

Tired and gassed from the travels, I flagged down a taxi and booked a room in a hotel near the office. The next morning, I went straight to Daisy and told her the story.

⋆✳⋆

Daisy was outraged and proactive. I loved seeing her all riled up. She got the Captain on the phone, and he apparently dropped whatever he was doing and showed up in the office about 15 minutes later.

"How much are you paying for that place?" Felix asked.

"Eighteen thousand a month."

"Ayyyy!" he cried. "That's too much! I thought you were paying eight thousand?"

"Nope."

"How much did you put down for a deposit?"

"Thirty-six thousand." (Roughly US$1,200)

"Ohhhhh," Captain Felix exhaled with a mix of defeat and disgust.

"Well, you can kiss that deposit goodbye," Daisy interjected.

Felix continued, "The first thing you're going to do is get all your stuff out of there."

"I don't have any stuff to get out of there. It was furnished. Almost everything came with the apartment. I had my passport, camera, and laptop with me, thank God, so none of the shit in the apartment was mine, except for a cheap stereo, some CDs, books, clothing, and a couple of kitchen utensils. Everything I own of value is in this backpack."

"That's great," Felix said, turning serious. "Whatever you do, *don't go anywhere near that apartment*. Don't even cross the street. Do you understand?"

"What should I say to the landlord?"

"Screw that landlord, Charlie," Daisy said.

"Yes," Felix agreed. "He's not a good guy. Screw him."

"Wait," Daisy said, "you didn't call the police, did you?"

I burst into laughter. "The cops! You kill me, Daisy."

"Oh," Daisy snorted. "I guess that's a 'no'."

"So that's it?" I said to Felix. "Just start looking for a new apartment? Forget the deposit? Forget the lease?"

"Meanwhile," Felix offered, "you can stay upstairs in the dorm. You can have my suite." This was a generous gesture. His ensuite had an attached bathroom and a balcony. Most of the other bedrooms did not.

"Only for a week or so," I said. "Until I get a new joint. Fuck, losing that deposit money is going to *hurt*."

"No problem," Felix said. "When you find a place, I'll loan you the deposit. Don't worry about money."

I wasn't about to forget about the deposit. Twelve hundred dollars was a lot of money to me. Fang had just fleeced me for upwards of three grand. *Nuh-uh, not letting this go*. So, I placed an ad on Craigslist, using pictures from before the break-in. Within a day, I heard from an American couple, Louis and Charlotte. I warned them that the place was in disarray, but if they liked it, I would tidy things up a bit. We agreed to meet the next day, so I cut out of work early, bought a 12-pack, and took a taxi down to the rooftop. I bagged up most of the trash, which was the easiest part, and removed some of the busted-up furniture. Miraculously, the bed hadn't been soiled by the intruder(s), so I gave the mattress a fresh set of sheets. I also managed to save some books and CDs, but the stereo was broken.

After eight beers, the alcohol took over. I attempted to clean the bathroom by hosing the walls down while standing in the utility area. Most of the shit washed down the floor drain, but I wasn't about to get in there and scrub the tiles. Overall, the place was on the cusp of livable again.

Early the next morning, I met Louis and Charlotte at the apartment. As soon as they stepped onto the patio, they didn't see the mess, destruction, or chaos—they saw an oasis, a home.

"This..." Louis said, "doesn't look all that bad. Nothing we couldn't fix."

Charlotte had already moved into the house. "I see you've got some cleaning supplies," she called out.

"Wait until you see the bathroom."

Charlotte wasn't fazed. "Ah, give me some bleach and a scrub brush."

After a few minutes of further exploration, Louis said, "I think we'll take it."

"Wait. I've gotta tell you about the kid who lives next door." I gave them a quick rundown of the situation.

"That's a bit concerning," Charlotte said. "This isn't a bad neighborhood, is it?"

"There's no such thing as a bad neighborhood in Taipei. It was bad luck. The kid doesn't like me. We had 'a thing.' He won't bother you. I'm the moron for leaving the front door unlocked. Keep the place locked up tight and you won't have any problems."

There was one final issue to resolve. *Would I sublet or hand them off to the landlord?* After some discussion, I finally said, "Look, I'm paid up for September, so forget about rent until October. If you guys kick down the deposit money to me, I'll hook you up with the landlord next month and you can take over the lease. It won't be a problem. That's exactly how I got the place."

"Done," Louis said. "Will you accept an international money transfer to your local bank account?"

"Even better," I said, "you can send it to my account in the U.S."

"Again, done."

"But don't forget about that kid next door, man. If you go out of town, make sure you have this place locked up fucking tight. Don't be a dummy like me."

And just like that, I was out of the rooftop—and into the dormitory at Knowledge Press HQ.

✳

The dormitory was pretty damn nice, and aside from early morning and lunch hour, the place was mine at night and on the weekends. The current housemaid wasn't a live-in, so she worked weekdays from 6:00 a.m. to 4:00 p.m. There might be an occasional guest from out of town, but they *usually* gave me plenty of heads up.

Daisy checked in about finding a new apartment and offered to help with my search. Captain Felix, on the other hand, was delighted to have me living upstairs and repeatedly told me that I didn't need to leave, nor should I want to. He said, "You have everything you need at your fingertips here. If I were you, I'd save my money and stay."

Nearly a month of cozy dorm life passed before I said to Daisy, "Give me your honest opinion. Should I move out?"

"I don't know," she replied, "but you can't stay in that suite forever. Felix wants you to choose a different room. You should move into that room on the far side, with the bathroom across the hall. Nobody ever goes down there. You'll be all alone."

"But your suite is on that side. Is that going to bother you?"

She hissed and said, "You're like my brother. And I'm not there very often anyway." Daisy hadn't stayed in the suite as long as I knew her. For the time being, no matter what room I lived in, the joint would still be mine. *An apartment can* wait, I thought. *I've got other plans.* And for a long time, that made a lot of sense—economically and/or otherwise.

Moving into the dormitory marked a major transition from living in a remote part of town to living in one of the more lively and upscale areas and home to Knowledge Press. My commute to the office went from 30 minutes or longer to several dozen steps from the dorm. Living in what was called the Anhe (Road) Corridor, I started hanging out at night markets and making many more reconnaissance missions into unknown parts of the city. Tonghua (Linjiang) Night Market was just around the corner, Taipei 101 could be seen from my dorm room window, and I could *crawl* home from the MRT stop. It simply increased my involvement with the city itself. Out on the Wenshan rooftop, sometimes I got lost in the wash of isolation. At KPHQ, I could get as isolated or social as I wanted without limits.

Oh. Except one. I couldn't bring anybody back to the dorms. No friends, and certainly, no lovers. It was completely off-limits to almost everybody. Captain Felix said my extended family and visitors from out of town were welcome, but as far as bringing girlfriends back to the crib? Forget it. "The dorm is not a fucking place," Felix said.

Something was going on between Captain Felix, Daisy, and the hotshot cram school teacher named Sherry.

Daisy had been acting weird since I returned from the final Zhuhai trip in October. Aside from my housing ordeal, she rarely started a conversation or acknowledged my presence in the office. There was palpable tension in every exchange.

Captain Felix didn't make a big secret about his attraction to Sherry, and since she was the most popular and profitable teacher at the cram school, he spoiled her with gifts and attention. At some point, he gifted Sherry a million-dollar apartment in another swanky part of town. Kind of an odd thing for a 65-year-old man to do for a 35-year-old woman who wasn't his wife, girlfriend, or mistress.

Two months older than me, Daisy was the opposite of Sherry, in looks and personality. Very plain, with a stern countenance, Daisy spoke excellent English and wasn't afraid to challenge Captain Felix on some of his scatter-brained impulsiveness. While generally supplicant to his whims, Daisy could put up a big stink when necessary. She was a very sharp and hawkish individual who claimed not to trust *anyone*, but she loved Felix—or at least felt like she owed him something. It was shaping up to be a truly gruesome love triangle. This thing was just getting started.

While I wanted to know what was going on, I knew it didn't have anything to do with me, so I kept my head down and waited for something to pop.

It was a Thursday night. I was waking up from a post-work nap in my dorm room when I heard someone enter the apartment. I figured it was the housemaid and didn't think anything of it until I heard footsteps pass outside my door and into Daisy's suite. The door slammed, and I realized it was probably Daisy, of course, nobody else slammed doors like Daisy. I don't think she realized how poorly she treated the doors in her life.

Anyway, it was odd because Daisy hadn't set foot in her suite since I started working there. Felix never stayed in his suite on the other side of the dorm, either. They told me the dorm suites were a "last resort" if something happened at the house they shared in Muzha. Daisy told me once that she would never voluntarily live in the dorm, and if she did, that would mean her relationship with Felix was over.

I poked my head outside the room and listened for clues. Daisy's bathroom shared a wall with my bathroom, and it sounded like she was running a bath. I closed my door, got dressed for the evening, and maybe five minutes later, walked out into the hallway, where I could hear the faintest whimpering of a woman crying. I ducked into my bathroom and listened intently. It was Daisy.

Within a matter of seconds, the whimpering turned to sobbing, and within a minute, Daisy was having a full-blown meltdown, howling and screaming and banging the side of the bathtub, which rang out like a bass drum across the varnished wood floors of the dormitory.

I quietly padded out of the bathroom and tiptoed across the apartment to the front door, where I slipped outside without a sound. Waiting for the elevator, I shook my head and stroked my chin. *Holy shit! That poor woman is going through something, man.*

When I returned later that evening, Daisy was gone. The next morning, she was already typing away at her computer when I arrived in the office. I sat down at my desk and said, "Hey, Daisy. Is everything alright with you?"

She stopped typing and stared straight ahead. "I'm fine. Why?"

"Well, it just seems like you haven't been talking to me lately, and I was worried that I said something to offend you."

"Of course not!" she shot back. "You're always very nice to me."

I groaned. "Not always. I've been known to push a few of your buttons."

"Nonsense." She made prolonged eye contact. "Can I trust you?"

"Of course."

Daisy got up and closed the office door. Her doctor found fibroids on her uterus, and he wanted her to have a hysterectomy. She didn't want a hysterectomy because she was certain that Felix was going to marry her, and she hoped that maybe they would have a child together. Captain Felix told her to go ahead with the surgery because he didn't want any kids. But it was more than that. She had conflicting and confusing thoughts and emotions, mainly about their relationship. Somehow, Sherry was involved. She didn't like how Felix catered to Sherry. They had been fighting about it for at least a week.

I took several deep breaths and said, "That's heartbreaking, Daisy. What are you going to do?"

"I don't have a choice." Tears welled in her eyes. "I'm having surgery next week."

"I'm so sorry, Daisy. I don't know what to say. Can I come visit you in the hospital?"

"Will you?" She began sobbing.

"Yes, of course. Please don't cry."

She left the office, and I didn't see her again for the rest of the weekend.

Daisy was out of the office on the following Monday, so Felix came in alone, just before lunch. He brought his standard high-energy persona. It was just another day. We had a light conversation about my weekend or whatever, and he casually mentioned that Daisy would be out for the week to deal with a health issue.

"Which hospital is she at? NTU, right?" (National Taiwan University Medical Center, the best hospital in Taiwan.)

"Oh, you know already?"

"Yeah, she told me on Friday."

"I want you to visit her in the hospital tomorrow."

"I was planning on it."

On Tuesday morning, I skipped out of the office around 10:00 a.m., went to the florist a few blocks away, bought a bouquet of carnations (her favorite flower), and took a taxi to the hospital.

Daisy was overwhelmed with emotion to see me. Her surgery was scheduled for later in the day, so I stayed for a couple of hours, just talking. I showed up the next day, too, and I accompanied Felix to pick her up when she was released on Thursday.

Even though Daisy and I already had a solid bond—Felix joked that she was my part-time personal assistant—visiting her in the hospital boosted our friendship to the untouchable zone. From that moment forward, I could do no wrong in Daisy's eyes, and she became fiercely protective and supportive of me, in and out of the office. As a result of our familiarity, Daisy told me *everything*. Unimpeachably loyal and bitterly vindictive, she was like a rattlesnake in the top drawer of your desk. I once told her, "You're the best friend and the worst enemy a person could have."

Captain Felix had many quirks and/or funny habits, like routinely asking if I had any travel plans "for the weekend." I used to reconcile this with the fact that he was constantly flying in and out of town, so it seemed logical to him that everybody else was doing the same thing. Another quirk involved asking if I needed any help. It seemed like every time he saw me, the first words out of his mouth were, "Charlie, do you need any help? Is there anything I can do for you?" Above all, Felix loved knowing the answer to the question he was about to ask.

We cruised through autumn without any major upheavals or catastrophes, both at work and in my private life. Following a month of radio silence, Fang resumed contact via text message or email, but I didn't engage very often. Otherwise, I wasn't dating anybody or doing anything special. I reckoned a break from dating and chasing women would do me good. And Martin was still coming through with the weed connection, so all my "needs" were met.

It was the day before Halloween when Felix came into the office around 3:00 p.m. He never showed up before 5:00 p.m. unless Daisy was out of town, which happened to be the case. She was visiting her son in the U.S. for a month. Anyway, Felix sat down and started talking about the best massage of his life—a Thai massage from a joint that recently opened down the street from the office. He went on and on about how the masseuse knew what she was doing, and man, he never felt so good.

I wasn't much of a "massage guy," so I just sat there and listened, nodding my head. Eventually, Felix got around to asking the question he already knew the answer to. "Have you been to Thailand?"

Felix knew I'd never been to Thailand because I told him at least three or four times during our year-and-a-half of acquaintance. But then again, Captain Felix wasn't known for his listening comprehension skills, and his retention of information was suspect, at best. He frequently couldn't remember the names of robots who'd been with him for years. He'd describe somebody as "that girl who sits near the copier" and shit like that.

"No, I've never been to Thailand."

Felix sat up in his chair, a big grin on his mug. Like meeting an old friend. "I will take you there! They have a lot of pretty girls, but you must be careful. Many diseases. Some of them are not very clean. But I know all the good spots. When would you like to go? I have some free time until Daisy returns from the U.S."

"Anytime works for me. I don't have any plans in the foreseeable future."

Felix smiled and slapped the desktop with both hands—another funny habit. "Alright! I'll set everything up."

The next morning was a Friday. Felix breezed into the office and said, "We leave in a week. Next Saturday. Does that work for you?"

"Works for me. And I'm excited. We haven't traveled together since April."

"Has it been that long?"

"It has."

"We'll start in Bangkok and make our way down to Pattaya. Have you heard of Pattaya? It's a real fucking place."

"*Oh yeah*, I've heard of Pattaya."

He got on the phone and started planning for the trip. Just before the end of the day, Felix had long since disappeared, Lloyd came into the office and handed me a round-trip ticket to Bangkok.

Felix didn't show up in the office that Monday. Or Tuesday. Or Wednesday. On Thursday, I tried calling him, but his phone was off. I panicked and called Daisy, who was happy to hear from me and excited to talk about her trip in the U.S., but she wasn't sure about Felix. "He could be anywhere," she said. "He's not answering my calls, either." When he didn't show up on Friday, I pretty much assumed that the trip to Thailand was off, and although I was disappointed, I didn't really care. *Easy come, easy go.*

After work, I went down to Carnegie's and drank alone. The night was very subdued for a weekend, nobody seemed to be out. It was around 9:30 p.m. when Felix called.

"Hello?"

"Sir, I have bad news for you. I'm sorry, but I can't go to Thailand with you tomorrow."

"That's okay. I kinda figured as much when you didn't show up in the office all week."

Felix paused for a moment. "Don't worry, I want you to go there and have some fun. You deserve it."

"Really? You want me to go by myself? Are you sure?"

"Yes, of course. Just be careful. And remember what I told you about hookers. Never sleep with the same one twice."

"Gotcha. But wait a minute. Where are you?"

"Where am I?" his voice trailed off. "I'm...in China. On business. We'll talk about it later. And don't say anything to anybody."

"Roger that, Cap'n."

8

One Night in Bangkok

Suvarnabhumi International Airport (IATA code: BKK)
Bangkok, Thailand
Saturday, November 7, 2009
11:00 p.m.

The flight wasn't even half-full, which was nice. I sat near the back of the cabin with a row to myself. God bless Bridget, the KLM flight attendant who made it her mission to get me as drunk as possible during the three-hour trip. From lift-off and the beverage service started until the plane touched down, I was never without a glass of red wine. The landing was so smooth I didn't spill a drop. It was almost midnight by the time I cleared immigration and customs at BKK. I jumped in a taxi and said to the driver, "Soi Nana," an area in downtown Bangkok known for its nightlife.

The driver let me out at the Nana Metro Station, and it didn't take long to find an open-air bar with some friendly foreign and local faces. I ordered a bottle of Singha and immediately struck up a conversation with a British guy standing nearby. This being my first visit to Bangkok, I was eager to make friends. The British guy was very friendly and happy to offer helpful suggestions.

"Where are you staying?" the British guy asked.

"I don't have a hotel yet," I replied. "Any recommendations?"

"It depends on how much you want to spend. This area is loaded with guesthouses and hotels. Walk two minutes in any direction and you'll find something."

We stood at the edge of the bar and people-watched. The sidewalks were teeming with people from every corner of the globe. A few minutes and another beer later, the British guy left to join his friends somewhere else. An exceptionally attractive girl from the other side of the bar caught my eye, came over, and spoke to me in English. She appeared to be in her mid 20s. *This girl is fuckin' hot, man.*

Please don't think I'm being condescending when I refer to her as a "girl" as opposed to a woman. It's just a figure of speech. It's the way I talk. It's the way most people talk.

"You just now come to Thailand?" the girl said as she reached for my hand that wasn't holding a beer.

"Yes, of course." I shrugged. The girl smiled and rubbed my hand.

"How long you stay in Bangkok?"

"I dunno."

"You buy me a drink?"

"Sure." I bought her a drink, a whiskey and soda, which she downed in two, quick, successive gulps. I signaled the bartender for another round. The girl moved from holding my hand to caressing my shoulder. We talked for five minutes or so. Our conversation covered the usual ground. *What's Your Story?*

"Where will you stay tonight?" she asked. At this point, I didn't know her name. She didn't offer and I didn't think to ask.

"I don't have a room yet."

"You can stay with me. I have an apartment."

"Really? Uh, OK..."

I assumed that she was a bar girl and just doing her job, which is separating stupid white guys like me from our money. However, I had no intention of picking up a prostitute tonight. I was tired and quite drunk, thanks to Bridget and KLM.

All I wanted was to find a hotel and get some sleep. Wake up tomorrow and decide what to do next. The problem was: The bar girl was getting more attractive by the minute.

★✳★

In a taxi on Sukhumvit Road
Sunday, November 8, 2009
2:00 a.m.

OK, stop. I was going to the "apartment" of a stranger in a city that's well-known for bad things happening to foreigners who have too much to drink. I admit to reckless naïveté. *What was the worst that could happen?* I thought, which I always seem to do when things get out of my control. And frankly, I'd been in many more dangerous situations.

The girl told the driver where to go and kissed me on the cheek. And things were now definitely out of my control. Almost immediately, I smelled piss somewhere in the taxi. I started to get nervous when we headed out of the city. The stink of urine became overpowering. At some point, the girl moved in even closer and we started making out. I put my arms around her and felt a dampness on her denim jeans. When I saw signs for Don Mueang, Bangkok's old airport, which is a good 20 kilometers out of town, I finally asked, "Where are we going?" The girl nuzzled against my neck and cooed, "My apartment. Don't worry. I like you."

I'm not worried. And I like you, too, but something really smells like piss in here.

By the time the driver pulled off the highway and into a lower-middle-class suburb (which I now know is called Si Kan) on the outskirts of the airport, I wasn't drunk anymore. And I knew one thing: somewhere along the way, this girl had pissed herself.

"Where are we going?" I repeated, with emphasis on where and going.

"It's oh-kaaay," the girl said.

"I don't even know your name."

"Poom." She kissed me, deeply.

The taxi stopped at a guesthouse that I thought was an abandoned gas station at first sight. It wasn't until I saw a guy sitting inside behind a desk that it occurred to me that this might be some sort of fly-by-night set-up. Still, I didn't panic.

As we walked toward the entrance, Poom leaned on my shoulder and said, "I am afraid."

"Afraid? Afraid of what?"

"I no pay my rent. The man be angry with me." She pointed at the desk clerk.

"How much is it?" I stopped in the middle of the walkway. Poom put her arms around me.

"Five hundred baht." Not a lot of money, equivalent to US$15.

"No problem. I'll pay."

A rundown guesthouse in Si Kan
2:45 a.m.

When I paid the clerk, it was with the last 500 baht I had on my person. The rest of my money was stashed in the backpack.

Traveling teaches you to minimize distractions and vulnerabilities. I don't own a wallet or a watch because those are the first things people try to steal.

- Nothing of real importance goes in the back pockets of your pants/shorts
- Keep as much cash as you can afford to lose in the right front pocket—never more than 100 bucks
- The remaining cash must be stashed in more than one place in the backpack
- ID and credit cards: no more than four cards on your person held together by a rubber band and put in the left front pocket

The overall idea was no two things in the same place. A crafty thief might get my camera, but he wasn't getting my passport. And the only way someone could get the entire backpack was over my dead body.

The clerk didn't ask for my ID or even make eye contact. Poom led me down a hallway to the door of "her room." She insisted that I enter first, which struck me as odd. Once inside, I made a quick survey. It didn't look like anybody lived there. *This is just another cheap guesthouse room.* Over my shoulder, I heard Poom lock and chain the door. I turned around to face her.

"What's going on?"

"How much money do you have?" Her arms were crossed against her chest, a wild look in her eye.

"What?"

"How much you pay me?"

"For what? I just paid for your room."

"This is not my room."

"What should I pay you for? We didn't do anything."

"Pay me three hundred dollars."

"*Three hundred dollars!* How about if I don't pay you *shit*, and I leave right now." I moved toward the door, but she blocked my progress. I backed off.

"No!" Poom said, her voice raising in urgency. "You pay me *now!*"

"For *what?!*" I said, my voice raising in urgency, too. I stepped back into the middle of the room and tried to reason with her.

"I don't have any more money." I reached into my pockets and pulled out the pack of cards held together with a rubber band. "See? No money. I need to go to the ATM."

"*No ATM! Pay me now!*" She tried to get at my backpack, but I pushed her away.

"I don't have any more money."

Poom went to the telephone by the bed and picked up the receiver. "You no pay me now, I call my brother and boyfriend. They come and kill you." She punched a series of numbers on the touchpad. Apparently, someone answered on the other end. Poom spoke excitedly in Thai. I had no idea what she was saying.

"Don't do that!" I pleaded. "I can get you the money. I need to use an ATM. I will pay."

Poom slammed the phone down and held out her hand. "Pay me, now."

"Please, just relax. We can work this out."

3:05 a.m

They say that time flies when you're having fun but I'm telling you that it reaches warp speed when you're scared out of your mind.

Poom started undressing, and by undressing, I mean she tore off her shirt. She was down to just her piss-soaked jeans and repeating a word in Thai, which sounded an awful lot like "rape" after the fifth time she screamed it at the top of her lungs.

"Don't do that," I said, calmly.

"*Rape!*" she cried. "*Rape!*" She banged on the outside wall and screamed, "*Help!*"

I sat on the bed, backpack still strapped to my shoulders, looked to the ceiling and said, "God, please get me out of here."

"I call the police. And you—" she made a cutting gesture across her throat, "—dead."

There was a firm knock at the door. Poom, half-naked, rushed to undo the lock and chain. She looked over her shoulder with a devilish grin. "See? Now you die."

Wow, her English is pretty good. Either that, or she's seen a lot of Hollywood movies.

It was the desk clerk, and he wasn't happy. Heated words were exchanged with the topless Poom. They were familiar with each other. The clerk stopped shouting at one point and looked at me as if to say, "Watch, I'm going to knock this crazy bitch out." I held my hands at waist level, palms up, head tilted to the side—the universal gesture for "I don't know what the hell is going on." The clerk faked a punch to Poom's face, stopping just millimeters from her nose. She flinched, screamed, and fell to the ground. He turned away and left.

Poom recovered miraculously from the non-punch. She was up and on her cell phone within seconds of the door slamming behind the clerk. I remained seated on the bed and lit a cigarette. She must have made five or six calls, all of them more urgent than the next.

Poom stood in front of me. "I call my brothers. Pay me, or they will kill you."

"I'm not giving you anything, dummy." Shaking my head. "Kill *me*. *Please*."

3:30 a.m.

Poom's attitude careened back toward friendly. *Bi-polar bitch.* It seemed for a while that I had things under control. Poom stopped screaming and demanding money and now said she wanted to be "happy-happy" with me. She produced a handful of "happy-happy" pills from her purse and threatened to take them at once. I took one look at the pills and said, "No, honey, please. No happy-happy."

This girl is fucking strung out. She went into the bathroom and from what I'm guessing, downed a handful of the pills.

Poom returned completely naked and dancing around the room to imaginary music. She made several efforts to undress me, but I refused, at least until I could get her into a shower. She finally relented and I managed to drag her into the bathroom where I hosed her down with warm water and soap and got very familiar with her body. And it was an amazing body.

As I soaped her down, I kept thinking that if I could just get her to stay in this mood, everything might be OK. *But then again, God only knows what she's on, and how fucked up do you have to be to piss yourself in a taxi?* I was still fully dressed and getting wet from the splashing. I handed her a towel and left her to dry off. I returned to the bed and started putting on my backpack.

"Honey," Poom called from the bathroom. "Are you ready to make love?"

"Yeah, sure."

Poom poked her head out of the bathroom just as I made a break for the door.

"NO!" she screamed, charging out of the bathroom and racing me to the door. "Pay me!" She continued to scream and tried to pull my nonexistent hair as I forced myself through the door. I made it past the desk clerk and onto the walkway. Poom, wrapped in a white bath towel, came out, crying hysterically. "Nooooo! Noooooo! *Pay me now!*" The desk clerk stood looking through the window as a passive observer. I continued walking toward the darkened street. Poom ran after me, reached from behind, and tore the glasses off my face. I turned around and she teased me with the glasses—repeatedly holding them out and pulling them away when I reached out.

"Pay me!"

"Keep the glasses," I said and continued toward the street.

I felt something light and plastic hit the back of my head. I bent down to pick up my glasses and saw Poom running back toward the guesthouse.

On a dark street outside the guesthouse
4:05 a.m.

I walked for a few minutes towards the highway, or what I thought was the highway, traveling by sense of sound, and it sounded like the highway was in the east. There were no streetlights, and except for a couple of stray dogs, the neighborhood was abandoned. Frankly, I wasn't really looking around—I was looking straight ahead. Scared out of my mind.

A few cars slowed down to check me out as they passed, and each time I thought it was either the police or Poom's brothers. And then in the distance, I saw the lights of a taxi headed towards me. I immediately began waving my arms to signal the driver. The taxi approached, passed me, and slammed on the brakes. The driver quickly reversed and rolled down the window. He was wearing a N.Y. Yankees hat.

"What *the fuck* are you doing out here?" the driver cried in perfect English. I detected an East Coast accent.

"I don't know."

"Get in, *now!*" I climbed into the taxi. "You are one lucky son of a bitch, let me tell you that," the driver said.

"Thank you so much for stopping." I sighed. "You have no idea what I've been through tonight."

"Yeah, well, where do you want to go? You can tell me about it on the way."

"Soi Nana."

9

Beer and Loathing on the Asian Riviera

The taxi driver was a decent guy. Following my brief outline of the previous incident with Poom, he said, "That's Bangkok, my friend. You're taking a big risk with the freelancers. If you want to get laid, go to Pattaya."

During the drive back to Bangkok, the driver proceeded to tell me his life story. His name was Tran, an American-born Thai. Wife and three kids back in Trenton, New Jersey—slight Jersey accent. He was taking care of his terminally ill father, who coincidentally lived in the neighborhood where the incident occurred with Poom. The taxi license belonged to his father, who was too stubborn to sell it off, which is exactly what Tran said he would do once the old man passed away. Meanwhile, he said he loved driving around Bangkok because "it's like driving in the U.S. minus the rules." I was his first fare of the morning, obviously, he said. Once we were back in the city, I only asked if he could take me to a decent hotel.

Tran dropped me off in front of a semi-posh hotel. I gave him 1,000 baht (US$30), which was three times the meter. He wished me well and repeated, "Pattaya is where it's at."

It was almost 5:00 a.m. when I walked into the lobby of the Grace Hotel. Three guys were on duty: a clerk, a bellhop, and a security guard. I asked for a room.

"One room, three thousand baht," the clerk said.

"Jesus," I sighed. "You take credit cards?"

"MasterCard only, sir."

"Look, I only want the room for a couple of hours. Can I get a discount?"

"I'm sorry, sir." He seemed disappointed *in me.*

"OK, no. I'm sorry. I was just asking."

"The rate includes a complimentary breakfast buffet, sir." He smiled. *Thailand. The Land of Smiles.* Three thousand baht is a lot of money in Thailand, like US$100, but I was tired and freaked out. I handed over my credit card. The bellhop escorted me to the elevator. The room was nice.

I decided to head for Pattaya as soon as possible, but first, I needed to shower, change clothes, and maybe get an hour of sleep. After a long, hot shower, I sat on the edge of the bed and realized that sleeping was impossible. The adrenaline was still pumping. Staying in the room seemed pointless. I didn't come to Bangkok to lounge around in a fluffy bathrobe and watch TV. My next thought was to have a couple of beers and relax. I quickly dressed and took the elevator to the lobby. The clerks gave me odd looks as I headed out to the street. I walked for five minutes before I found a beer bar still doing business.

Bangkok is an eerie place to be drinking at dawn. Many of the outdoor beer bars stay open 24/7. The law says you have to turn off the music and any unnecessary lighting if you want to stay open. So, mostly what you hear is chatter from the bar girls and the occasional "Welcome!" said to passing men.

There were a few grizzled Westerners at the bar, very clearly inebriated and not interested in me. The feeling was mutual. I ordered a beer. A bar girl immediately appeared next to me. "Hello, welcome," she said.

"Thanks," I said. "I just want to have a few drinks."

"OK OK." She went away. I managed to choke down three beers before the sun came up.

The walk back to the hotel was surreal. The first light of morning is special no matter where you go. Walking through Bangkok at dawn is when you see the casualties of the previous night. All the debris and puddles of unknown origin.

Back in the hotel room, I spent an hour reading and re-reading the section about Pattaya in *The Rough Guide to Thailand*. Suddenly, I got hungry, so I packed and left the room. The place was so nice I was tempted to go back and smooth out the bedcover where I sat.

I walked out of the elevator and into the second-floor restaurant. If I had been holding something, I would have dropped it. I cried out loud, *"Are you fuckin' kidding me!?"*

The place was crawling with Arab guys in white cotton *dishdashahs* and winter-season *shumagg* headdresses. A few women were covered head-to-toe in black fabric. I stopped in my tracks, and so did everybody else in the joint. If a record had been playing, the needle would have scratched across the vinyl. The last time I felt so instantly uncomfortable was when I stumbled into a gangster bar in Taipei. Only this time I didn't flee the scene. The initial shock of being the only bald American in the room was brief. I made a very cursory pass of the buffet spread. Almost everything was *halal*. I wasn't hungry anymore. I drank a glass of orange juice and beat it down to the lobby. I dropped the key card on the front desk and walked out. One of the dayshift clerks chased me out to the street with my receipt. "You need a taxi?" he asked.

"No, thanks."

The bone-rattling bus ride to Pattaya could have been worse. There could have been a screaming child or a carsick pregnant woman in the seat next to me. The driver could have leaned on the horn or slammed on the brakes every time he passed a semi-truck at 100 km per hour. No, wait. *That's exactly how it was.* I stared out the window and pretended I wasn't hurtling down the road toward my death. There isn't much to see on the ride from Bangkok to Pattaya, but it's a damn good thing I was paying attention to where we were going. The guidebook and the woman who sold me the ticket said it was a two-hour ride to Pattaya. The bus seemed to stop at random places along the way. Three hours into it, I noticed that the bus had long since passed a sign for Central Pattaya. It occurred to me that the terminal stop of the bus was not Pattaya but somewhere much further down the road. I got off the next time the bus stopped with a vague idea of my location.

A motorcycle taxi approached with a freshly lit cigarette dangling from his mouth. I said, "Pattaya" and he said, "Three hundred baht." Roughly US$10. *Deal.*

Scared and melting are not conducive. I lost count of how many times I almost fell off the back of the bike. My thighs were burning from clamping down on the seat frame and my knuckles were frozen in rictus from gripping the rear sissy bar. Twenty hair-raising minutes later, the driver dropped me off on Central Pattaya Road. I walked around for a long, sweaty hour. I wasn't ready to settle on a hotel room just yet. Maybe I'd go back to Bangkok. Pattaya is serious sex tourism. I wasn't certain this was a place I wanted to be. Beer bars as far as the eye can see. Even in the afternoon, sex was dripping from the power lines overhead. And the humidity was killing me. After making a loop of Beach Road, I stopped in a Thai version of 7-Eleven for a bottle of water. I was passing through Soi 7 when I came across a couple of backpackers. They were taking a break in the shade. I noticed that the guy was reading the *Lonely Planet Thailand* book. I approached and said, "Hello! How you guys doing today?"

Reg and Diane were an early-30s married couple from South Africa, at the end of a year-long backpacking journey around Asia. They had just crossed over from Cambodia and were making their way towards Bangkok for Johannesburg. They were both deeply tanned and reeking of patchouli and body odor. Diane said they really weren't sure why they were in Pattaya but that's where the bus stopped and...

"I bought the wrong bus tickets," Reg said apologetically toward Diane.

I took off my backpack and sat in the shade next to Reg, comparing notes about hotels. Reg and I bantered for a while as Diane did some sort of yoga stretching. Their M.O. was budget-level guesthouses, less than 600 baht a night. Diane vividly recalled the jungle hut they had previously occupied in Cambodia, and waking up to find a "gorgeous snake" curled at the foot of her sleeping bag.

The three of us walked back to Second Pattaya Road where Reg pointed at a guesthouse and said, "That place looks kekker." Five hundred baht per night. The rooms were situated above a beer bar. The people were super nice, but the room was awful. I didn't even ask about internet access. At that point, I was happy to have a place to put my backpack. Reg and Diane took the room next door, and I could clearly hear their conversation as I got in the shower for a cold-water splashdown.

It was late afternoon, and Reg was already in the beer bar enjoying a cold Singha when I popped in with my laptop. The beer bar itself was quite small; the size of an average Asian storefront. The sound system was good. A young girl approached and handed me a full-blown menu. I pointed at Reg's beer and said, "I think I need one of those."

"What?" the girl said.

"I'm sorry," I said. "A bottle of Singha, please."

"Ohh-kaaay. Seventy baht." She held out her hand. In Pattaya, you pay for the beer in advance.

With my laptop in tow, I tried to poach the bar's wireless connection, but it didn't work. Oh well. I had a hard time getting the beer down and paying attention to Reg's story about Laos in which they saw a guy on a motorcycle get decapitated by a truck door that swung open unexpectedly.

A few girls began to appear and loiter from the sidewalk. The *mamasan* came over and Reg waved her off, so she sat next to me and held my hand. She asked if I had a girlfriend yet and how long did I want to stay in Pattaya? Reg was very amused. Eventually, the *mamasan* gave up and left me alone. Diane showed up and suggested we have dinner together; Reg had a taste for green curry.

Just about the last place I expected to find a decent Thai green curry was at an Austrian restaurant called Domicil on Second Road, but that's where we wound up. I ordered the Chef's salad. Reg raved about the curry. Diane had the schnitzel and said it was quite tasty. They were both interesting people and I enjoyed their travel stories. Their use of South African slang was simultaneously endearing and confusing. After dinner and another beer, I began to wind down.

"We're just now scheming to make a round of the bars in the gully," Reg said. "You're welcome to join us."

"Thanks for the invitation but I'm going to turn in for the night."

"Shot, bruh. Then we'll catch up with you in the morning." We settled the bill, and I bid them good luck and farewell. I didn't plan on ever seeing them again.

It was 8:00 p.m. when I went back to the guest house and fell asleep face down on the bed. I didn't know what time it was when I woke to the sound of Reg and Diane arguing loudly. I could hear every word. It was a lot of "Well, fuck off then" and zippers to backpacks opening and shutting.

"Don't give me that kak. You're a rotten wanker."

"Ag, fuck off, you've been a chot since Ho Chi Min."

And they left, slamming the door on the way out. I lay there in the dark for a while before stirring. Then I got up, turned on the light, double-checked to make sure I wasn't forgetting anything, and left the room. The clock above the check-out desk said 7:50 a.m.

"Your friends leave," the clerk said as I handed her the key.

"Yes, thank you."

Out on Second Road the morning heat was already oppressive. I walked up and down a few side streets (*soi*) until I came across a decent-enough-looking joint called Flipper House. I don't remember what floor the room was on, but it was 1,200 baht a night (US$40); there was a sweet rooftop pool with a swim-up aqua bar. The towels were nice. I showered, put on my surf shorts, and made a beeline for the pool. I hadn't been in a rooftop swimming pool for quite some time, so I was excited about doing something. It was 9:00 a.m.

I had the pool to myself for half an hour. The bar wasn't officially open but there was a team of kids to hustle items from the restaurant on the main floor or make you a cappuccino. Around 9:35 a.m., a mixed couple with an infant son sat on the lounge chairs across the pool from me. The man was short, stocky, white, balding, hairy like a gorilla, British, wearing green-tinted sunglasses and in his late 40s. He had a bottle of beer in his right hand. The woman was also very short, but thin, brown, with a full head of black hair and certain facial features that said she was Southeast Asian and hardly spoke a word of English. The child was healthy and happy, and his skin tone tended toward the brown. The woman and child played in the pool while the man lay there smoking and drinking. Occasionally, he would scold the woman and say, "Don't let 'em put that in his fucking gob, for chrissakes." She was indifferent and only paid attention to the child. The man signaled a server. Two young, uniformed Thai kids came over and stood attentively. "Yeah, I'll 'ave another Heineken." He then said to the woman. "Right, tell the bloody sheep what you want."

Enough pool time.

I was walking south on along the beach side of Beach Road. It was 10:15 a.m. A short Thai dude wearing a Bob Marley shirt approached and said furtively, "I got the smoke, I got the smoke."

"How much?"

"Three hundred baht, small bag." (US$10)

"Give me two."

We stopped in front of a jet ski rental operation. I handed him the money, he handed me the weed. I put it in my pocket and started walking north. I stopped in several convenience stores on the walk back to the Flipper House, looking to buy rolling papers, to no avail. Then I remembered the first place I stopped to buy a bottle of water; the phony 7-Eleven.

Back in my room, I surveyed the product. The quality was shit but there was a lot of it for 20 bucks. I made short work of rolling half a dozen joints. I smoked one and felt pretty good. I took my third shower of the day, and it wasn't even noon. Then I walked out of the hotel, made a left, toward the beach, and stopped at the first beer bar, Rosie O'Grady's Irish Pub. I ordered a lemonade. An attractive, busty young woman approached. We talked for a few minutes before she asked if I wanted short-time or long-time. "Short-time," I said.

I paid the bar fine and we went back to my room. Afterward, the woman told me to come back and see her tonight; something about being her "butterfly" and we could have long-time. *No, I don't think so.* I paid her and we parted with a dry kiss. *Let's cross Rosie O'Grady's Irish Pub off the list.*

The Reuben sandwich at Domicil was delicious when washed down with a few beers. I returned to the hotel and smoked another joint before heading back out. I walked around for ten minutes before stopping at a place called Eager Beaver and saddled up to the bar. November in Pattaya is sort of a transition period from low to high season, so I was the only white guy in a beer bar on that side of Soi 7 as far as I could see. When you're the only customer in a Pattaya beer bar, expect a lot of attention. Even the *mamasan* asked if I'd buy her a "lady drink," which is fucking ridiculous, but I said, "OK, sure" and the next thing I knew, I was surrounded by girls. It was like feeding birds in a park. Word gets around fast.

We pause here again to clarify some prostitution lingo and protocols. A "lady drink" is an overpriced beverage that you can purchase from the bar, for the prostitute (or bar girl), which all but guarantees the "lady" in question has accepted your invitation for social interaction and will keep you company for 20 minutes or however long it takes her to finish the drink, at which point, you will make a decision. One, buy her another drink. Two, forget about it and move on. Or three, inquire about the bar fine and negotiate a rate for the lady. On average, lady drinks cost twice the usual price.

Two of the bar girls were late-20s hardened hookers and didn't press. They were interested in doing business, but after all, it was only four in the afternoon. They let the third girl, a fresh-faced rookie named Suripon, do her thing. She called me "darling" and made gratuitous body contact. Her English was poor but the *mamasan* was eager to translate if I kept those lady drinks coming. During our conversation, Suripon rubbed me into a hard-on, which she announced to her co-workers by saying "Wah!" with a raised left fist, her right hand grabbing the mid-forearm.

The *mamasan* waddled away and returned with an elaborately carved, upwardly bent wooden penis. "You are good!" she said. As it were, the wooden penis was attached to an ashtray and the *mamasan* implied that I was to use it during my next cigarette, which, not coincidentally, was hanging from my lips. Suriporn produced a lighter and said, "Darling." I repeatedly pushed the wooden penis ashtray back toward the *mamasan* and said, "I don't want this thing." They were all amused.

Suripon wanted to play a game of pool, but I refused to get up off the bar stool. She was teasing. She knew I didn't want to stand up with that hard-on. She repeatedly made fun of the pre-cum stain developing near the left front pocket of my olive green six-pocket shorts. "Do you want long-time or short-time?" the *mamasan* asked.

"Short-time."

"Why not long-time? Suri is a good girl. You are her first customer."
I waved her off. "Short-time only."

After a few beers, I paid the bar fine and we went to my room. Two hours later I paid her, and she left. Suripon was great. I really liked her. She was 26, from the north somewhere around Chiang Mai, and I don't doubt for a minute that I was her first Pattaya customer. As I was getting dressed to go back out, I had a change of heart. *Damn, she would have been a good long-time.* But I'd already been laid twice in under eight hours.

After dinner at Domicil (Chef's salad, again) I took a *songathew* (small bus) down to Walking Street, which is infamous for go-go bars.

Go-go bars are distinct from beer bars with bar girls. Go-go bars generally feature scantily clad dancing women, sometimes on stage or the bartop. Most go-go bars have showtimes and various "spotlight" performances. It really depends on where you are, but almost *nobody* goes to a go-go bar to "hang out." You go there to ogle the "talent" and pick a hooker. It's kind of like a retail showroom. Aside from the bartenders and *mamasans*, every woman working in a go-go bar has a price.

After a cursory loop around Walking Street, I beat it back to the main road, feeling queasy. Along the beach promenade, there were a shocking number of underaged girls, about 50 for every bald, pot-bellied loveless bastard on the prowl. *This is madness! What am I doing here?* This...this was not right. It was wrong. A 15-year-old girl shouldn't be out here offering to blow scumbags for 20 dollars, and I shouldn't be out here saying, "No, thanks, honey. Maybe next time."

And you know what would make me feel better right now? *Ladyboys.*

Crossing the First Road, I made my way to Boys Town and posted up in the first ladyboy bar on the path. The bartender was on the mannish side of the spectrum, but the rest of the boys were *on fire!* It just cheered me up. These guys were not fucking around, for real. If you met one of these ladyboys in a straight bar, you wouldn't know they were boys until you took 'em home or did a spot check on-site.

I ordered a beer and a minute later, a gorgeous ladyboy came over, and stroked my shoulder.

I said, "I'm just here to hang out."

"OK, G.I." he/she said facetiously. "You're bald and ugly anyway."

He/she started sashaying away when I said, "But I have money. And you...aren't getting any of it." The pretty boy spun around, winked and smiled.

The ladyboy fascination lasts about ten minutes or one beer. Whichever comes first. In this case, it was one beer. I left and walked back towards Flipper House, stopping for beers at a series of bars on the way—five or six bars. I met a few people. I don't remember anybody.

Back at the hotel, I smoked a joint and went up to the deserted rooftop pool. I floated on my back in complete silence for at least an hour. At midnight, one of the hotel security guards came by, rapping his flashlight on the aluminum exit ladders, and told me the pool was closed for the night. I got out, dried off, and went back to my room.

The next morning, I woke up simultaneously refreshed and spent. With two more days, I didn't know what to do with the time. Day drinking was on the table.

After wandering around the mall, I went back down to the Eager Beaver to see if Suripon was there. The *mamasan* told me to come back at 2:00 p.m. when Suripon began her shift. I heard her say "butterfly." In Thai prostitution lingo, a butterfly is a man who develops a crush on a certain hooker and routinely seeks her services. For example, in China, I was Fang-fang's butterfly.

Leaving the Beaver, I went back to the beach, stopping in a few beer bars along the strip. I talked to a handful of sexpats, got depressed, and went back to the hotel. I got high and hit the rooftop pool. There was a group of deeply tanned, middle-aged Aussies, who took up half of the east end of the pool. They were talking about their escapades from the previous night and a two-day trip to one of the nearby islands, Ko Samet. At the far end of the pool, a pair of Brits were sunning themselves on lounge chairs, barking like tattooed sea lions. After an hour or so my skin began to tingle so I left. I didn't bother to change out of my wet surf shorts or put on a shirt as I padded down to Domicil once again for lunch. I had the schnitzel. Not bad. From there I returned to the Eager Beaver to find Suripon.

No sooner than I reached the pool table, Suripon called out, "Darling!" and approached with a wide smile and gave me a tight embrace and warm kiss.

"You want long-time with me?" she asked.

"Yes." I paid the bar fine on the spot. We drank at the bar for an hour or so before returning to Flipper House.

★✳★

Pattaya is the Asian Riviera for sex tourism, a sleazier, tropical version of Amsterdam. Pattaya deserves some sort of Nobel Peace Prize because God only knows what the world would be like if there wasn't a place for fat, bald, middle-aged deadbeats to get some love. *All these hopeless men. All these unfortunate women.* It's a twisted, false paradise for everybody involved.

I was fascinated and heartbroken by the collection of working girls. Estimates ranged from 6,000 to 20,000 women working in Pattaya. Most were farm girls from the northern parts of Thailand, Laos, Cambodia, and Vietnam. Most sex tourists at this time were Northern European. I met a few Americans, Aussies, Kiwis, Canadians, and a Chinese tour group at the airport. Throw in a few creepy Middle Eastern thugs and Soviet Block retirees wearing expensive and tacky attire. Russian fashion seemed to be, "I want to look as ridiculous as possible for as much as you can charge me."

I'm not "good-looking" by any metrics or measurement, but I had never seen so many ugly, awkward men in one place. An all-day parade of prehistoric caveman archetypes slouching toward genetic extinction. Everybody has an acceptable level of shame by association, but just *being in* Pattaya, never mind participating in the business, scratched that self-loathing itch.

★✳★

The morning after the long-time with Suripon, I moved to the Golden Beach Hotel a few blocks away for my final night in town. I'd leave for Bangkok early in the morning and catch a late-night flight back to Taipei.

The Golden Beach wasn't a bad spot. I went for a swim in the pool, had some *pad thai* in the restaurant, and took another long nap. I woke around 8:00 p.m. and didn't feel like traveling far from the hotel. There was a beer bar next door, so I settled in at a table near the front window and started drinking. It was only a matter of time before the bar girls on the sidewalk came for me.

The sound system was bumping current and classic rock music, which was nice. I wouldn't *not* go into a bar because they were playing "It's Getting Hot in Here", but if the joint next door was blasting "Welcome to the Jungle", that's where I'd go instead. Tonight, the music made me feel just a little less morose; strange to say, but side one of *Appetite for Destruction* was somehow comforting.

Watching all the characters passing by—mostly hookers and johns—I felt a slight twinge of relief. *Not me, tonight. I'm getting the fuck out of here tomorrow.* A cute chubby girl approached from the sidewalk and made conversation. Despite making it clear that I wanted to be left alone, she wouldn't stop. *Where are you from? What are you doing in Pattaya?* Et cetera. We talked for a while, and I focused on asking her questions in the same manner. Turns out she was 19, from somewhere up north.

I asked, "Why are you doing this?" as in, why are you a bar girl and turning tricks? And she replied, "I'm doing this to support my family. My father died and we are very poor." You could bank on that story from *every single hooker in Asia*. They were the most altruistic fuckers on the planet. So many life-saving fundraisers for grandmas who need a kidney.

The girl seemed genuine or naïve, can't be sure. I bought her a lady drink but never asked her name. Fifteen minutes or so passed and she bluntly asked if I wanted to pay the bar fine and take her upstairs? She was extremely sweet and relatively wholesome for the trade, but *too young*. Nineteen might make her a woman, but she had about two years of life on her. I politely declined, and she looked hurt, albeit in some small way. I'm sure it was the money.

The *mamasan* came over and they spoke in Thai. The girl got up, said goodbye, and went back to working the sidewalk, trying to drag other foreigners into the bar for a drink. The bar girls in Pattaya are trained to never take no for an answer. It's pretty annoying and aggressive. You gotta be like, "No, sorry, fuck off" if you want to make any progress down the street.

A numbness started to creep, so I ordered one last beer and paid my tab. I sat there watching the girl out on the sidewalk. Now and then she shot me a most disappointed and plaintive look. It gave me goosebumps. An unfamiliar song started to play, and something about it just hit me in the chest from the very beginning. It was "Use Somebody" by Kings of Leon, who I'd never even heard of.

I've been roamin' around, always lookin' down at all I see
Painted faces fill the places I can't reach
You know that I could use somebody
You know that I could use somebody

The music moved me to overwhelming sadness. The women, the scene, the previous night, my life—everything. If I were not in public, I probably would have wept openly. For the first time since I left San Francisco for Taiwan, I felt a staggering sense of self-loathing, buttressed by the reconciliation between right and wrong.

★ ✱ ★

My story is particularly contentious because it involves right and wrong, good and evil. My conscience is equally divided; half the time, I think it's a terrible story to tell, and the other half, I think it's the responsible thing to do. The twain shall never meet. Perhaps it's possible to be all things at once. Maybe my conscience will allow these two equal and opposite ideas to co-exist in the absence of objective merit.

Traveling and doing a bunch of greasy and illegal shit in foreign countries is not a noble pursuit. It makes for good storytelling, but otherwise, I walked in limbo between a missionary and a mercenary. This version of tourism was exhilarating and frightening, but it's not worthy of an "Attaboy!" or a pat on the back. Therefore, I'm not concerned that writing about it might seem self-congratulatory. I'm telling you the story and you can make of it what you will.

When things got dark, I kept repeating one of the Captain's mantras: "Don't think too much." *You think too much, Charlie.*

The Year of the Tiger symbolizes resilience, optimism, and fearlessness.

10

Guangzhou's Shooting Star

Felix didn't really *ask* about Thailand when I returned to the office. He signaled toward Daisy and said, "Charlie! You're back. So good to see you." A few minutes later, Daisy went to the kitchen for a cup of tea. The Captain leaned over and said, "Tell me all about it later."

★

As the year-end holidays approached, once again, Felix and Daisy were bugging me about travel plans. They were headed to Beijing for two weeks. Felix thought I should return to the U.S. for Christmas, but I refused. Daisy said she didn't care what I did as long as I wasn't "spending the holidays alone." Ultimately, I spent Christmas and New Year's Eve in Taipei, hanging out in the dorm, writing during the day, and prowling around the bars at night.

January was a blur. There were books to write and dictionaries to edit. I didn't have time to think about traveling. Fang kept popping up in text messages, but I hardly replied with anything of substance. Captain Felix kept leaning on me about Chinese New Year, just around the corner. The Year of the Ox would meet the Year of the Tiger. I finally told Captain Felix I would return to see my friends in Guangzhou. He wasn't enthusiastic about the decision, but he didn't give a shit. A round-trip ticket to Hong Kong was on my desk before the end of the day.

Drugs were the main motivation for returning to Guangzhou. It had nothing to do with my "friends," who didn't exist. During last year's lunar holiday, I met a group of dudes in a bar called Elephant & Castle. I hung out with them for several nights over a week. They were fleeting acquaintances, but I remembered a few by name. I hardly expected to see them ever again. Guangzhou was the one place in Asia where I could get my hands on some weed or hash, which became increasingly imperative because Martin went missing in action at the end of December.

∗✱∗

For the previous year and a half, Martin was my sole source of weed in Taipei. We hooked up once a month like clockwork. Martin was a rich kid from a rich family with a rich wife. His gangster connection was solid but pricey. After our second "drop" in public, Martin trusted me enough to pick up the weed at his home in Ximen. He introduced me to his wife Josephine and their two young daughters. We had several family dinners together. The whole thing was *beautiful.*

Not long before Martin helped me with the Fang situation in Zhuhai, he started to show some off-kilter behaviors here and there. He was more paranoid than usual. I chuckled when he casually mentioned a "porn addiction." But I didn't know him well enough to make a judgment call.

One night in October 2009, we met at Martin's place to make the drop. His wife and daughters weren't there, which was odd. Martin said they were at his in-laws' house in Taoyuan. He had deep black circles under his eyes and the usually pristine, modern apartment was a junkie mess. I didn't want to press him, so I gently asked if everything was alright. His response was a gut punch.

"Dude, my wife hates me. My dad and I aren't getting along. My brother wants to kill me, and my in-laws want to help him."

"What *the fuck* is going on, man?"

Martin paused. "Meth."

I was shocked. "*Meth!?*' M-E-T-H, *methamphetamine?*"

"Dude, I've been doing a lot of meth."

I took a massive deep breath. "Are you high right now?"

"No, I'm clean. I stopped using when Josephine took the girls to her parents' house. She says she's not coming back unless I've been clean for two weeks."

"How long has this been going on?"

"A year."

"When did Josephine find out?"

"Dude, she was using *with me*. After Miu-miu (his youngest daughter) stopped breastfeeding."

"Is she clean now?"

"What do you think she's doing at her parents' house?"

My heart sank. "That's no fucking joke, man."

He waved me off. "I'm the one who's been using for a year."

I exhaled several times and shook my head. "*Martin...*"

"It's totally fucked up. But I'm gonna stay clean and fix things. I'm not about to lose my daughters."

We met again in November and Martin said he was still clean. Josephine and the girls were home, and the five of us had take-out dim sum in their dining room. Martin said he mended fences with his dad and brother. In December, he didn't want to meet at his place, so he picked me up in his BMW and we drove up to Elephant Mountain, where we smoked a joint and talked for a while. Everything seemed back to normal.

Two days after Christmas, Martin called around 6:00 p.m. and offered to make an early pickup for January.

"Sure," I said. "I'm always happy to score."

What a fucking dummy. I should have noticed the red flag. We *never* spoke about weed on the phone. **Never.** It was rule number one. We used code phrases like 'have dinner' and 'go for a beer.'

Martin said, "It's gonna be a little different this time. I'll come pick up the cash now and drop off the weed later tonight."

Second red flag: Martin *never* mentioned money over the phone or asked for cash in advance, which would have meant we had to meet twice for every transaction.

"Sounds like a plan."

An hour later, Martin picked me up outside the dorm. We drove around the block, and I gave him the cash. He dropped me off in front of the dorm and said, "Alright, I'll be back in about an hour. I'll call you."

I never saw or heard from Martin again—ever. When he didn't show up that evening, I figured he got hung up somewhere, so I didn't worry about it too much. But when he didn't answer my texts and calls the next day, I knew something bad was afoot. *Maybe he got picked up by the cops?* I kept trying to get in touch through the New Year, but like I said, he never replied. Sometime in early January, I went to his apartment building and asked the security guard to call upstairs. The guard called, spoke to someone, hung up the phone, shook his head and said, "Beat it, pal. They don't want to see you."

Several weeks later, I was talking to Wilson, who had originally hooked me up with Martin. I told him the story and Wilson said, "Oh yeah, man, Martin is known for ripping people off. I should have warned you about that. Sorry."

"Do you know what happened?"

"He relapsed, bad. I think he wound up in rehab for a while. I'd stay away from him if I were you."

"Given that he owes me money and isn't returning my phone calls, I don't think that's going to be a problem."

A week before I left for Guangzhou, Fang called and asked about my travel plans for the Chinese New Year. In the most non-committal and passive tone, I told her I'd be in Guangzhou for a few days and probably go somewhere else. She said she'd fly from Ningxia to Zhuhai on February 17. Did I want to see her? I said yes, I'd like to see you, but my travel plans haven't been settled. "Really? You want to see me?" Her tone was scolding and unconvinced.

"I'm flying to Hong Kong on the fifteenth. I'll know more then." This was a lie. My flight left on February 13.

"Keep me posted," she replied.

I had no intention of calling her. But if she called me...?

★ ✱ ★

Saturday, February 13, 2010

The first day of a nine-day holiday and Chinese New Year's Eve. I flew into Hong Kong and took the train to Guangzhou, which was almost as easy as flying direct. The Guangzhou airport was located way out of town. Traffic to and from the city center was atrocious. I booked two nights at the Ocean Hotel on Huanshe East Road, very near the intersection of Jianshe Sixth Road—where the drug dealers hung out—and from there I would play it by ear. Once I scored some decent stuff, I would decide whether to move on or stay put.

The flight to Hong Kong was scheduled for 8:30 a.m., so I had to get up at 5:30 a.m. to make the flight. I jumped in a taxi just before dawn. There was a soft purple light over Taipei. Traffic to the airport in Taoyuan was minimal. and I was pleasantly surprised by the lack of crowds in the departure terminal. The flight was almost empty. I could have counted every passenger on the A330—a sizable aircraft. Landed in Hong Kong at 10:30 a.m., cleared immigration and customs around 11:00. Took the Airport Express MTR to Jordan/Kowloon and walked down to Tsim Sha Shui. It was a cold and blustery morning. The soft light of the sun was now dull and gray.

I booked an advance ticket on the 2:47 p.m. fast train to Guangzhou, so I had time to kill in Hong Kong. *Again.* So I headed to Chungking Mansions and made one pass of Nathan Road to see if I could score some hash. At least a dozen guys tried to sell me a suit or a watch, but no hashish. I wandered among the cell phone booths and Pakistani food vendors for 20 minutes or so. Nothing better to do, I wound up walking to the Hung Hom Rail Station, which was crawling with humanity—the New Year's travel madness I was expecting. It was 12:30 p.m.—still two hours to kill—so I cruised around the main floor of the departure hall, looking for a place to sit and read a book. No such luck. As a last resort, I went upstairs to McDonald's, ordered a double cheeseburger meal, posted up on a shockingly cozy chair, and turned to the first page of *Then We Came to the End* by Joshua Ferris.

The train to Guangzhou was relatively uneventful. We arrived at the Guangzhou East Rail Station just before 5:00 p.m., by which time I'd wiped out 200-plus pages of the Ferris novel. After clearing immigration, there was a secondary security check—a single X-ray machine and two uniformed security guards standing at opposite ends of the machine. Several hundred converging bodies funneled into a two-meter-wide lane, trying to get their luggage on the conveyor belt at the same time. There was a lot of pushing and a bit of shoving involved. I joined the scrum for a few minutes before I noticed a few guys casually stroll past the crowd and the security guards without having their luggage screened.

The guards were beyond overwhelmed—their faces pinched and helpless. I wedged out of the throng, walked around the metal rails of the lane, and passed the guards without making eye contact. I noticed the X-ray machine video monitor wasn't even turned on. Against my better judgment, about 20 yards past the checkpoint, I looked over my shoulder to see that almost everybody else in the line had followed my lead.

The taxi line was long and unruly. A tout approached and offered to take me to my hotel for 100 yuan, which I laughed off.

"*Tai gui le ma!*" I said. (Too expensive!)

"How much do you want to pay?"

"I'll give you 50 yuan."

He laughed in my face. "Chinese New Year's Eve price. You won't find better."

"No thanks."

Walking toward the McDonald's on the corner, a green taxi pulled up with his window down. "A hundred yuan," he said. It was cold and raining and even though I knew it was a 20-yuan fare to the hotel, I agreed and climbed inside the sedan.

It was 6:00 p.m. when I checked in to my business suite at the Ocean Hotel, a four-star lodging on Huanshe East Road, across the street from a Holiday Inn. I don't know what this room went for during the high season but I'm sure I couldn't afford it. I booked it online for US$50 a night, which was a steal. I took a shower, re-dressed, and walked down to Jianshe Sixth Road. Ten minutes later I paid 100 yuan (about US$15) for a gram of hash from a short, glassy-eyed Nigerian street dealer in a leather jacket. There was very little chit-chat. We saw each other coming and made eye contact in front of the Starbucks.

"I got the good stuff," the dealer said, eyes flashing as we met. He quickly turned and walked alongside me.

"What you got?"

He grinned and shrugged. "What do you want?"

"Hash."

"I got hash."

"How much?"

"One hundred for a gram. It's all I have on me."

"Meet me on the bridge," I said. The dealer made a quick U-turn and headed in the opposite direction. I climbed the stairs to the pedestrian bridge over Huanshe East Road and waited. A minute later, the dealer showed up and handed me the compressed black tar in a small baggie. I put it to my nose and caught a wispy aroma of opium. "If it's good," I said, handing over the cash, "I'll be back for more."

"Take my phone number," he handed me a small scrap of paper with his name, Marcus, and an 11-digit number. And we parted ways.

Sometimes it's unnerving when everything goes exactly as planned. I proceeded to the other side of the bridge and into the Elephant & Castle, which was empty. No sign of the Nigerians. I was vaguely hoping to see Monty or Steve, two pub regulars I met last year, but you know how that goes. Though I'd only hung out with them for a few nights, Monty said, "If you make it back to Guangzhou, you can find us here."

Trixie (the bartender) recognized me, so we made small talk. I wished her a happy new year and snuck off to the bathroom to get a better look at my purchase. It was good stuff. *Excellent. This will be a good trip after all.*

Two Duvels and three cigarettes later, I was sitting alone at the bar, watching a Filipino dance show on TV. Two foreigners entered and headed back to the pool table. They looked vaguely familiar, but I couldn't be sure. Rather than bumrush their game of pool, I stayed patiently at the bar. Sure enough, a third white guy walked in. It was Monty, the affable California expat who was always making a joke or laughing. He stopped at the bar to buy a beer, and I said, "Hey Monty. Remember me?"

"Oh yeah," Monty said. "I recognize your face, but the name escapes me."

"Charlie. I met you and Steve here during the last Lunar Festival."

"So, you only come around once a year. You're like a comet. You're Guangzhou's shooting star!"

We decamped to the back room where Monty introduced me to the other two foreigners, Eric and Graham. Eric was an American from Ohio in his mid 20s. Nice kid; considered the authority on rolling joints. Graham was an Aussie and a longtime resident of Guangzhou. I liked them both immediately. The four of us switched off playing a game of pool called killer, similar to cut-throat, and drinking beer for an hour. Eric announced, "Monty, it's time to roll one." We convened at a table and they began rolling a nice fat joint of weed. Eric passed the dank green buds under my nose. I offered to share my hash, but he declined, saying it would affect the burn of the joint. Graham and I had a forgettable conversation about expat life.

The rest of the night was mellow and effortless. Nobody mentioned that today was probably the most important Chinese holiday of the year. It was just another night. A few more of the Elephant & Castle crew showed up, plus a British guy named Jeremy. But there was no sign of Steve. We sat around the pool table, drank pint after pint of Carlsberg and Tsingtao, and got high several times. Sufficiently drunk, I got up, said goodbye, and stumbled back to the hotel.

Sunday, February 14, 2010

At 9:00 a.m., I parted the curtains and took in the view from the 15th floor. The sky was uneasy and gloomy, a reciprocity of my attitude. Sensing the onset of a delayed hangover, I made a beeline for the restaurant on the 26th floor just before they shut down the free buffet. Got me a couple of fried eggs, a lukewarm pile of stir-fried noodles, and some toast. Then it was back to bed until mid-afternoon.

Around 3:30 p.m., I woke and immediately smoked more hash—just a little bit. Mildly buzzed, I set off walking toward the far end of Huanshe

East Road, where it turns into Huanshe Middle Road, in search of several recommended Turkish restaurants—not the least bit hungry. This was simply a reconnaissance mission. I came across several places that were closed for the entire holiday. The only place still open, a joint called Bosporus, seemed inviting enough to peruse the menu. It was 4:30 p.m. by the time I found it, with enough of an appetite to sit down for a meal. I had some hummus, curried lamb kebabs, and a meze platter with olives, tomatoes, cucumbers, and slices of Kasseri cheese.

Wiped out again by the time I returned to the hotel and smoked a larger portion of hash and really felt it. Another power nap. I woke around 9:00 p.m. and hit the Cave Bar, just across the street from Elephant & Castle, for happy hour until 10:30 p.m.

I don't know why I went to the Cave Bar. It was too early—the place didn't get busy until midnight. A dozen bar girls were sitting in the booths, and one local guy was at the bar. The staff was disinterested at best and outright hostile at worst. It took 20 minutes for my bottle of Heineken to arrive, and I had to ask for it three times. The girl almost didn't even open it—she set the bottle in front of me and turned away before having a second thought. Other customers straggled in. Not one bar girl approached me, and only a few made meaningful eye contact. As I finished my second beer, a striking couple bounced into the bar and stood near the stools to my left. The guy was tall, East Asian of some ethnicity, I guessed Indian, with a huge shock of wavy black hair, receding quite a bit. He exchanged *"Xin nian kuai le!"* (Happy Chinese New Year) with at least half of the bar staff. A minute later, he was wrapped in a growling bear hug with a little Cantonese guy. His girlfriend-slash-companion was also tall, a Euromutt of unknown pedigree, with sparkling blue eyes and an ugly face, and I'm never the first guy to call someone ugly because I own a mirror. She *oozed* of personality, put it that way. I was tempted to introduce myself since they seemed to be friendly folks, but then I heard the guy say, "Hey, not too bad tonight. Not so many fucking foreigners."

The woman sighed. "Yeah, where do they all come from?"

You fucking assholes are foreigners, too. I knocked back the beer and made a hasty exit.

Eric and Monty were at Elephant & Castle, along with a Chinese guy I met last year, Albert, and an Irish guy named Sean. They said I just missed Steve, who was supposedly on his way to pick up a hooker on Jianshe Sixth Road and take her back to his place.

A few minutes later, a Canadian guy named Calvin showed up, sloppy drunk, also a memory from the last trip. Calvin was funny as shit but not in the sense that you're laughing *with him.* He was a short, stocky dude in his mid 30s and resembled the Little Caesar's "Pizza! Pizza!" cartoon character. Most of all, he loved to hear himself talk. He was harmless when sober, but borderline psychotic when drunk.

Eric's roommate, Tyrone, a British-educated Pakistani national, showed up, trailed by the golf pro from Arizona whose name will always escape me. Again, the whole crew decamped to the pool table while Eric and Monty tag-team rolled a joint, with a bit of good-natured bickering about the right amount of tobacco to mix with the hash. Out of nowhere, a Nigerian guy named Sonny appeared. Albert stood up and made a deal for a gram of hash. I noticed Sonny gave it to him for 75 yuan. Curious, I approached Sonny and asked, "Do you have any more of that?" After a bit of haggling, he offered to sell me four grams for 200 yuan. *Deal.*

Monday, February 15, 2010

I woke up around 10:30 a.m., too late for the complimentary breakfast at the rooftop restaurant. I quickly dressed and left the hotel. *Goddamn, it was cold,* around 3°C/37°F, frosty by Southeast Asian standards. It hadn't been that cold in Taipei all winter. It was a brisk 10-minute walk down to the Starbucks at Jianshe Sixth Road. I got a large black coffee and recognized the ugly white woman from the Cave Bar last night, sitting alone, smiling into a cell phone. No sign of the hyper-kinetic Indian guy. *Why does she look so fucking satisfied with herself?*

From there, a 15-minute walk to the brand-spanking-new Taojin MTR station on Line 5, heading for Zhujiang Xincheng (Zhujiang New City). I was looking for a restaurant called Gail's, which was supposedly *the* place for authentic American comfort food in Guangzhou. Emerging from the subway exit, I found myself in a deserted office district. I walked for 30 minutes in two different directions and didn't find Gail's. An hour later I found myself in Tianhe, standing in front of the semi-famous

Tee Mall. Hungry and dismayed by the rote selection of crap fast food (Kung Fu, KFC, McDonald's), I got back on the subway and returned to the hotel. The restaurant on the 26th floor was empty at 1:30 p.m.

After lunch, I went down to the lobby and extended my room for another two days. Then I got high and crashed for the afternoon.

My cell phone started buzzing around 4:00 p.m. and I knew it was Fang. Nobody else in mainland China had my number. Finally, around 5:00 p.m. I got up and checked the call log. She had called a dozen times and left three messages. I called her back and she answered furiously, "*What are you doing? Where are you?*"

"I was sleeping."

She was not amused, spitting out a long stream of Chinese, none of which I caught except, "I'm in Guangzhou now. Where is your hotel?"

Apparently, she decided to change her plans and just show up in Guangzhou instead of Zhuhai—and two days earlier.

From there, the situation descended into a morass of miscommunication: dropped cell phone signals multiplied by our basic inability to communicate across the language barrier. I had no choice but to go down to the front desk and sheepishly ask one of the clerks who spoke English to give directions to Fang's taxi driver. I went back to my room and paced, awaiting her arrival. Fang called again and said they were stuck in traffic.

Fang arrived at 6:30 p.m. and we immediately had sex.

Afterward, in the shower, she asked, "Are we going out tonight?"

"Yes. Where do you want to go?"

"Let's go to the place *you* want to go."

"You work here [in Guangzhou]. Let's go to one of *your* places."

She pinched my arm and said, "We're *not* going *there*."

I was reluctant to take Fang to the Elephant & Castle and felt that bittersweet "I knew this was a bad idea" as soon as we entered the bar. The crew was very polite to Fang, but she wasn't having any of it. Eric spoke good Mandarin, but she rudely brushed off his attempts to start a conversation. Albert sized her up and didn't bother. Fang refused to join us in the back room at the pool table, saying, "Go, have fun with your friends. I'll just sit here and talk to the bartender." I looked at Trixie and said, "You'll take care of her, right?" Trixie rolled her eyes and turned away.

I spent the first hour bouncing back and forth between the back room and Fang at the bar. Monty approached me. "What's up with your lady, man?"

"I dunno. She's in a mood."

"Where'd you find her?"

"You don't want to know."

Monty laughed. "I don't think I do!"

Fang was obviously unhappy, and Trixie seemed annoyed. I was pounding beers because Fang wasn't going to last much longer, and I wanted to get a solid buzz before we returned to the hotel. The night was over. We certainly weren't going to the Cave Bar or the Gipsy Club afterward. Fang had a scary-calm look of irritation.

I was in the back room saying goodbye to the crew when Eric said, "Hey, don't leave yet. I just rolled a joint and we're going to spark it up."

"Alright, I'll have a few tokes."

Fang was *pissed* when we left the bar. She slapped my hand away and stayed two steps ahead as we walked to the hotel. Standing in the elevator, she turned and said, "*Ni you xiguo dama le ma?*" (Were you smoking marijuana?)

"*Shi de. Meishenme dabuliao de.*" (Yeah. It's no big deal.)

She stomped her foot and turned away, disgusted.

Back in the room, she got on the computer and opened a translator. She wrote, "I love you and I want to marry you, but drugs are a dealbreaker."

I didn't know what to say, so I said, "I understand."

She grabbed her phone and went into the bathroom, where she stayed for at least an hour. First, she took a bath. Then I heard her talking in hushed whispers. I drank a few beers from the minibar and watched TV. She came out of the bathroom in her pajamas, said, "Good night," and crawled into bed. I looked over my shoulder and shrugged. It was the first time since we met that we didn't have sex before falling asleep.

Tuesday, February 16, 2010

During breakfast, Fang informed me that she didn't need to return to Zhuhai after all. Aside from that one time in September of last year, I never asked Fang-fang about her "work." She told me that she worked in Guangzhou and Zhuhai, but she never explained what "work" meant. I briefly wondered where she got money because she didn't ask me to pay for her flight from Ningxia to Guangzhou. But then I figured it out.

After breakfast, we returned to the room, and Fang immediately got on the computer, logging on to QQ, the Chinese version of Facebook. I sat Indian-style on the bed, tapping away on my laptop. A few minutes passed and I was confident that she was engrossed in the QQ version of Farmville and chatting with her friends, so I fired up a chunk of hash and got high. Since we're both cigarette smokers and Fang was puffing away on a Shaanxi, I knew she wouldn't notice the smell. And she didn't.

Around 2:00 p.m., Fang got up, undressed, kissed me, and took a shower, our unspoken code for "let's have sex now." I joined her in the shower and that was that. At 4:00 p.m. we got out of bed and resumed our previous positions. An hour later I went down to the lobby shop to buy some beer. We drank the beer, and I went back to writing.

Fang loved Bollywood movies, particularly the music and the dancing. She watched hours of that crap. I inferred that her interest in Indian culture stemmed from one of her encounters with an Indian client. I figured she met some Indian guy who she really liked and suddenly became fascinated with all things Indian.

At 6:00 p.m., Fang said, "I'm hungry, let's eat."

"How about Indian food? There's a place called Ashoka down the street that looks good."

As usual, Fang complained about everything at the Indian restaurant. After dinner, I said, "Let's go for some drinks."

"I don't want to go back to that place."

"Let's just go back to the hotel."

"Fine with me."

I stopped in the lobby shop and bought an armful of beer. Fang went up to the room without me. She was watching a Bollywood movie when I got to the room. I offered her a beer, but she said, "I don't feel like drinking tonight." So, I opened my laptop and resumed writing. When the beer was finished, I climbed into bed and fell asleep. I don't know how long I'd been out when Fang shook me awake and said, "You didn't even say good night!"

"Good night."

Wednesday, February 17, 2010

I was awake before dawn and took a long hot shower. The wheels of my mind needed a serious realignment.

Fang woke up as I left the bathroom. "What are you doing today?" she asked.

"I have work to do. And we're moving to a different hotel at noon." She drifted back to sleep while I got online and booked two nights at another hotel on the other side of town. An hour later she got up, showered, dressed, and stood in front of me. "Are we going to eat?"

"You go ahead. I just want some coffee."

"They have coffee in the restaurant."

"I know. It's too expensive and doesn't taste good. I'll go out and get it at Starbucks."

"But I don't want to eat alone."

"Honey," I pleaded. "*Just go.*" It took a few more minutes of persuading but she finally agreed, and we parted at the elevator.

The travel services office in the lobby sold train tickets to Hong Kong, so I furtively bought one for Sunday morning. The ticket lady said the ticket would be sent up to my room later in the afternoon. I explained that I was checking out at noon, so I needed it before then. "OK," the ticket lady said, "Come back in one hour."

I walked down to the Starbucks on Jianshe Sixth Road and bought a coffee. An hour later I returned to the Ocean Hotel, but the ticket hadn't arrived. "It will be here in thirty minutes," the ticket lady assured me. I went back to the room and Fang was packed and ready to check out.

"Not yet," I said. "We have to wait."

"Why?"

"There's a problem with my credit card."

Twenty minutes later there was a knock at the door. A bellhop handed me the train ticket and a signature form.

"What was that?" Fang asked.

"The hotel bill."

Fang was not pleased about moving to a different hotel and repeatedly asked why. I told her the new hotel was just as nice but cheaper and closer to the airport. Hotel Elan was cheaper and closer to the airport, but it was nowhere near as nice as the Ocean. The minute we walked into the IKEA-furnished room at the Elan, Fang couldn't hide her displeasure, and frankly, neither could I. There was no reality in which we could spend two days cooped up in that shoebox together.

Dealing with the Hotel Elan front desk staff was like rapping my knuckles on concrete. I had to pay (cash) for both nights even though we checked out 15 minutes after checking in. Of course, I wound up losing money on a move that was supposed to *save* money. We tried to negotiate. The desk clerks intentionally spoke Cantonese, something of an insult when Mandarin was available.

We took a taxi back to the Ocean Hotel and checked back into the same room. Following our ritual afternoon sex, we took a long nap that was interrupted by Fang's cell phone. She answered and I could hear a man's voice and heard her say *baba* (father) a few times. When the call ended, she said, "My father wants to know when you will come to Ningxia."

"Uh, I don't know."

I left the room, went down to the lobby, bought a couple of beers from the shop, and smoked several cigarettes in the lounge area. Fang-fang called and asked, "Where are you?"

"In the lobby."

"What are you doing?"

"Nothing. Having a beer."

"Come back upstairs."

I finished the beer and went upstairs. She was back on QQ, with a Bollywood movie on the TV in the background. We didn't speak for a long time. Finally, I said, "Let's go eat." We went to the Turkish restaurant, Bosporus, still barely acknowledging each other. After dinner, I said, "Look, I know you don't like it, but I want to go back to the Elephant & Castle."

"Fine. I don't care."

The bar was deserted when we arrived, just Trixie and the off-duty cop. We sat at the bar and drank beer for a while. I kept expecting some of the crew to show up, but nobody came. The front door didn't budge. This went on for an hour or so. I couldn't get the beer down my throat fast enough.

Fang grabbed my arm and pulled me to face her. "Are you going to marry me?"

"I need to think about it. I need to ask Felix what he thinks about it."

"Why? Why would you ask him?"

"He's my boss. I *have* to ask him. It's not a choice."

She took a deep breath, leaned back, and shook her head. "I know you're not going to marry me."

"Just relax."

"I told you about the professor from Taiwan. He will marry me. You're not serious."

All I could say was, "Ahhh..." and shake my head.

For a minute, it looked like she was going to cry. There was a fleeting glimpse of hurt in her eyes. She regained composure and finished her beer.

"Let's go," she said. "This place is boring."

Thursday, February 18, 2010

Overnight, I had a series of uncomfortable and irrational dreams, some of which involved my mother. I wished I could talk to her. She would have had some good perspective on the current situation. Fang woke me at 9:00 a.m. and said, "Let's go eat before it gets too late." We went up to the restaurant where I drank coffee and chain-smoked, watching in amazement as Fang devoured her breakfast. She must have cleared five or six plates from the buffet.

We got back to the room and Fang was sullen. She made a few calls while lying on the bed. Occasionally, she sighed heavily. Hardly a word passed between us since breakfast. She sounded very unhappy when talking to her friends and I heard her make a couple of derogatory remarks, but I couldn't be sure. I suspected that last night's talk about marriage was not sitting well with her. I got the feeling that she had realized this relationship would never work out.

I sat down on the couch across from the bed and said, "What do you want to do today?"

Fang shook her head and looked away from me.

"Aren't you bored?"

"What is there to do?" she snapped and looked out the window. "Where is there to go?"

"I'm leaving tomorrow. It's our last day together."

"I know."

My mind was flooded with all the things I would have said if we both spoke English or if I could speak better Chinese.

It was 12:48 p.m. when I looked up at the clock. *I have less than twenty-four hours left with her.*

Fang didn't like to walk more than 30 minutes at a time. She didn't want to *see* anything. She didn't want to *go* anywhere except shopping for clothes and jewelry that I couldn't afford. All she ever wanted to do was sit around the hotel room, eat, drink, smoke, and sometimes, fuck. That still left us with 16 hours a day and nothing else in common.

And whenever we went out, she was rude to everybody, especially the restaurant staff, which offended my sensibilities as a former food service worker. No matter where we dined, Fang found something to bitch about. She routinely summoned the server to complain. She never liked the table we were offered and always demanded to sit somewhere else. She made strange faces at half the dishes that came to the table. This type of behavior would be typical of a very spoiled, high-maintenance woman from a well-to-do family in Shanghai or Hong Kong, and not a country girl from Ningxia who disliked working so much that she found it easier to sell her body.

At 5:00 p.m. I went down to the lobby shop to buy beer and smokes, when I noticed a white woman working behind the front desk. ***What the fuck?!*** I looped around the lobby and approached. The woman greeted me warmly with an Eastern European accent. Her name was Katarina.

"Listen," I said, "I'm in 1508. I'm checking out tomorrow."

Katerina nodded and began typing and mousing on the computer. "Yes, Mr. Charles? What can I do for you?"

"Well," I said, pausing to phrase it as simply as possible. "I'm trying to get on a flight out of Guangzhou tomorrow at noon, but I might not be able to get a seat."

Katerina nodded again and said, "I see."

"I'm going to check out and pay tomorrow morning, but can I make a reservation for the same room for the same price, on Friday and Saturday night?"

"That is not a problem. If you get a flight out of Guangzhou, please give us a call to cancel the reservation."

"I'll do that."

Katerina confirmed the reservation, and I thanked her.

"By the way," I said. "What the hell are you doing here?"

"Do you mean in Guangzhou?"

"Yes."

"I study International Business and Chinese at Guangzhou University, and this is part of my training program."

"Where are you from?"

"The Ukraine."

"Wow. I'm impressed."

Katerina smiled and said, "Thank you. Is there anything else I can do for you?"

"Nope. You've been great."

Fang and I went back to Ashoka for dinner. The only topic of conversation was our departure times tomorrow. Her flight left at noon. I told her that my train to Hong Kong left at 2:30 p.m. There was no point in asking if she wanted to hit Elephant & Castle, but I was dreading the thought of spending the rest of the night in the hotel room. Suddenly, I remembered Shamian Island, the place I stayed last year, pre-Fang. It was an idyllic oasis on the south side of town. There were more than a couple of cool little places we could go for a drink. Fang seemed to perk up when I mentioned it.

We took a taxi to Lucy's, my favorite spot on Shamian Island. Even though it was quite chilly, Fang wanted to sit outside on the patio so we could look at the lights across the river. It was such a weird experience. We sat close, drank, smoked, and every so often, she sighed. At one point she said something like, "This world, it just isn't fair."

Back at the hotel, we climbed into bed and lay there facing each other. I wanted to tell her how sorry I was that things didn't work out, but my Chinese just wasn't getting us there. Eventually, she put her finger to my lips and said, "Just hold me, Charlie. That's all I want."

We fell asleep, entwined for the last time.

Friday, February 19, 2010

Fang was already upstairs in the restaurant for breakfast when I woke up, and I had a minor panic attack, thinking she had packed up and left. Instinctively, I went to the safe and checked for my money. It was still there. Fang wasn't a thief. I felt bad for thinking she might have pulled a runner.

She returned from the restaurant and we started packing.

I had exactly 6,217.50 yuan (US$850) in cash. I took 2,000 yuan and stashed it in my backpack. I put 4,200 yuan in my left front pocket and the rest in my right pocket. I didn't wait for Fang to ask for money.

"This is all I have left," I said, holding out the 4,200-yuan stack of cash. She didn't look up.

"Just leave it there on the nightstand," she said, annoyed. We both knew exactly how much money I had.

At the front desk, I went through the entire charade of paying for the room and giving back the key. The clerk called us a pair of taxis: one for Fang and the airport, one for me to the train station. The first taxi arrived, and I said, "You take it." We hugged for a solid minute, and she said, "Call me when you get back to Taipei." Then she got in the taxi, and they drove away. She didn't look back or wave.

The second taxi arrived. I don't know why, but I had the guy take me to the train station. I had conflicting feelings of despair and sadness versus freedom and release. I knew I'd never see Fang again, but I wasn't sure how to feel about it. "Happiness" wasn't part of the equation.

It was a blinding sunny winter afternoon—the first time I'd seen the sun since arrival—not too chilly or windy. Arriving at the train station, I decided to walk back to the Ocean Hotel, which took about an hour. With a crafty bit of foresight, I switched off my phone and removed the Chinese SIM card because nobody except Fang knew the number.

Katerina was at the front desk when I arrived at the hotel. "Hello, Mr. Charles. I guess you didn't get a flight home? Would you like me to put you in 1508?"

"No, I'd like a different room. Is that possible?"

"Of course."

⋆✶⋆

When you arrive at Taoyuan International Airport (TPE) and deplane at the arrival and immigration gates, one of the first things you see is a massive banner that reads, "Drug smuggling in Taiwan is punishable by death." The punishment for drug possession in China was equally severe. You could face a firing squad or, if you got lucky, simply get deported and blacklisted from entering the country. However, none of that mattered in Guangzhou. The cops on the street were there to protect the customers, not arrest them. Everybody knew exactly what was happening on Jianshe Sixth Road.

During the week, I bought roughly five grams of hash and smoked maybe a gram, leaving me with four grams to bring back to Taipei. Hell, it was the whole point of visiting Guangzhou. Despite all the hype about the dangers of smuggling drugs into Taiwan, I wasn't concerned in the slightest. I'd already traveled back and forth with various quantities of weed and hash with no problems. I knew exactly where to put the dope and how to behave when going through customs.

Four grams is nice, but why not more? Does it matter one way or the other? If I got caught, the quantity didn't matter. The government had a zero-tolerance policy, so I'd be fucked to the wall for a crumb or a pound.

And four grams of hash would only last a month, at best. I didn't have any idea where I might find another connection.

The dealers on Jianshe Sixth Road didn't come out before sundown, but I decided to take a chance instead of spending the day indoors. After several hours of walking and loitering in the plazas between retail shops—not an African guy in sight—I gave up and took the long walk back to the hotel. I stopped in the lobby shop, bought two 500 ml bottles of San Miguel, and returned to the room. I took a shower, drank the beer, and watched part of a "zany" Hong Kong comedy I'd seen a couple of times before, so I kinda-sorta knew the plot, but *I didn't understand the actual plot.*

The scheming matriarch had lobsters dropped down her dress. She got "pinched." Her heart-of-gold but tough-as-nails daughter got the money and the guy. All Cantonese comedies end with a shot of the entire cast looking into the camera, throwing money in the air, and shouting, "Waaahhhh!" like they just won the lottery.

As I turned off the TV, a soft pang of guilt struck my conscience, and, for a moment, I felt Fang-fang's absence. Suddenly, I understood her motivation and empathized with her disappointment. Cutting through all the bullshit, life is mostly maintaining the status quo. I couldn't feel too bad about lying to Fang when she was lying to me anyway. It almost didn't seem to matter at all, which is horrible. A slideshow of every dishonest memory flashed across my mental screen. Lies stacked on top of lies. The meaning of every word, every action, every thought, clouded in a haze of self-doubt. *Does it even matter?*

One of the worst things that could ever happen to anybody is losing your sense of meaning. Make no mistake, when you get to that place where nothing matters, you must want to be there. Nobody stumbles across nothingness by accident.

Back on Jianshe Sixth Road at 7:00 p.m., well past twilight, I got as far as McDonald's before a dealer approached. Two uniformed cops stood on the opposite side of Jianshe.

"What about them?" I asked the dealer.

"No worry 'bout them," the dealer said. "Follow me."

We stepped down from the sidewalk into the sunken courtyard in front of a currency exchange booth. Another dealer came over to stand guard, and we got right to business. I bought three decent-sized chunks of hash—roughly 5 grams for 300 yuan. The drug dealers on Jianshe were the best I'd ever dealt with anywhere. They were smart and they spoke English. They weren't pushy and they didn't make small talk. They knew exactly how much product they could get caught with and not spend a significant amount of time in jail. If they liked you, they'd give you their cell number when the deal was done.

The transaction couldn't have been any easier, except I dropped the money when handing it over.

"Sorry," I said sheepishly. The dealer quickly bent down to scoop the cash and said, "No problem, mon. Catch you later. I'm out here every night."

Tracing my steps back to the sidewalk, I spied that ugly white woman from Cave Bar and Starbucks watching the whole transaction from street level, glaring at me, like, "How dare you, sir?" She took a few steps toward me as I emerged from the courtyard, looking like she was going to say something, so I cut her off.

"Haven't you ever seen a drug deal?" I snapped, brushing past. "Mind your business, dummy."

I kept walking toward the Elephant & Castle. As I rounded the corner to the steps of the pedestrian bridge, a white guy in a blue jacket cut across my path and mounted the steps three at a time. It was Steve, the one character I hadn't run into yet. I followed him for 30 seconds before I called out, "Hey, Steve!" He paused, turned around, and barked, "What!?"

We kept walking across the bridge, and I immediately went into my You Might Not Remember Me speech.

"Oh yeah. You're the guy from Taiwan. What was your name?"

"Charlie."

"Right, well, Charlie. I'm trying to find this *fucking idiot*, so..." He was visibly agitated, looking everywhere but at me. "This fucking cunt says meet me at the bank," he was speaking at rant level, "then he says meet me at KFC, then he says he's *fucking all the way over here!*"

"Will you be at the pub later?" I asked. We had almost reached the other side of the bridge, and I could see the lights of the pub.

"Oh yeah," Steve said. "As soon as I hook up with this—" he turned, leaned over the railing, and shouted, "YOU ARE SO FUCKING STUPID! DO YOU KNOW THAT? YOU ARE FUCKING STUPID!" at a black guy on the street walking in front of the pub. "This guy is so fucking stupid," Steve said to me. "Don't ever deal with him." The black guy stood at the bottom of the stairs. Steve began screaming at him, "YOU ARE SO FUCKING STUPID! WHO THE FUCK DO YOU THINK YOU ARE DEALING WITH? ARE YOU REALLY THIS FUCKING STUPID?!"

I stopped walking as soon as Steve started screaming. He reached the bottom of the stairs, but I was only halfway down. I got a look at the dealer. *Yikes! There's no way in hell I would ever talk to him like that.* Yet, the dealer didn't seem annoyed at all, in fact, he just nodded his head while Steve said, "You know what? You wanna fucking jerk me around, I'll *never* do business with you again."

Leapfrogging the rest of the stairs, I slipped past and made a beeline for the pub.

Monty, Eric, Tyrone and I were sitting in the back when Steve marched in, dropped a golf-ball-sized chunk of hash on the table and said, "Here, motherfuckers." Eric and Monty pounced on it, immediately haggling over who would split it up, who would roll the joints, etc. Steve sat down next to me and said, "I almost killed that fucking guy."

"What happened?" Monty asked.

"Aw," Steve spit in disgust, "these fucking guys have to get their acts together, man. I'm fucking sick of their inconsistent, incompetent bullshit."

"Was there a problem?" asked Monty, looking at me. "Oh no, don't tell me." He started giggling. "Did Steve go postal on a Nigerian street dealer again?"

"Dude!" I said, incredulous. "He was *fucking screaming* at the guy."

"He pissed me off," said Steve, matter of fact. "Don't fucking call me every three minutes and change the fucking location, all right? I'm not a fucking pigeon. I'm not a fucking toy. Listen, do you know how many of these fuckers I've dealt with over the years?" The question was rhetorical, so I just shrugged.

"Ohhh," chimed Eric. "Did you go through Sonny's boy, Natrone?"

"No, jackass," Steve snapped. "It was that stupid fucker from the Gipsy Club."

"*That guy*," Monty said, "has some serious shit."

"This *is* really good shit," agreed Eric.

"Man, Steve," I said, "sorry I didn't stick around. But you seemed to have things under control, and you know, what could I do?"

"Don't say you're sorry. *You didn't have a fucking thing to do with it!*" Steve raged. "Why are you sorry?"

"Was it hardcore?" Monty said, patronizing.

"The hardest of cores," I quipped.

Eric said. "When he gets like that you just have to bail." He gave me a knowing nod. "I've seen that shit go down. Not good."

Steve seemed at once satisfied and irritated with himself. "You know what? I should have made him walk back down to KFC. Stupid...mother...fucker."

Saturday, February 20, 2010

I woke to an email notification from Fang. "Where are you?"

I wrote back, "In Taipei."

"Your phone is off," she replied.

"I forgot to pay the bill. It won't be back on until Monday."

"Call me then."

After a walk down to Starbucks, I spent the morning and afternoon in the hotel room, writing and getting high. The skies were cloudy again, and the outside temperature hovered above freezing. At 4:00 p.m., I went to the sauna and soaked in the hot tub until my skin started to prune. Back in the room, I piled on every layer of clothing in my backpack and went for a long, aimless walk until 7:00 p.m., when I posted up at Elephant & Castle.

Steve was sitting at the bar. We made small talk for a while. Monty and Eric showed up later. Many of the other characters rolled in. It was nearly identical to every other night. We drank, smoked, and played pool. Eric rolled the joints and kept me company while Steve and Monty went out to Jianshe Sixth Road for hooker reconnaissance.

"Where's your lady?" Eric asked, referring to Fang.

"She went back to Ningxia. Mercifully."

"A ray of fucking sunshine, isn't she?"

I chuckled softly and shook my head. "Fortunately, that relationship has run its course."

"When are you going back to Taiwan?" he asked.

"Tomorrow."

"Didn't you buy a shitload of hash yesterday?"

"Yeah."

"What are you gonna do with it? You couldn't have smoked it already!"

"I'll bring it with me."

"For real?"

"Hell, yeah. I've done it before. It's easy."

"Dude, I wouldn't. Listen, I'll buy what you've got left."

"Nah, man. I'm good. I know what I'm doing."

"What are you gonna do? Keister it?" Keister is prison and drug smuggling slang for stuffing it up your ass.

"Noooooo. Uh-uh. I just keep it in my pocket or my backpack."

Eric leaned back and stared at me for a moment. "Good fucking luck with that."

"Luck certainly has something to do with it."

Sunday, February 21, 2010

After checking out of the hotel, I made a beeline for the train station. The hash was in the front pocket of my backpack, wrapped in a piece of paper. The baggage scanner at the train station didn't give me a second look. Once again, I noticed the video monitor of the scanner wasn't even turned on. I arrived in Hong Kong, took the MTR to the airport, which was swamped with travelers, checked in for my flight, and decamped to the bathroom. I took the hash out of the wrapper and dropped it into the bottom of the backpack's main compartment.

Arriving at security, I removed my laptop and other digital devices from the backpack and put them in a separate tray. My heart rate remained steady, and I moved with confidence, not looking around or over my shoulder, not making eye contact with anybody in uniform. Just another normal, weary traveler trying to find his way home after the long holiday. The backpack was otherwise clean, containing only my clothing, no batteries, liquid, sharp objects, or other prohibited items, aside from the hash, of course. Those were the two keys to successful small-scale drug smuggling. Don't act suspiciously and hide the contraband in plain sight.

I didn't flinch while the backpack scrolled through the scanner or smile when walking through the metal detector, and I stood with legs and arms spread as a guy passed a theremin-type wand around my body. The backpack emerged from the scanner, followed by the container with my laptop, passport, money, belt, and credit card. I stuffed the laptop into the backpack, grabbed my belt and other items, and moved to one of the tables where other passengers were reassembling their travel gear.

That was it. There wouldn't be a final hurdle at TPE because I didn't have any checked luggage, and therefore, I strolled right through baggage claim. The drug dogs were busy sniffing bags on the carousel and didn't notice me, so I breezed through customs without blinking an eye. It was that easy.

11

Intersecting Layers of
Utility and Complexity

The irony of risk was not lost on me, dear reader. We know that two years earlier, I fled San Francisco because my drug and alcohol routines were getting out of hand. And part of the reason I moved to Taiwan is I figured it would be difficult to score dope there, and it was, for the most part. But again, there I was, finding loopholes and back doors to continue the cycle. Granted, weed and hash weren't serious drugs, but they were strictly forbidden, using and possessing them could have put me in jail for a long time. *I didn't care.*

The smuggled hash would last two months, at best, so I needed a new connection in Taipei. Martin had been a reliable source (with an occasional dry spell when we had to wait a week or two for the shipment), but now, he was out of the picture. And frankly, there was never a time when I *wasn't* looking for another source. When it came to scoring drugs, options were preferable to slavish dependence on one guy.

There was only one place or type of place in Taipei where I knew for a fact that drugs were available: *nightclubs*. Martin and Wilson told me repeatedly, *explicitly*, in very certain terms, that I should never, ever try to score drugs in Taipei nightclubs. Every drug bust in the news involved a nightclub. Martin said, "You might make a connection in a nightclub, but you *always* make the deal somewhere else, some other time."

Even after nearly two years of halfheartedly scanning the nightclubs for a dealer, I never found one. I met a bunch of people who said they *might* be able to hook me up, but none of them ever came through. And I hated the nightclubs.

Down to the last crumbs of the Guangzhou hash, I fortunately met a local dealer named Chang, and, more importantly, a guy named Ken Sloan, an American expat who worked for one of the government ESL testing programs and played percussion in a local cosplay skiffle band.

Chang was a pony-tailed vendor who sold pipes, rolling papers, and other paraphernalia at Tonghua Night Market. His stall was just a few yards from the east entrance at Linjiang and Keelung Road. I briefly spoke to Chang a few times and eventually bought a pipe, but he never offered anything. It seemed too obvious—at first—to ask him. It didn't seem possible that he sold weed or other stuff from right there in the lane, with thousands of people passing by every day. On the other hand, he had a ponytail and a stoner vibe. It was another situation where I failed to "read the room." Fortunately, my simple-minded persistence paid off.

One night in late March, I went down to the night market at prime time on a Friday and posted up around the corner from Chang's stall, just watching the scene, drinking beers, looking for cops, that kind of thing. It was easy to blend into the backdrop if you didn't make any sudden moves or draw attention to yourself and wore mostly all-black clothing in the winter months.

About half an hour into my surveillance, Chang made a transaction with a local woman in a long, flowing dress—I could smell the patchouli backdraft as she whisked past my position. They greeted each other with a hug, which the woman used as a pretense to slip him a folded packet of cash. Chang handed her a small paper bag. They hugged again, and the woman breezed off. So, that was a major *Aha!* moment. I stuck around for a while and watched Chang make two more deals, both high-speed fly-bys, meaning regular customers with pre-arranged orders. I made a quick exit with plans to return the following evening.

The next night, I went down to the night market around 10:00 p.m., already buzzed from a six-pack and the last remnants of my stash. I approached Chang's stall, giving him a nod and a smile before idly browsing the pipes. Before I could speak to him, a pair of expat guys showed up, clearly buzzed as well, and bought some rolling papers. The taller of the two expat guys spoke Mandarin with Chang, and the gist of the conversation seemed to be that Chang wasn't currently holding but would have some tomorrow. The tall expat guy said, "Maybe I'll come back and see you tomorrow," and they left.

Chang caught me eavesdropping and gave me a dirty look. Flustered, I walked away and bought another beer at the OK Mart down the lane. As I stood out front drinking the beer and having a smoke, the same two expat guys came up, and the tall one, Ken, stayed outside while the short one, Ted, went in to buy beers. I nodded to Ken and said, "Sup, man?" He returned the nod and said, "Weren't you just down at Chang's?"

I introduced myself and asked about his conversation with Chang. Ken told me he would *never* buy dope from Chang. He called it a "honeypot" and said other foreigners had been pinched. "Stay away from that guy," he said. I pointed out that he'd just bought rolling papers from Chang. Ken said, "There's nothing illegal about that, is there?"

Ted came out with their beers, and they invited me to a nearby park to smoke a joint. I spent most of the time asking about their weed connections, but they stonewalled me. Otherwise, we had a lot of things in common, and it was a pleasant exchange. When it was time to part, Ken gave me his phone number and email address and said, "Drop me a line sometime. I might be able to help you out."

Despite Ken's warnings, I went back to Chang's the next night and didn't waste any time. After greeting him, I asked if he was holding. He said he was, but it was for someone else. If I wanted, I could wait around to see if the guy showed up. If he didn't show by 10:45 p.m.–15 minutes after their appointment—the shit would be mine. So, I posted up in the usual spot and had a few beers. Sure enough, at 10:30 p.m. sharp, a foreign guy came and collected his stuff. Afterwards, Chang said, "Come see me next Thursday," and he'd hook me up then. The rates were TWD$10,000 (US$330) for 10 grams. *Bring cash.*

A few days later, Ken Sloan hooked me up with some hash, so I didn't need to visit Chang, and I avoided that side of the night market for a while.

Three weeks went by, a fair enough cooling-off period. I was down to my last few hits of the hash from Sloan, who said the next drop wouldn't happen for another week at the earliest. So, I reluctantly went back to see Chang.

Tonghua Night Market is a 500-yard section of Linjiang Street that runs perpendicular to the namesake Tonghua Street, with two dozen alleyways shooting off in all directions. It's easy to get lost back there if you're unfamiliar. Once you get to know the area, you can pretty much avoid the market altogether by cutting through the alleys.

Taking a roundabout way behind the market, I wound up at the east entrance with a clear view of Chang's operation and his neighboring vendors, but far enough away that I could blend into the traffic. From the Keelung Road entrance, I looked for CCTV cameras. There didn't appear to be any pointed at Chang's operation. Then I looked for cops— not in uniform. Undercovers. A couple of vendors looked highly suspicious, particularly this one guy selling socks who was way too clean-cut and healthy-looking to be selling socks. He also had a clear view of Chang's. Directly across from Chang was a snack vendor who didn't seem to have any snacks for sale. He sat patiently staring at Chang, who didn't seem concerned at all.

After five minutes of observation, I approached Chang's stall. He smiled and remembered me. "Hey, where you been, Charlie? I've got good stuff." *This fucker remembered my name?*

My heart rate kicked up. A younger guy in his 20s with obvious gang tattoos moved behind me and took a seat next to Chang.

"This is my friend," Chang said. The red-lipped and unfriendly gangster guy gave me a blank stare, chewing his cud of betel nut. "How many do you want?"

"I want one," I said. 'One' meant one 10-gram portion of high-grade weed.

"Wait here!" Chang shuffled off to his storage space to retrieve the dope. Turning around to check for onlookers, the sock seller and the no-snack vendor were staring at me. I turned back around and pretended to be looking at the pipes, my heart pounding and adrenaline spiking.

The gangster said, "*Gei wo qian.*" (Give me the money.)

"Umm...what?"

He patted his hand on Chang's workspace behind the display. "*Zheli. Fang zai zheli.*" (Here. Put it here.)

"No. I'll wait for Chang."

"*Just do it!*" he spat in English and my eyes almost popped out of my head. I furtively removed the money from my pocket, ten $1,000 notes, folded in half, and placed it on the counter. The gangster took the money and slipped it into his pocket.

Chang returned with an "OK!" and placed a small silver canister on the workspace. "Go ahead. Take it."

My heart was throbbing mercilessly. Slightly nauseous, I slipped the canister in my pocket and said, "Everything is good?"

"No problem," Chang replied, smiling. "Be more careful from now on."

The gangster spat a wad of betel nut juice and garbled something in Taiwanese.

The ensuing five-minute span, essentially the time it took to wind my way through the alleys and get home, was always unpleasant but thrilling, nonetheless. The adrenaline coursed through my body, and it didn't feel like my feet were touching the pavement.

Over the next few weeks, I stayed in touch with Ken Sloan and saw his band a few times. The next shipment of hash came in, so we were flush with dope. When I mentioned the buy from Chang, Sloan said, "Dude, *don't do that anymore!*"

"Look, Chang must be paying somebody off down there. Otherwise, wouldn't the cops have shut him down by now? I don't think it's a honeypot like you say it is."

Sloan exhaled. "Listen, just be patient. I've got a solid connection with all the benefits and none of the drawbacks. It will happen when it happens."

Ken Sloan turned out to be a cool guy for a while. Our friendship lasted several years, but Sloan didn't know that I routinely zipped down to the night market and bought weed from Chang. It went on for years until one day, Chang disappeared.

***

My work and status at Knowledge Press Ltd. had many intersecting layers of utility and complexity.

Technically, what it said on my business card, my job title was Head Writer and Editor, and I created a mountain of material for the company. Tests, books, essay prompts, reading passages, conversations, short stories, speeches, voiceovers, etc. Anything related to the English language. Even the marketing ads landed on my desk for approval. Perhaps more importantly, according to Captain Felix, I was "The Real McCoy," i.e., the perfect American. I couldn't have been more American if I tried, but I tried to be as *non-American as possible*, which meant being polite and keeping my voice down in public, just for starters. Felix said, "When you walk into a room, everybody knows you're an American."

This was only partially true. A ton of Asian people mistook me for European, usually German or British until I opened my mouth.

Semantics didn't matter to Felix because I had a white face and an undeniable American accent. "Every publishing company and cram school in Taiwan wants Americans," Felix told me. Canadians were acceptable, too, and U.K. expats were equally welcomed. But *as far as he was concerned*, the Captain wanted a genuine U.S. citizen to create his materials and be a figurehead for marketing. Just having an American on staff gave his company an automatic façade of authenticity, authority, and credibility. I was the "token foreigner" or "white monkey" (*bai houzi*) of the operation. The gig at Knowledge Press was unique, but I wasn't exactly blazing new professional trails. Expats have been working the rent-a-foreigner circuit in Asia for decades.

The tricky part of my job was dealing with Felix and his ideas, many of which emerged from the cosmic radiation of the people around him. A meteor shower of "fuck, no." People from outside the company pitched the Captain with improbable, backward, and foolish ideas or a combination thereof. The people *and* the ideas, mind you. But I was the sounding board. Felix bounced every KPHQ-related idea off me because I *wouldn't tell him what he wanted to hear.* Felix didn't always listen to my feedback, but he always wanted to hear it.

✶✳✶

The cornerstone of the Knowledge Press educational system was simplicity, epitomized by the Captain's **Non-Stop English** program, a conversational teaching method that emphasized speaking in patterns of three. Everything had to be in short sentences with basic vocabulary. *Easy to memorize.* Meanwhile, the bread and butter of the empire were the schools and the students—that's where the Captain made his money. He told me on several occasions that the publishing company had been in the red from day one. Therefore, students were cooed and coddled like newborns. More than one student complained that a teacher was too strict, that teacher was gone. If a teacher said a test was too hard, they called me to dumb-it-down. And sometimes, this principle or idea of simplicity got carried beyond grammar and syntax. Case in point: The Universal Essay.

In preparation for future proficiency exams, students of English as a Second Language wrote myriad short essays. The topics ran in the following vein:

Some people prefer to live in a small town. Others prefer to live in a big city. Which place would you prefer to live in? Use specific reasons and examples to support your answer.

Or....

How do movies and television influence people's behavior? Use reasons and specific examples to support your position.

Some little genius at one of the schools got an audience with Felix and said, "The students need one essay they can memorize to answer any question. Like a template."

Felix had been in the ESL game longer than I'd been alive, so he should have said to the kid, **"There's no such thing."** Or "If such a thing were possible, my friend, somebody would have already written one." And those *would have been my exact words* when Felix came into the office and announced, "I want you to write a Universal Essay! Something the students can memorize to answer any question."

"If such a thing were possible..." I began to say.

Felix didn't let me finish. "I want you to..."

At this point, I knew the battle was over. Felix wasn't asking, he was telling.

"How long do you want it to be?"

"Use the Non-Stop English formula. Nine sentences."

"*Nine sentences*...that will answer *any* question?" I shook my head in disbelief. Three hundred words is pretty much the standard minimum essay length on writing tests and evaluations.

"It must be compatible with Non-Stop English. The students will memorize it. Like a template."

Cold silence. I bit my tongue and tasted fresh blood. My cheeks flushed, and beads of sweat formed on my brow. Felix came around the desk and put a hand on my shoulder. "It's a tough job. You're a genius. Try your best."

I ignored the rest of whatever he said and returned to what I was doing before the Universal Essay was mentioned. And I didn't give it a second thought until the next afternoon when Felix asked, "How's the Universal Essay coming along?" and eagerly approached my desk, expecting to see a nine-sentence answer to all the problems in the world today.

"Um..." I quickly opened a blank page in Microsoft Word and typed the title: **The Universal Essay.**

Felix stood next to me and read it out loud. There was an awkward pause, and I then typed:

There is no easy answer.
This is a very complex subject.
It may be a matter of opinion.

I think I have an open mind.
I want to remain objective.
I will look at it from every angle.

The evidence is not conclusive.
More data needs to be collected.
Until then, the problem can't be solved.

Felix read each line as it appeared on the screen. "You're a genius! You can do anything! But can you change the last section?"

"Change it?"

"Make it better."

I quickly tapped out:

I want to do what's best for everyone.
I want to help others at all times.
I want to make a difference.

"No, that's not it," Felix snapped. "Keep working. You can do it." I saved and closed the file and went back to playing online solitaire. The next afternoon was a repeat performance. I quickly opened the file and began to write:

Think before you write.
Develop a clear theme.
Know your intended audience.

Be original.
Make it stand out from the rest.
Use your creativity.

Show, don't tell.
Use stories, examples, and anecdotes.
Be specific and make a strong impression.

"I like the first one," the Captain said, disappointed. "Let me see that one again."

"But *this* one," I begged, "is much better. It doesn't answer *any* question; it helps the student remember *how* to answer any question. Like a template."

The phone rang. Felix got distracted. That was the end of it for the day.

Of course, the *next* afternoon, he came in and asked to see the first version. He read it a few times and said, "It needs to answer any question. Take a bit from here and there. Nine sentences that answer any question."

I sighed and stared at the computer screen, pretending to be engrossed in solving the puzzle. Opening a new blank document, I typed: **This too shall pass**, highlighted it, and clicked **Copy** until my wrist started to hurt. Captain Felix laughed and repeated his mantra of encouragement. I knew this fucking Universal Essay thing wasn't going to be forgotten anytime soon. I had a feeling that it would join all the other money-hemorrhaging ideas I failed to talk him out of: the illustrated children's books, *The Dictionary of Three-Word Clichés*, *101 Ways to Say Hello!*, *Speeches for Almost Every Occasion*...and he was showing signs of following through with it. And I'm sure he would have if an unnatural disaster hadn't come along and wiped it off the map.

But in the meantime, I was losing sleep over this fucking Universal Essay bullshit. I tried to look at it from all angles. I took it out of the box and couldn't get it back in. I researched a thousand questions and made charts and graphs. I chopped it up, moved the pieces around at random, and stuck them back together. Then, I tried to list the nine most frequently asked essay questions on standardized tests. No matter how I approached it, I knew deep down in my soul that it was futile. There is no Universal Essay. It couldn't be done by me—that was for damn sure. So, I folded my arms over my chest and waited. And waited. And sure enough, a week later, a man-made typhoon of drama inundated the Knowledge Press world, mercifully drowning the Universal Essay in its ebb.

12

Summertime and the Living is Queasy

The trip to Guangzhou changed me in ways that took months to acknowledge and understand. A new reality emerged from the ambivalence of asking myself, "What the hell am I doing?" and never having an answer. There were a *finite* number of times I could feel so utterly lost, foolish, confused, and hopeless, and I reached the terminal number. I've read similar stories about people who decided to stop drinking or using drugs. One day, they woke up and said, "Enough is enough." They didn't need rehab or support groups. It was entirely possible to *just stop.*

The first transformation was physical. *You gotta start taking care of yourself.* I joined a gym, worked out 3-4 times per week, started eating properly and getting decent sleep. The second transformation was emotional and/or psychological. *I'm done with hookers. Done.* I didn't care about getting laid anymore. And I stopped trying to meet or date in Taipei. That whole "sleazy" aspect of my persona was dead. Yet, a biological clock started ticking, and I was just now hearing its movement. Maybe it was residual trauma from the Fang situation, but I wanted something more stable. *I just want to find one good woman and settle down. Maybe even start a family. I don't want to keep chasing this fucking dragon anymore.*

It might seem fraudulent or incredible for someone like me to change, but everything from the last two years—hell, my entire adult life—led to this point. So, again, it wasn't exactly an overnight transformation. Of course, some things didn't change—the need to smoke pot wouldn't go away until many years later—but I rarely smuggled dope across international borders again. The booze kept flowing, but I suddenly had a mission or a direction. *Find a partner, start a family, and do something meaningful with my life.*

* ✱ *

Captain Felix operated on another level sometimes. If he was playing chess and we, the robots, were the chess pieces, getting captured and taken off the board was often a relief. Almost every Felix decision was filtered through his Machiavellian character and a close reading of *The Art of War*. When he wanted to say "fuck you" to somebody, he never said fuck or you.

Daisy came into the control center late one afternoon just before quitting time and said, "Charlie, I have news for you! The Captain's niece is coming to work at Knowledge Press."

"Yeah, so... What does that mean to me?"

"She's from the States. She just graduated from UCLA. Felix gave her a one million Taiwan signing bonus!" (Roughly US$30,000)

"What's she going to do? Translate? Edit? Teach?"

"I don't know. That's up to Felix. I think she's a writer." With a suspicious smirk of warning, she added, "But don't worry, she's not coming to replace you. Felix wants to be her mentor, and maybe one day, she will take over the company."

"That's great. Good for her."

"Are you busy tonight? Felix wants you to have dinner with us so you can meet her and the rest of his brother's family."

"I'm free." *Yeah, free dinner in a nice restaurant*, I thought.

"We'll have dinner upstairs at five-thirty."

"Upstairs?"

"Yes. The housemaid is making dinner for us."

I snickered, "*That's* her welcome dinner?"

Daisy leaned back and sighed, "Felix doesn't get along with his younger brother. They're not close. His brother is a doctor in Pasadena."

I arrived at 5:30 p.m. on the dot and they were all waiting for me. Felix introduced me to his niece, Lindsey. "This is Charlie. He's the straw that stirs the drink around here."

Lindsey was fucking gorgeous, like, one of the most genetically gifted women to hit the deck at KPHQ. Twenty-two years old, fresh out of college, full-figured, Asian American sorority girl with a California accent, wide toothy smile, and smoldering eyes. *Haha!* I chuckled. *She's not going to be around for long.*

Dinner was routine but remarkably frosty. Nobody except Felix and maybe Lindsey was happy to be there. We sat and listened to Felix and his brother begrudgingly agree to disagree about Lindsey's prospects in the company. There was *clearly* no love lost between the brothers, and Lindsey's mother was grinding her teeth. On the other hand, Lindsey was outspoken and assertive. She announced that she would live in the dorms until she got her bearings in Taipei. Though her father (and Felix) were originally from Tainan in the south, she said, Lindsey had only visited Taiwan a few times. She couldn't wait to start her Taiwan experience!

Daisy shot me the side-eye. *This fucking chick is capital-T trouble.*

After dinner, Felix pulled me aside and said, "Don't help Lindsey with anything. Let her figure things out on her own."

Lindsey moved into the dorm that Friday night, taking the room closest to the main dining room. I vaguely noted all her luggage in the lobby. There were four or five pink Rimowa roller suitcases and several designer tote bags. As I left the building, Mr. Chu was wrangling her stuff into the elevator. These minor details seem meaningless and ephemeral, but they sometimes circle back around.

I lived on the other side of the flat, so Lindsey and I hardly crossed paths that weekend. I saw her on Saturday night as she was leaving the building. She appeared to be dressed for a night of clubbing. I said hello as we passed, waving slightly. She was smiling, like, "Oh yeah, buddy. I've got this shit dialed in." And she did. Have it dialed in.

On Monday, Lindsey appeared in the office at a cubicle in the main room. Daisy arrived and groused about Felix. "He says (Lindsey) is going to take over the company when he retires," she scoffed. "I told him many

131

times. This girl isn't a teacher. She's a party girl. Did you know her Chinese is terrible?"

"Honey, I don't know a goddamn thing about her."

"The signing bonus was a waste of money. This girl isn't going to amount to anything. Mark my words."

Later that evening, I was leaving the dorm when I met Lindsey coming off the elevator. She was carrying a box with a brand-new iMac. She smiled and I nodded in acknowledgment.

I didn't know what Lindsey was working on, but one day, Captain Felix handed me a piece of paper and said, "Read this and tell me what you think." It appeared to be a translation of a reading passage from the college entrance exam.

"Uh, it's kind of awkward in spots. Did a native English speaker write this? It doesn't seem like it."

"It's a translation by Lindsey."

I didn't want to make trouble for Lindsey. "Oh, well, it's not bad."

It seemed like Lindsey had only been at KPHQ for a week or two when I noticed that she never came back to the office after lunch. I didn't think anything of it because...who knows what Felix had her doing? Maybe she was going down to the cram school in the afternoons? It didn't matter. I just noticed her absence. But then one evening, I clocked out and went upstairs to my room. Lindsey's door was open, and she appeared to be working on her iMac. I didn't say anything but made a mental note.

The next morning, Daisy came into the office with a bad attitude. "That girl (Lindsey) doesn't know what she's doing."

"For fuck's sake, Daisy. Give her a chance. She's only been here for a week."

"*It's been a month!*"

"Oh. Haha."

"She can't write. She can't translate Chinese to English. Or English to Chinese, which is even worse! What is she doing here?"

"I thought you said the Captain is going to be her mentor, and she'll take over the company."

"That girl isn't taking over anything."

Felix arrived a few minutes later. "Charlie, have you seen that girl? My...niece..." he stammered to remember her English name. "Lindsey?"

"Have I *what* now?"

"She's not in the office. Do you know where she is?"

"Felix, why the fuck would I know where she is?"

"Gretchen said Lindsey hasn't been coming to the office in the afternoon. Something about 'she's working from home.'"

"She lives upstairs. Can't *somebody* go knock on her door?"

Gretchen came into the control center, which ended my involvement in the discussion.

I took a trip to Hainan Island for a long weekend and returned to the office on Tuesday morning. Lindsey approached my desk before I had a chance to power up my PC. *Fuck, this girl is hot.* There is not a single doubt in my mind that before Lindsey arrived on the KPHQ scene, Captain Felix told her, in explicit terms, "*Stay away from the foreigner.*"

"Hi, Charlie!" she flashed a million-Taiwan-dollar smile. "I'm sorry I haven't, like, spent more time getting to know you. I've just been, like, super busy." She fanned herself.

"No problem, Lindsey. How's it going? Do you like the job? How's Taipei treating you so far?"

"It's been, like, so amazing, oh my god. Such a whirlwind! But," she paused, "I need to ask you about a few things."

"Go ahead. Shoot."

"Well, like, I have an iMac upstairs in my room, and it's like, so much more comfortable for me to work up there. I...I don't really like the office environment. I hate the overhead lights."

I coughed and nodded in agreement. "You and me both. I hate these fucking lights."

"I know, right? But, I guess, there's, like, a problem...with me. Captain Felix said I can't work from upstairs. Do you know anything about that?"

"I don't."

"Like, I'm *really working* upstairs in the afternoon. I just don't understand why I can't work from there. I mean, like, if I get the work done, what does it matter?"

"Take a seat." I motioned for Lindsey to close the door. "It's OK, you can sit in Daisy's chair." She closed the door and sat down.

Maintaining eye contact, I said, "I also have an iMac in my room upstairs, and I've been asking Felix to work remotely since I started here. Unfortunately, he won't allow it. Now, in your case, I can't say for sure because that's something you'll have to work out with him. But every time I bring it up, he says, 'I need you in the office, where I can see you. Where I can reach out and touch you.'"

Lindsey frowned and shifted position in the chair. "So, like, you're saying he won't let me work from upstairs?"

"I'm saying you should talk to Felix about it."

"I tried, but like, he told me the same thing, like, word-for-word, oh my god."

I leaned back, sighed, and said, "I can't help you, Lindsey. If he allowed me to work from home, I wouldn't be here right now."

She pouted and smiled sadly. "See ya 'round."

That was our only conversation. I never ran into her upstairs in the dorm because she had been staying at her boyfriend's apartment since the second week. She told Felix the dorm room was her "private office." Felix didn't like that. Not one bit.

Daisy arrived just before lunch, sullen and combative, again, grousing about Lindsey (among other things). "That girl has to go. She's not doing anything for the company."

Felix was out of town, so nothing happened until Friday afternoon when he finally showed up at KPHQ. He signed all the documents on his desk from accounting, then asked if Lindsey was in the office. Daisy told him that Lindsey didn't come back after lunch. Felix didn't respond.

That Sunday afternoon, I returned from a trip to Fulong Beach and arrived at the dorm around 3:30 p.m., where Lindsey's luggage was sprawled about the foyer and dining room. Her door was closed. I shrugged and went about my business like I always do. An hour later, I headed out to the supermarket. Some of Lindsey's luggage was still in the dining room. As I exited the elevator in the lobby and walked toward the gate, Lindsey was dragging one of her roller bags across the courtyard toward a taxi. There was a huge pile of clothing on one of the lobby couches. A curling iron, blow dryer, and cosmetics were spilling out of an overturned tote bag. Several pairs of shoes were lying about. Another roller bag was parked in the middle of the courtyard. Her iMac was in its original box, sitting on the curb.

I stopped in the middle of the courtyard for a moment when Mr. Chu came around the corner and headed toward the lobby.

As I exited the gate, passing Lindsey on the sidewalk, she thought I was *there to help*. "Oh, hi Charlie. Don't worry. Mr. Chu is going to deal with the rest of my stuff."

"Is he? Good luck with that." The taxi driver and I telepathically wondered if all her luggage would fit in his sedan. And I kept walking.

Felix knew Lindsey was leaving, and he explicitly instructed Mr. Chu:
1. Do not help her move anything.
2. Have the locks changed immediately after she's gone.
3. Give a copy of the new key to Charlie.

Unfortunately, the good Captain didn't tell me about the situation. I should have at least received a heads-up from Daisy.

It was my Sunday routine to hit the posh supermarket in the basement of the Shangri-la Hotel about five minutes farther down Anhe Road instead of my go-to supermarket. And I wasn't sure what I wanted to buy (except for wine), so I spent more time browsing than usual. All told I was gone from the apartment for an hour and a half. It was 5:15 p.m. when I rolled up to the dorm. Lindsey and her luggage were long gone, and my key to the door didn't work.

It took me a few minutes to add it up. *They changed the fucking lock.* I called Mr. Chu but he didn't answer because he was still on his scooter, headed for Zhonghe where he lived. That cunt wasn't calling me back anytime soon. Felix and Daisy were unresponsive, too. It was hopeless. I said to myself, "You might be locked out of the dorm tonight."

With nowhere to go (on a Sunday evening) and two sacks full of groceries that might go bad, the options were limited. I put the groceries in the KPHQ office break room refrigerator, walked down the street, and checked into a room at the HD Hotel next door to Carnegie's.

Monday morning, Felix couldn't decide if he was more pissed off that Mr. Chu helped Lindsey or locked me out of the dorm.

"What was I supposed to do?" Chu cried. "Leave her there with all that shit?"

Felix snapped, *"That's exactly what I told you to do!"*

Daisy kept saying, "This is what I mean. He screws everything up!"

"This guy," Felix said, pointing at me, "had to stay in a hotel last night. Who's going to pay for that? *You?*"

Mr. Chu was immediately transferred to the cram school, and Susie's husband, Jerry Mouse, took over as the main gofer at KPHQ.

Taipei has a wide range of bars in classes or categories. Lounges, cafes, speakeasies, nightclubs, dance clubs, sex clubs, sports bars, wine bars, cigar bars, music venues (aka live houses), sausage markets, and a dozen subspecies of locals-only establishments. You could hang in a locals-only joint if you spoke decent Mandarin. Otherwise, fuck off.

The Anhe Road Corridor in the Daan District was accessible, active, and affluent, with three foreigner-friendly bars in a 0.5-km radius of the dorm. Naturally, I went out drinking almost every night at one or more of a dozen bars within a 10-minute walking distance. For roughly the first six months, I made the rounds at Roxy Rocker, Saints & Sinners, Bobwundaye, Carnegie's, and one strictly local pub called Gorgon. Tuesday night started at Roxy 99 for Ladies' Night. That shit gets expensive, and between the traveling and my weed consumption, I had to scale back. But I still went out drinking every night.

Taiwan is one of a handful of places in the world that doesn't have any open-container liquor laws, so it's completely legal (and generally permissible) to drink just about everywhere except while *in transit* on the most prominent forms of public transportation, mainly city buses and subway trains. To be fair, some expat asshole has rocked up on the MRT

Blue Line with a beer in his paw, but it wasn't me. Responsible public intoxication has its limits.

However, I frequently purchased a tallboy of Asahi Dry from the 7-Eleven *inside* the MRT station and pounded it just before scanning my Easy Card and stumbling through the turnstile. The Taiwanese are non-confrontational people, but they're masters of the accusatory stare. If I properly disposed of the can in one of the nearby recycling bins, which I did religiously, nobody ever gave me the stink-eye.

Most taxis and long-distance buses and trains are fair game for boozing as long as you're relatively discreet and cool about it. During my residency, only one taxi driver told me I couldn't drink a beer in his ride. It was late at night, I was hammered, and the driver said he wouldn't take me home if I didn't dump the beer. "I don't want you puking in the back of my car," he scolded. So, I found another, less judgmental driver.

Drinking is acceptable in public places in Taiwan because alcohol doesn't have a negative connotation in society. To a certain extent, various degrees of intoxication are acceptable, or nobody really cares. It seemed to me that Asian cultures had the booze puzzle figured out. *I loved it.* There was no stigma or "loss of face" for getting sloshed on a Tuesday night. Likewise, the Taiwanese were familiar with me and my kind: a middle-aged white guy walking down the sidewalk. *American English teacher,* they thought. *Probably drunk.* To their credit, I was probably drunk.

Let's get one thing straight: Taiwan didn't turn anybody into an alcoholic; we were all like that before we arrived. Felix always said, "You're a good person, Charlie. Your only problem is you smoke and drink." It posed a paradox: If the Taiwanese thought so lowly of us, why were they cool with letting a bunch of drunks teach their children?

One of the first words I learned in Mandarin was *bianlidian.*

bianlidian [bee-un-lee-dee-en] Convenience store, minimart; e.g., 7-Eleven.

Home to more than 13,000 convenience stores, Taiwan has the world's second-highest density of convenience stores per person: one store per

1,769 people (population: 23 million). According to statistics from the Ministry of Economic Affairs, Taiwan's ratio of convenience stores is only topped by South Korea, and barely ahead of third-place Japan—interestingly, neither has open-container laws on the books. As of this writing, Taiwan also has the world's highest density of 7-Elevens per person: 6,712 stores, approximately one store per 3,400 people. To put that in perspective, there are only 9,492 7-Eleven locations *in the entire United States.*

In Taipei, it's not unusual to see two 7-Elevens across the street from each other, or better yet, several clustered together on the same block. Plus, there are a variety of competitors; you have 7-Eleven, Hi-Mart (aka Hi-Life), OK Mart, and Family Mart.

While I'm certainly a creature of habit who enjoys routine, I'm equally fond of variety. When I needed to cut spending, I often walked around aimlessly at night, sometimes walking from one end of town to the other. I might look at a map and say, "I haven't been to the Datong District in a while." These walkabouts invariably included frequent beer stops at the *bianlidian.* Urban alcoholic multi-tasking, so to speak—seeing the sights and building a solid buzz.

Meanwhile, the overarching utility of the convenience store was not lost on my expat brothers in booze. A tallboy of Taiwan Beer at 7-Eleven was maybe US$1.50, tops. A bottle of beer in a bar started at US$3.00. We did the math. While I preferred to keep moving, many guys posted up at one minimart and got smashed. Locals did it, too. The *bianlidian* was also a popular "pre-game" spot for budget-minded expats. We'd routinely have three or four beers at Family Mart before heading into Roxy Rocker.

To put an even finer point on the ubiquity of convenience store culture, one of the most enduring and accurate jokes told in Taiwan expat circles goes like this:

Q: What's the best bar in Taipei?
A: The nearest convenience store.

After a while, I started making a game of it—but only at night. I followed what I call "The Sundown Rules," one rule with a few minor exceptions:

No drinking while the sun is above the horizon, except on major holidays, my birthday, and vacations. Set the clock and daily routine to match the sunset. The rule also applies to daybreak; once the sun peaks above the horizon in the east, it's time to call it a night, a solar "last call."

Anyway, I developed a term for these nightly beer crawls: The Bianlidian Relay. To start, pick a random minimart, for instance, the 7-Eleven at the corner of Fuxing South Road and Xinyi Road. [Loud voice from a megaphone]: "Start walking north and finish this beer before you get to the next convenience store." And yes, I frequently spoke to myself in the second person.

Arriving at the Family Mart at Siwei Road, I'd buy another beer, take a right, and keep walking. The process would repeat itself until I got too sloppy to walk. And I got really good about reciting my address in Mandarin while drunk. Maybe six taxi drivers in Taiwan spoke proper Drunkard English.

The Bianlidian Relay had a major flaw. There were simply *too many* fucking convenience stores. The first couple of times, I didn't make it out of my neighborhood before I was stumbling and slurring. I felt like a pledge at a fraternity party. *How in the hell did I drink ten beers already?*

I tried to fix the problem with a *bianlidian*-specific solution. Since 7-Eleven was by far the most common convenience store in Taipei—there were three within 100 meters of KPHQ—I declared a moratorium on 7-Elevens. From there on out, I would only count on the lesser stores: OK Mart, Family Mart, and Hi-Life. But even by excluding 7-Eleven, you'd be surprised how many Family Marts are across the street from each other. It got to the point where I had to say, "From now on, only minimarts on *one side of the street*." Eventually, my second-person voice said, "Fuck it, tonight's an OK Mart Bianlidian Relay Night."

I saw a great deal of the city on foot, and I could pretty much act as a GPS when a travel companion asked if there was a convenience store nearby.

Taiwan didn't embrace me as much as it tolerated me. With a lot of luck, I found a decent gig and, slowly but surely, settled into a long-term lifestyle in Taipei. Six months turned into a few years. People came and went, but the Bianlidian Relay remained constant. While there may come a time when I miss other aspects of my life in Taiwan, the Bianlidian Relay occupies a special place in my heart.

★✳★

A new bar called Sam's Club opened across the street and around the corner from the dormitory. It was a tiny place, occupying a former coffee shop on Linjiang Street at the western entrance of the Tonghua Night Market from Anhe Road. The area was popular with tourists from the Shangri-la Hotel just a frisbee toss down the street, and long-term expats in Taiwan. The entrance to the night market got a ton of foot traffic via Linjiang Street.

Sam's Club was owned and operated by a Taiwanese guy named Sam and his business partners-slash-part-time bartenders, Simon, Arthur, and Xingxing. They were all in their early-to-mid 30s and super nice guys. Sam and Xingxing spoke excellent English, while Simon and Arthur weren't quite as fluent.

After one visit, I started going to Sam's Club every night and stopped crawling around the other bars. Sam's didn't open until 9:00 p.m., so I'd always start the night with a Bianlidian Relay. After a month of nightly visits, I got to know Sam and the boys. We became friends. I was warmly welcomed into their lives. They invited me into their homes. I became a popular fixture at the bar. They took me out to dinner on Sunday nights when the bar was closed. When Simon was bartending, he'd *make me dinner* (he was a chef by trade). If someone brought in some snacks from the night market, they always set me up with a spread. Not everybody had Sam's English skills, so I started speaking a lot more Mandarin every night, which was a win-win for me. And I finally found "my spot."

As a long-term expat, I have "kinks" about bars and restaurants. Whenever I'm in a new city or neighborhood, looking for a place to drink, everything kind of seems the same, and one of the few things that will *demand* my attention is the presence of another foreigner. So, for example, when I was in Zhuhai, if I walked by a joint on Bar Street and saw another foreigner, I would either make a beeline for that bar or make a mental bookmark and return later. The mere presence of a foreigner in a drinking establishment will attract at least the passing attention of any other foreigner just walking by. It's a conscious and sometimes subconscious recognition like, "Oh, there's one of *me* over there. That place must be cool. They probably speak English." It was an inevitable magnetism that I couldn't control or resist.

On the other hand, the presence of another foreigner is repulsive to some expats. They'll go the other direction by default. But I know I'm not alone because we put my "foreigner magnet" theory to the test at Sam's Club.

I went out of town, so I was absent from the bar for a week. When I returned, Sam said, "Hey Charlie, I've got a business proposition for you."

"I'm listening."

"You come here every night, don't you?"

Brows furrowed, shaking my head, I looked him in the eyes. "..."

Sam laughed nervously in recognition. "I know...I know. OK, OK. From now on, you only pay 50 Taiwan dollars for a bottle of beer." The usual price was TWD$90 (US$3) for Taiwan Beer and TWD$120 (US$4) for Heineken.

"That's nice, but what's the catch? Where's the business?"

"Keep coming here every night. And sit on the patio more often." And that's how I became the *de facto* marketing tool—the "bar boy" for Sam's Club.

Sam's had a small patio in front, with two tables facing Linjiang Street, just feet from the pavement. Most of the time, I sat inside at the bar but remained visible through the windows from the street.

It started happening within the first week. A foreigner or a group of foreigners would walk past Sam's Club, see me sitting at the bar, and they'd take notice. Many kept walking. In some cases, they would loop back around and enter the bar. In other cases, they would stop, have a brief conversation with each other, and cautiously step inside. The outlier was the foreigner who walked by on Tuesday night and returned on Wednesday night.

Without exception, the new foreign faces were warmly welcomed by Sam, the boys, and yours truly, and almost everybody seemed to enjoy themselves. In the beginning, it was mainly visiting businesspeople staying at the Shangri-la, but a rainbow of expats wound up having a few drinks at Sam's, and some of them became semi-regulars.

Business picked up noticeably when I sat on the patio. Much to my surprise, Sam said it worked on Taiwanese, too. "They see a foreigner and they get curious," he said. People would walk by and ask, "Hey, is this place any good?" and I'd say, "It's awesome! Come on in."

I lost count of how many people I met and drank with at Sam's Club, but a few stand out from the pack.

Boris and Michael were a tag team of mainland Chinese businessmen with local ties. They were in their early 40s—the same age as me—and owners of a logistics company in Shanghai. I met them one night as I loitered on the patio of the bar. There was a small pop-up seafood stall with outdoor seating across the street. The clientele was strictly local—I'd never dined there. Not a word of English on the menu and some sketchy food preparation hygiene issues that could be seen from the 7-Eleven on the corner. Even Sam and the boys thought the seafood stall was garbage and off-limits.

I was sitting on the patio, smoking and drinking, minding my own business. Michael, Boris, and a few other mainland types were eating at the seafood stall. They were zoned in on me, and I returned their stares occasionally. This went on for maybe five minutes or so.

Suddenly, Michael shouted, "Homosexual!" across Linjiang Street, and obviously in my general direction. I did one of those *Who, Me? Are You Talkin' to Me?* moves with a finger pointing at my sternum and laughed. I raised a bottle of Taiwan Beer in their direction. The other men at the table laughed. Michael continued shouting "homosexual," waving a lit cigarette for emphasis. I gave him a few nods and thumbs up and put out my cigarette.

A minute later, the chunky and sweaty-faced Boris approached and said, "Excuse me, sir. Are you an American?" His English, though somewhat stuttered, was pretty damn good.

"Yes. Why? What do you want from me?"

"My boss [Michael] invites you to have a drink," Boris said. I peered across his shoulder to see Michael lording over a table full of half-eaten dishes, empty beer bottles, and cigarette packs, surrounded by his cadre.

"OK," I said. "I'll drink with him."

Glossing over the deeper complexities of Taiwanese society, let's just say that the highest probability of anybody calling out a foreigner, let alone with such a controversial term, and sending his valet over to make an introduction, would be from a rich, powerful, and obnoxiously drunk mainland Chinese guy like Michael. It's one of the few ways to know for sure that somebody is out of their mind. Grandiose displays of wealth and power in Taiwan tended to generate envy and disdain instead of favorable impressions. Most Taiwanese think flashing wealth is tacky, and rudeness in public is a loss of face. It was one thing to have nice clothes, shiny new cars, and fancy apartments. Those are A-OK. But uncivilized and particularly mainland Chinese-like behavior was *seriously* frowned upon. Felix and Daisy would have been jumping out of their skins if they heard and saw that shit. Therefore, it was obvious to me, *way* before I accepted the invitation, that Michael was someone "special." I didn't care that he was calling me a homosexual. I just wanted to know what kind of asshole had the stones to do it.

I went over and met Michael and his crew. Following the introductions, it was clear that Michael had a tenuous command of English. Boris or one of the other lackeys had to translate for him. My Mandarin was passable in discrete survival and conversational situations but hardly good enough to pass in a roundtable discussion about my sexual preferences.

And so, on that note, Michael insisted that I sit next to him. He draped an arm across my shoulder, handed me a glass of beer, and said, "My friend, *ganbei!*" (Drink up!) and we tossed back the beer. The next words out of his mouth were, "So, you are homosexual."

My sexual preferences have been questioned and/or challenged in the past. There were two things I never did: protest too much or escalate the tension by returning the accusation (gaslighting). In this instance, I merely laughed and said (in Mandarin), "*Bu zhidao. Wo shi ma?*" (I don't know, am I?) which, of course, raised an uproarious amount of clucking from the peanut gallery. For the next five minutes I sat and drank and answered the usual questions about my country of origin, purposes in Taiwan, and the ubiquitous, "Do you like Taiwanese girls?"—which I also never failed to answer the same way.

"I like *all* girls—who like *me*."

The five minutes of relative comfort were up when Michael once again leaned into me, arm around my shoulder, baring a smile and flashing red-stained betel nut teeth, and said, "So, you are homosexual." It wasn't as much of a question as much as a statement. There was no upward tonal crescendo on the back end of *sexual*. There was no lingering doubt.

Bored of the conversation, I turned to my left where Boris sat hunched over yet smiling. Grabbing him by the sleeve, I said, "Hey, I need you to translate something for me."

I set into a lengthy diatribe, pausing every 15 seconds to let Boris do the translation.

"*No, I am not a homosexual but...your homophobia is projection. Why are you asking? Are you looking for a gay man? Are you in the closet?*" I got a little heated, said some things that weren't very nice.

Out of my peripheral vision, I saw Simon observing the situation with arms folded from the bar patio. I smiled and waved to him, as in, *I'm fine. No problem here.* Simon quickly came over, towering above the table, and said, "Charlie, are you OK? Do you need any help?"

Simon was a formidable presence: six-foot-one, 220 pounds of Taiwanese gangster tattoos and attitude. Michael and Boris immediately assured him there was no imminent threat to my safety. I thanked Simon and said I would be fine. Simon kept staring at me over his shoulder as he walked away. It felt good to know I had backup.

Surprisingly, Michael seemed to understand the translation of my spiel. He was amused, to say the least. After Boris rattled off the last bit, Michael waved, something like an umpire calling a runner safe, and said I was missing the point. He jabbered at Boris for a minute while I simmered and accepted another Mild Seven cigarette from one of the other dudes.

Finally, Boris turned to me. "Charlie, he is not serious. He is only joking and wanted to see your reaction. Do you understand?"

"Whatever, Boris. I don't give a fuck."

Boris hesitated for a moment, and Michael chimed in, "So, you are homosexual."

And that was the end of that. I stood up, thanked them for the hospitality, and started to leave when Michael and Boris protested and tugged on my arms. "Please, don't be offended. Stay."

"No, thank you but I've had enough of this for the night."

Simon and Arthur came out of Sam's Club looking serious and pissed off. Arthur put his arm around my shoulder and led me back to the bar while Simon stood berating Boris and Michael. He returned to the bar and said, "I hate those fucking mainland cunts."

A few nights later, Boris and Michael were back at the seafood stall across the street from Sam's Club but without the cadre of associates. It almost seemed like they were waiting for me to show up. As I crossed the street to enter the bar, Michael called out, "Hey, Charlie!" He motioned for me to join them. I reluctantly turned around and approached their table.

"What? No homosexual tonight?"

They both had quizzical looks. "What do you mean?" Boris asked.

"You don't remember?" Judging from their blank stares, they didn't remember all the details of the previous evening.

"Sit down," Michael said. "Let's have some drinks."

They poured me some beer and made light conversation. Michael was relatively sober compared to the other night, and he said as much. "I was very drunk that night. I'm sorry if I offended you."

"Forget about it."

Boris said, "What are you doing tonight?"

"Drinking at Sam's Club, like I do every night."

"Would you like to come to KTV with us?"

"Um, no thanks. I don't sing."

Boris laughed.

Michael said, "You don't have to sing at this KTV!"

"You like Taiwanese girls?" Boris asked.

"Yes, of course. I like *all* girls. Especially the ones who like me."

"Good!"

There are several types of karaoke houses and bars in Taiwan (colloquially known as KTV), and most are strictly aboveboard, i.e., good clean fun. They took me to a relatively infamous place in the Zhongshan District called CEO, which was somewhere between a Japanese hostess bar and a high-priced brothel. The women were initially contracted for social companionship, but you could always negotiate for more. In this particular place, you weren't allowed to "take them outside." They had special rooms (at extortionate rates) where you could take things further if both parties agreed.

We pulled up in Michael's black Mercedes sedan to the podium in front of CEO and were immediately greeted by two valets, one of whom was wearing a headset. Michael was driving; I was alone in the backseat. A few minutes of negotiation. Boris gave me the play-by-play. "We don't have a reservation, but the boss is a V.I.P. The next round of girls comes at ten o'clock. We may have to wait...only twenty minutes..."

Finally, we got out of the car and entered the lobby, which was decked out like a five-star hotel. A host took us downstairs to a waiting hall with plush couches. Every few minutes, a parade of hostesses came prancing by on their way to the next "lineup." Michael got impatient and collared some kid in a uniform, and the next thing I knew, we had a bottle of Scotch and two buckets of ice.

A parade of women eventually appeared before us, and Boris said, "This is our lineup." Michael selected a trio of women, and we were escorted to a room with three leather couches, two knee-high lounge tables, and a massive flat-screen TV on the wall. The karaoke machine was built into the opposite wall. A couple of male attendants popped in and out with the Scotch and a bucket of beers for me. I wasn't much of a whisky drinker. Michael sat on one couch off to the side while Boris and I shared the largest couch in front of the screen.

The women entered without negotiation or hesitation and automatically sat next to the three of us. I wasn't sure if Michael had made the assignments in advance or if they just decided amongst themselves. At any rate, the youngest-looking and skinniest of the women sat next to me, rubbed my arm, and immediately refreshed my glass of beer.

This was a new experience, so I followed their lead. Every so often, Boris leaned over to explain what was happening and how things worked.

"These girls are companions. Michael is paying for that. No sex unless you both agree to it. In that case, you must pay for her services. Michael isn't paying for that. But I wouldn't do it. A private room is very expensive. Just enjoy her company. We have the room and the girls for two hours. The girls will do all the singing. Just sit back and relax. Your girl will take care of you, pour your beer, light your cigarette. You can touch and kiss her if you like, but nothing more."

My companion was very attractive and nice, but she didn't speak English, so we did our best in Mandarin. She was 22 years old, from southern Taiwan, and relatively new to the KTV scene. It was her first week in Taipei since dropping out of college in Pingtung, allegedly.

All three women took turns on the microphone, doing sappy and maudlin Taiwanese and Chinese pop ballads. The women were attentive and very nice to look at, but within 15 minutes, I wondered if this was it. *We just sit here, drink, and watch them sing? What a waste of time!*

Michael was getting pretty familiar with his companion. *Now we're getting somewhere!* And I hoped that he would take the woman to a private room so I could fuck off and get the hell out of there.

An hour passed before Michael got up, went to the door and summoned one of the uniformed attendants. They spoke briefly. A few minutes later, the attendant returned to the room and handed something to Michael, who slipped the small package into his front shirt pocket. I made eye contact with Boris, who smiled and nodded his head. I had no idea what was happening.

Michael came over, bent down, and whispered in my ear, "Have you ever done ketamine?" He produced the packet from his shirt pocket and waved it in my face.

"I've done it a few times."

Michael blinked slowly. "Let's do it."

The ketamine was dumped onto a tray. One of the companions started cutting small lines while another began removing tobacco from the tips of several cigarettes and shoveling small amounts of the powder into the paper. My girl stayed glued to my arm. It seemed like this was all new to her.

Boris asked, "Do you prefer to smoke or [sharp sniffing noise]?"

"Either way is fine with me." I did a couple of lines and smoked one of the cigarettes. Michael's companion also partook in the festivities.

My head was buzzing and spinning, and I lost track of time and space. Michael and Boris kept offering lines, and I kept sucking them up. Eventually, all the ketamine was gone. Michael went back outside and grabbed the attendant, who returned five minutes later with another packet of ketamine. That happened twice more within an hour, which felt like an eternity. Everybody except my companion was doing lines, and it got quite greasy in there for a little while.

At the two-hour mark, the women got up without warning, said goodbye, and left the room. I was fucking *blasted*, but Boris and Michael seemed fine. A couple of attendants cleared the booze and ashtrays from the table. The lights came up, the host presented the bill to Michael, and that's when things went south.

I didn't have the vaguest idea how much it cost to get a room, three women, a bunch of booze, and four packets of ketamine in this KTV establishment, but Michael *lost his shit* when he saw the bill for TWD$75,000 (roughly US$2,500), screaming at the host with threatening gestures. I sat there in a daze while Boris tried to soothe Michael. I'm not sure what happened after that. A couple of bouncer-types entered the room and left with Michael and Boris. Following several minutes of stunned, motionless stupor, I was startled when my former companion returned with a sympathetic look and said, "I think there's a problem, and you should leave now." Another attendant walked me upstairs to the front door. The valet asked, "Where do you live?" I told him, and he said, "Do you want me to call you a taxi?" I said that would be very helpful, thank you.

I woke up the next morning with the worst three-day hangover I've ever had in 40 years of substance abuse.

I didn't see Boris or Michael for a long time after that. Several years later, long after Sam's Club closed, I ran into Boris at the night market. We reminisced about the KTV incident.

"What happened to you?" asked Boris. "Where did you go?"

"Where did *I* go? You fuckers left me sitting there like a dummy."

"We went to negotiate the bill with the owner. Michael was very upset."

"Where is he these days?"

"In Shanghai." His eyes flashed. "He's gay, you know?"

"Mmm-hmm."

Boris nodded. "He has a boyfriend now."

* * *

An unusual expat named Chuck appeared one random weeknight. He was already at the bar when I showed up at 9:00 p.m. Xingxing was bartending. *Da xingxing* in Mandarin means gorilla. He was six-foot-two, 300 pounds, with a shaved head and a goatee. Nicest guy in the world but extremely intimidating. Xingxing vaguely nodded toward Chuck when I walked in, like, "Check out this guy."

Chuck was ethnically Indian, tall and skinny, with straight jet-black hair down to his chest. He was also wearing sunglasses. I sat a few stools down the bar, closer to the window, and waited for Xingxing to bring me a bottle of Heineken. Chuck was concentrating on his cell phone and didn't notice me. This gave me a chance to size him up. He had an expensive watch, nice business casual all-black pants and shirt. I'm not a shoe guy, but his leather loafers looked like they cost more than I made in a week. He was staying at the Far Eastern Shangri-la—no doubt.

Xingxing and I talked for a while. *Sam's coming later? Where's Xiaomei?* (Sam's girlfriend). *Is Zizi coming?* (Xing's girlfriend) *How's work?* Etc.

A few minutes later, Chuck turned to me and said, "Hey, man, you're an American."

"Yep. I'm Charlie. What's your name?"

"Chuck Das."

I've had a weird affinity with other guys named Charles, Charlie, Chuck, and Chas. It's a common name, but I've had many more friends and acquaintances named Charles than any other. At least we always have a conversation starter. I wonder if other names have the same experience. Chuck Das and I hit it off right away. The initial conversations were intense. We talked for two hours that first night. Sam, Xiaomei, and Zizi showed up and I didn't even say hello to them.

Chuck spun a web of impressive and almost unbelievable origins. His family were billionaire-class Indian but living in Sri Lanka, and he was somehow a U.S. citizen, too. He just bought a castle in Scotland and he owned a shady "shadow banking" investment firm. He was in Taipei for a few nights on a business and spent the previous week in Manila. He referred to himself as "asset rich but cash poor." *This guy is probably telling the truth.*

Chuck left to meet an associate at a nearby nightclub but asked if I'd be at Sam's Club tomorrow night.

"I'm at Sam's every night."

The next night I was finishing up the ribeye steak that Simon cooked for me when Chuck Das returned. We picked up the conversation where it left off. Chuck asked if I owned any property. I said no.

"Why not?" He already knew that Captain Felix paid me in peanuts.

"Cuz I can't afford it!"

"Well, you would if you worked for me."

"To be honest, Chuck, I don't know a goddamn thing about international finance. I'm terrible with numbers."

"You don't have to be good with numbers. You just have to know one thing."

"What's that?"

"How can you help me?"

"That's basically what I just said, Chuck. I don't know if I *can* help you. What kind of skills do I have that will make a difference? I can't think of any. I'm a writer and editor. I'm good at finding shit."

"You're looking at it the wrong way. *How can you help me? What can you do to help my company?* Think about it."

"Right on, I will."

Eventually, the conversation came around to women and sex tourism. We shared experiences in China and Thailand. Chuck asked about getting a hooker in Taiwan. It was one of the few places he had never indulged. Of course, he knew how to use the internet and get the names of some hotspots, but he couldn't get a handle on it.

"What do you have for me, Charlie?"

I told him what I knew. Prostitution in Taiwan is weird, very cloak-and-dagger stuff. The best place to get a hooker in Taiwan was online, but unless you read and write Mandarin, forget about it. In most cases, you needed a local "in." There were two maybe three areas to pick up freelancers from the streets, but I strongly discouraged Chuck from that option, and he wasn't interested anyway. He was talking about top-shelf escort stuff, which, again, wasn't readily available to foreigners except in certain nightclubs.

"You're staying at the Shangril-la," I said, "which is just down the street from Carnegie's. You could post up there tonight and I almost guarantee you're going to find a girl—or vice versa. A nice one, too."

"I was wondering about Carnegie's."

The next night, Chuck was already sitting on Sam's patio when I arrived.

"Hey, Chuck. How'd it go last night?"

"Dude…" he said smiling. "You were so right. I'm buying your beers tonight."

We had a long conversation about international sex tourism. At some point, we talked about the Philippines because Chuck had spent a lot of time in Metro Manila and Angeles. He gave me the rundown on the scene. All that greasy shit was so fascinating to me, even if I didn't partake anymore. It was really good to compare notes with someone other than Felix.

Chuck returned to Taipei several times over the next few years, and we stayed in touch for nearly a decade. For the most part, Chuck Das was a "real person." I *thought* he was telling the truth, but I wouldn't know for sure until many years later.

A local woman named Elaine started hanging out at Sam's Club that summer. She worked as a production manager for *Apple Daily*, the island's premier local gossip magazine and generally one of the most amusing pieces of shit I've ever seen as far as throwaway weekly tabloids are concerned. Imagine a cross between *People*, Perez Hilton, TMZ, and

The New York Post, with a dirty comic strip at the back, next to the horoscopes, something that wouldn't be out of place in *Penthouse* or *Playboy*. The publisher claimed 'to keep people honest' by exposing their dirty laundry. Its motto was: "Don't Put on Airs: Just Seek the Truth." *And bring a fucking camera, chop-chop.*

Elaine was cool. There was no sexual tension between us. Her English was amazing, and she was patient with my Mandarin. We had several great conversations, especially about Captain Felix. I wasn't telling Elaine anything she didn't already know because Felix was a famous teacher. *Everybody* knew Zhang Yi. His face was on billboards, and he frequently appeared on television news, either as a commentator or the subject of some "scandal" or something. At the same time, Sherry had been in the tabloids, so Elaine was very familiar with the workings of Knowledge Press and Zhang Yi English Academy.

One night, Elaine asked, "Is your boss sleeping with Sherry?"

"Probably not, but he hasn't given up yet." What I didn't know at the time was Felix and Sherry *had* slept together multiple times.

"Oh? What do you know about their relationship?"

I laid it all out for Elaine, starting with the high-end condo Felix had given Sherry and ending with Captain Felix in serious courting mode, taking Sherry out to dinner whenever possible.

Elaine raised her eyebrows. "Does Sherry have another boyfriend?"

I replied that she did, some other blowhard teacher, I don't know his name. Some married guy. Or maybe he's divorced. *Some guy.*

We continued talking until I ran out of gossip tidbits and changed the subject. The next night, I rolled up to Sam's Club and found Elaine sitting with a dude named Rocky, who also worked for *Apple Daily*. After exchanging some pleasantries, Elaine said, "Listen, I don't want to put you in an awkward position, but would you mind telling Rocky what you told me last night? About Zhang Yi and Sherry?"

"Sure, no problem." I repeated the story to Rocky, and that was the last time Elaine ever mentioned Captain Felix or Sherry, for that matter.

13

Goodbye, Golden Goose

My desk at Knowledge Press was situated in the northwest corner of our private office, which gave me a quirky sightline to the main robot room. I could crane my neck slightly to the left of my PC tower and see most of the cubicles in the main room and the hallway leading from the front door. Otherwise, I remained out of general sight. Whenever I heard the main door open and somebody enter, I'd lean over and get a preview of who it was. Ninety-five percent of the time, it didn't matter who had arrived, but it became a habit.

One morning, Sherry came into the office, and I watched like a voyeur as she beelined to her cubicle, immediately followed by Felix, who entered the control center, sat down, put his feet up on his desk, leaned back, and gasped, "Ahh, Sherry. She's so dynamic. Don't you think?"

Lifting my hands from the keyboard, I looked him over, knowing his satisfied glow, and asked, in a hushed tone, "Sir, did you just have sex with Sherry?"

Felix grinned and sighed, looking up at the ceiling. "Ah, she's such a dynamic woman. And me, I'm just this ugly old man." He made eye contact. "Life is a sea of trouble."

I leaned back in my chair and stared at him. He wasn't going to admit that he'd just banged Sherry, but... *What the fuck does that mean?*

Later that evening, I went out to dinner with my old friend Veronica, who used to be a teacher at the cram school. It was purely platonic. Veronica was engaged and way out of my league. I just liked hanging out with such a gorgeous woman; she just wanted all the latest gossip from Knowledge Press and ZYEA. Even though she no longer worked for us, the experience still occupied a big part of Veronica's psyche. She got her first big break from Felix and respected him in some perverse way. And she could hardly contain her excitement when I told her the story about Felix and Sherry from this morning.

We dined at a Japanese restaurant in the Songshan District, not far from Veronica's apartment. She chose the place. I rarely went to that part of town.

As Veronica and I were exiting the restaurant, she pointed toward the right and said, "Look, that's Sherry's building."

It was a swanky condo building. Looked super pricey.

"Oh. I didn't know you lived so close to her. Is that where Felix bought her an apartment?"

"It *is*."

"Really? Let's go down and have a look."

As we started toward the building about a block away, a taxi pulled up at the entrance, and two people got out of the back seat, embraced, and kissed while standing on the sidewalk.

"Holy shit!" I cried. "It's Felix and Sherry! Quick, let's get out of sight before they see us."

We ducked behind the pillar of a nearby arcade and watched as Felix and Sherry exchanged an intimate moment. They appeared to be having a pleasant conversation at first, but Sherry started shaking her head. Suddenly, she was dropping her head as she spoke—of course, we didn't know what she was saying—and Felix spread his arms out, pleading with her. We could almost hear what Felix was shouting. Sherry spun around on her heels and bolted into the entrance of the building, leaving Felix standing alone on the sidewalk.

"Oh my God!" Veronica gasped. "She just rejected him!"

I chuckled with mischief. "Sure looks like it."

The Captain pulled out his cell phone, made a brief call while hailing a taxi, and disappeared into the night.

✳

The definition of good changes over time. In the beginning, this adventure in Taiwan was "everything" because it was too messy, scattered, and overwhelming to compartmentalize. I filed every experience into one big folder labeled **Everything**. Everything was good, turned kinda bad. I went away for a while. When I came back, everything was not as bad. Soon, everything became bearable. And it became comfortable. Sometimes, everything was boring. Sometimes, everything was exciting. Everything was pathetic and fascinating, desperate and miraculous. Everything was a drug that enslaved and redeemed me. Everything was warden and wet nurse. Everything was bad and good and everything in between.

We can only exist in our microcosmic head spaces. Look at the so-called gray areas of your life. The things that aren't necessarily bad and not necessarily good—but you do them anyway. There's a lot of flesh in those areas. If I were to take one countable event in my life, for instance, the affair with Fang, I could spend macrocosmic amounts of time picking it apart and seeing individual aspects of this event as good or bad, starting with: *Did I deserve it?* Fuck the mental gymnastics. The Math of Everything begins and ends with a zero.

Everything can be good and bad and everything in between if you allow it to be. The definition of good (or bad) doesn't change over time, but time has perspective. I don't think my exact age is crucial to the story, but let's just say that statistically, I've already lived about 65-70 percent of my life, meaning I'm not an old man, but I'm not a young man anymore, either. There are good and bad aspects of both sides.

★✷★

It was usually a *bad* sign when I stumbled into the office at 10:30 a.m. and saw the Captain's shoes in the foyer. That meant: (a) he got there before I did, which he loathed but never directly confronted me about, and (b) I had approximately 30 seconds to prepare myself for his ever-changing moods. *Which version of Felix do we have today?*

I stepped into my *lanbai* slippers and steeled myself to face the Universal Essay issue. But no. That morning, I found them—Captain

Felix, Sherry, and Gretchen—clustered around his desk, locked in a lively but vaguely contentious discussion. They appeared to be plotting some sort of Capture the Flag offensive. The sight gave me pause and a chortle. There was no sign of Daisy; she was out of town for the week. But wait. From experience, whenever I saw Sherry in the Hot Seat next to the Captain's desk, she was either: (a) trying to rat out a co-teacher or an insubordinate robot or (b) asking for money or an expensive favor.

Sherry and I hadn't made eye contact in months. Gretchen sat there and clucked like a chicken too fat to walk, so I never paid attention to her anyway. Captain Felix didn't acknowledge me, so I plunked down in my chair, powered up the PC, and went about my business. If it was truly a sensitive or serious discussion, Felix would politely ask me to leave and return later, which always resulted in some sort of cash bonus. I never took offense because I never considered it my office in the first place. And whatever Felix had cooking was infinitely more important than any marshmallows I had roasting over the campfire. And generally, none of the day-to-day bullshit around KPHQ involved me. On this occasion, a bad sign turned into a good sign, or at least, *null and void*. And that's where I wanted to be.

From what I could gather, Captain Felix was not-yet angry but poised to be furious about someone or something for reasons to be explicated in due time. The three of them were talking about crafting a response to the breaking news. That's all I could get. I kept my head down and out. A few minutes later, Jerry Mouse came toddling in with a foot-high stack of *Apple Daily*, the local gossip magazine. The cover of the latest edition featured *paparazzi* shots of Sherry and her new boyfriend, Kao Kanhua aka Kevin Kao, making out—*on the cover of the magazine*. Felix grabbed a copy and leaned back in his chair. The blood drained from his face as he leaned forward and rested his elbows on the desktop, holding the magazine closer to his nose.

Captain Felix bounced in his seat when agitated. One of his legs started tapping at 200 bpm. He rocked back and forth—just a little bit, remaining in control, but just on the edge. He had two modes of distinction: deescalate or explode, opposite ends of the spectrum. In moments of agitation, he could go either way. There was no in-between. I watched him peruse the magazine in my peripheral vision. Every five seconds, I tried to sneak a direct glance. Again, I briefly caught sight of

Sherry on the cover of the magazine. The bouncing began. Then Felix discarded the magazine to his right, tossing it disdainfully onto the stack of books that bridged our two desks together, face up. And that's when I saw what the news media dubbed "The Tongue"—Kevin Kao sticking his tongue down Sherry's throat while driving behind the wheel of his Mercedes-Benz.

Taiwan is a small place. What accounts for local headline news wouldn't make decent gossip in a retirement home cafeteria. The scandals were flashy and dramatic but typically light on one thing: scandalous behavior. On the other hand, the ESL racket in Asia is no joke, and schools are a big fucking deal. The guys who run the schools are fiercely competitive, and Captain Felix was unquestionably one of the last surviving Old School kingpins.

Despite her slight and tawdry personality, Sherry had long been considered the Golden Goose of the cram school operation. She made headlines about a decade earlier when she was a stewardess and gave birth to a child out of wedlock, and the father was rumored to be a high-ranking and very married government official. He *wasn't* the father, but the gossipmongers ran with the story anyway. Nobody was out to get Sherry *per se*; she was a throwaway pawn in the story. However, the Vice-chairman of the Ministry of Finance had some fearsome enemies, and he took a big hit on that one. Anyway, years later, Sherry's nickname among the familiar was "the sexy (or slutty) cram school teacher." And she wasn't a dummy, even though she could barely complete a sentence in English without a visual aid. Physically, she was an aging KTV hostess, dolled up in clothing so revealing you would never in a million years guess she was a cram school teacher, and her classes were packed to the rafters with nascent adolescent high school boys. There was a waiting list to join her classes. Zhang Yi had to build bigger classrooms to accommodate the demand. She was a genuine Golden Goose, laying the golden eggs.

Given their disparate levels of perceived attractiveness, it was obvious to **everybody** that Sherry had been fleecing Felix for everything she could get. The depth of their relationship wasn't yet crystal clear, but *something* fishy was going on between them. Word in gossip circles at Knowledge Press was that Captain Felix was sighted on several occasions leaving Sherry's apartment building late at night. *I could confirm that one.* And I had long and conflicting suspicions that Sherry was either (a) the Captain's lover or (b) an illegitimate daughter. Sometimes, I saw them together and saw the same person. I didn't believe any of the rumors—I believed *all of them.*

Forgive me if you think I'm judgmental for saying that Sherry was total trash. Certain characters—drug dealers, cops, politicians, models, actors, rock stars, and prostitutes, all sociopaths and liars, basically—have an essence, an intangible quality of presence, and **I know them when I see them**, in or out of uniform, so to speak. Over time, I observed Sherry's vindictive scheming and steered clear. When she tried (and failed) to cause trouble for me, she became an enemy.

The blood started draining from my face, too, when I realized that *Apple Daily* was involved. I flashed back to my conversations with Elaine and Rocky at Sam's Club. *Holy shit, did I trigger this impending catastrophe?* It sure looked like Rocky took my information and ran with it.

The people at *Apple Daily*, for reasons not entirely beyond my grasp, had *paparazzi* follow Sherry around for a couple of weeks, and they got many entertaining photographs. Why they chose Sherry is almost beside the point. At any rate, they did. And as I mentioned earlier, they had wonderful shots of her making out with her boyfriend in the front seat of his car. And checking into a love hotel. And checking out of the love hotel. Meanwhile, the boyfriend bragged to his friends with X-rated cell phone shots he'd taken during those love hotel romps. And of course, we all got a good look-see at those, too. And it went on and on...

These photographs of Sherry's love life would hardly be scandalous—shocking, maybe, if you didn't know her—unless the new boyfriend, Kevin Kao, happened to be—*uh-oh*—a recently divorced and famous-in-his-own-right teacher and owner of a rival school, who not coincidentally was a principal antagonist behind the shutdown of our schools over some building code technicality. It was what I called Total Chopstick Bullshit. Those ESL guys loved to play games like that. This Kevin Kao chump was the one who used his muscle in the government to force Captain Felix to spend half a million dollars on an updated fire sprinkler system that had aged beyond legality. In other words, this Kevin Kao was supposed to be the Captain's mortal enemy.

Legally, it appeared nothing was amiss. Had Kevin Kao still been married, there might have been reason for scandal—adultery is a crime in Taiwan, and justice is served with cash. An extramarital affair was a seven-to-eight-digit figure in the local currency. At any rate, Sherry was also divorced. So, where was the scandal? Two famously talented and single people got together and talked about teaching methods. Exchanged ideas. Maybe a few bodily fluids. Jay-Z and Beyonce. Sean Penn and Madonna. Brad Pitt and Angelina Jolie... To me, there was nothing to see here.

Where Captain Felix was concerned, Sherry had finally crossed the line—fucking the competition. Unfortunately for Sherry, that ephemeral and arbitrary line was crossed on the cover of a gossip magazine available in every *bianlidian* and supermarket in the country, as well as feature stories on the local TV news. Felix wasn't going to give her up that easily.

Jealousy is a bitch. Anybody who knows jealousy knows what it's like to die. It's worse than death because it just doesn't end. The pain goes on and on. When you can't have the one thing you want more than anything else, sometimes, you will stop at nothing to make sure no one else gets it, either.

★✱★

If I had known about the breaking scandal, there was no way in hell I would have come into the office unless Felix or Daisy called and said, "Where the heck are you?" or I knew with absolute certainty that Felix was out of town and not coming back anytime soon. This had nothing to do with me, but sitting there, trying not to pay attention, felt wrong. It felt **bad**, like I was seeing something I shouldn't be seeing. Like I might have started a fire that burned down the building. Or it was something I didn't *need* to see—like, for instance, the live birth of a foal or a real-time amputation. *That* definition of bad hadn't changed since I was old enough to realize my penis did more than get caught in my zipper.

The talk was fast and contentious, and I couldn't keep up. Robots came in and out of the room. Felix stood up, left for a while, returned, stood up, and placed a call on his cell phone that wasn't answered. Sherry and Gretchen sat nervously on the Hot Seat, still uncomfortably close.

Felix sat down and said, "OK, here's what we're going to say," and the three of them conspired to write a response—ostensibly to the magazine. Captain Felix dictating, Sherry transcribing, and Gretchen clucking her encouragement. Sherry appeared to be deeply concerned, beyond worried. Her repeated apologies seemed to be sincere, but I could see that Felix wasn't buying it.

The gist of the response went like this. Felix accused Kevin Kao of trying to steal Sherry and put her to work in his (Kao's) operation, which was perplexingly taboo in this society. Rape, murder, embezzlement, wire fraud; those things were waved off like a parking ticket. Trying to jack someone's Golden Goose was *verboten*. And given Sherry's massive popularity with students, this wasn't just about love. In Taiwan, it was essentially a declaration of war.

Coco the fax machine girl came in waving a message from a TV station. The Captain would be allowed to respond at 4:30 p.m.—on live television. This shit was blowing up island-wide. Captain Felix made a hasty exit. He *evaporated*. Sherry and Gretchen split. Soon the office was back to its normal, deadly quiet self.

I went about my business like any other day. At 9:00 p.m., I shuffled down to Sam's Club and watched the evening news report on TV. I saw the rebroadcast of Felix's interview and another featuring Sherry with Kevin Kao at her side—which was weird. Just a few hours ago, she was at KPHQ, apologizing to Felix. *Something happened* between her presence in the office and the media interviews taking place. She must have fought with Felix.

The Captain's statement was clear and concise compared to Sherry's rambling and sobbing profession of love for the enemy. She all *but* announced that she was leaving our school for Kevin Kao's school. She stuttered and cried and said how she didn't want this to happen, she was sorry—coached by Kevin Kao—and tried so very hard to be contrite, because that's what the TV-viewing public wanted to see. They wanted formal apologies and tokens of respect. All that kowtowing bullshit.

Sherry finally said she would make an "official announcement" soon—after consulting her mother, who also happened to be real tight with Captain Felix. *More intrigue.* Even if she had wanted to, Sherry couldn't just come out and say, "Yeah, fuck Zhang Yi. He's a chump. I'm outta there!" Overall, though, it was bad news for Felix and ZYEA. *Very bad* for the Captain. He was on the verge of losing his Golden Goose. I wondered how he could spin this to his advantage. I wondered if it would help sell books.

The next morning, KPHQ was almost empty. Only a few robots were at their desks. The office had a cold, evacuated feeling. Several cubicles belonging to Sherry's little team of assistants were cleared out.

Wow! They've all defected. And I was kind of worried there for a minute. For my job security, of course. *What if Sherry could single-handedly bring down the empire, and take my red carpet existence with it?*

At any rate, Daisy had been out of town for the last week and was due back that afternoon. And she *loathed* Sherry, too. We bonded over our shared hatred of the woman. While I was anxious to hear what Daisy had to say about things, in a way I was glad she wasn't around. The last thing Felix needed was *Daisy* screeching in his ears.

Later that morning, Felix arrived and was set upon by robots looking for signatures. He didn't even look at me. I typed and said nothing. Sometime later his phone rang. The way he answered I knew it was Daisy. As usual, I could hear her voice loud and clear. Felix held the phone about six inches from his ear. Struggling to eavesdrop, I gleaned that Daisy: (a) heard about the scandal and (b) was going to stay wherever she was until the weekend, at least.

Near the end of their conversation, Felix said in English, "No problem. They need you. Everyone wants your help. You are needed there. You are in the demanding. Stay there. You are demanding."

I knew he was trying to say "in demand" but didn't interrupt. The fact that he even spoke to her in English was for my benefit. My friends and I called it 'banana boating,' a phenomenon that happened frequently in public. Taiwanese and Chinese loved to show off their English skills if they had any. Sometimes, pushy parents forced their kids to speak English with me. Other times, walking through the night market, some young doll on her cell phone saw me in the vicinity and broke into English. I always laughed because I knew the guy on the other end was saying, "Why are you speaking English? Is there a foreigner nearby?"

The call ended and Felix turned to me. "Sir, do you need any help? Is there anything I can do for you?"

"No, thank you. I'm good."

"That's great. So, you saw the news? Do you know what's going on?"

"I do, and it's none of my business. By the way, you wanted to say, 'You are in demand,' not 'You are demanding'. It's kind of an insult."

The Captain's face lit up. "You're right!" He laughed and smiled and patted the desktop. "Thank you for reminding me!" There were rare occasions when I corrected his English, and he was happy. It was the weirdest thing. I rarely ever did it unless I heard him make an egregious error, like telling Daisy she was *demanding* rather than *in demand*.

"Tell me the difference between the two."

"Well," I said, standing up from my chair. "When someone is *in demand*, it means they are popular. There's not enough of 'em to go around, you know? When someone is *demanding*, that means bossy."

"I see." He was genuinely pleased. "Thank you for your help. Stay right where you are. Don't move." He called Daisy as I stood and watched. He always wanted me right there when these little events occurred, like a witness. Another peccadillo was Felix rarely ever said "Hello" when he called. Daisy answered and he boomed, "You are *in demand*! You are not demanding." He paused for a moment. "They need your help. There is not enough of you to go around. You are popular—in demand. *Your mother...is demanding.*"

The call ended pleasantly. I went back to work. Some time passed before Felix said, "I envy you. You are free. I have so many monkeys on my back."

I heard the monkey comment at least a dozen times before. I knew what he meant. I could see all the monkeys on his back, and I knew how they got there. Now I understood what he meant by "life is a sea of trouble." He had a world of shit to deal with. The empire and everything that went with it. Everybody wanted a piece of Captain Felix. Hardly a minute went by without someone calling, entering, asking, informing, inciting, apologizing, or, my favorite, delivering a gift basket. Politicians reaching in every pocket. His messy divorce ordeal—I didn't even get to that part yet. A week didn't go by without a kowtowing robot coming in with an elaborate red and gold box of Japanese pears or whatever fruit was in season or considered an auspicious traditional gesture. It was no wonder we went on those mainland hooker junkets. The guy needed to disappear every so often just to escape the hell of his design. His business and personal affairs were so entangled I couldn't decide if he was a total genius or a pure sociopath. In Taiwan, he was both good and bad, and nobody had a problem with it.

Felix was getting ready to leave for the day when he absently remembered that I was sitting there. He smiled as he doffed the same baseball cap he had worn since we met and said, "I'm sorry. I'm not ignoring you. I've been very busy lately."

"I know. I'm busy, too."

"Good. You are working very hard. Thank you for your hard work."

"Thank *you*."

✱

Another weekend in yet another drunken fog. The scandal rocked the local news coverage and made headlines in the papers. On Sunday, Sherry made a blubbering official announcement that she was leaving our company and joining forces with Kevin Kao. *Total defection.*

Everywhere I went, the neighbors asked my opinion about the scandal. I told them all the same thing: *I don't know.* And that made them visibly frustrated because they were so used to foreigners (me) being frank and open about their (my) feelings and opinions. Like when the neighbor asked me to tutor their 17-year-old son who was trying to get into the top university, and I told them, "Sorry, I'm not a teacher." It knocked them off balance and they said, "What the fuck do you mean you're not a teacher?" My neighbor Julia said, "What the fuck do you mean you don't know anything about Felix and Sherry?"

On Monday, I stumbled into the office around 11:00 a.m., expecting to see Felix but relieved to see only Daisy. She said hello quite a bit more cheerfully than I expected. Frankly, I was surprised she came back at all. I sat down at my desk and tried to focus.

"Welcome back," I deadpanned.

"Did you see the news last night?"

"Yeah, I saw it."

"She's leaving the company."

"Quite a convincing performance."

"So, what do you think?"

"About what?"

"You know." She squinted, smiled, and stabbed a finger toward the Captain's desk. "*Him*," she hissed.

"I have no idea what you're talking about."

"*What do you mean you don't know!?*"

"I mean, this shit is none of my business," I replied calmly. "And nobody cares what I think."

"Nobody cares what *I* think!" she half-shouted.

"Oh yes, they do. You'll see. You're next. They're coming for you. It's only a matter of time."

Daisy's cell phone rang, and she answered it before the first cycle of the ringtone could complete. It was Felix.

"*Laoshi, ni hao,*" Daisy purred. "Where are you?"

Their conversation went on for a few minutes. I lost interest once it was clear that Captain Felix wouldn't be around until mid-afternoon. I was happy since that meant I could fuck off until then. Well, I could fuck off whenever I wanted, I just had to be on my toes when Felix was around—make it look like I was doing something. Felix didn't care unless I was on a deadline. Either way, he rarely looked over my shoulder.

Finally, the call ended. Daisy turned back to me. "He's so excited!"

"Really? I would have thought he'd be upset. I mean, she was the quote-unquote sexy cram school teacher, the most famous teacher on the island, as advertised. The Golden Goose."

"They had a big fight on Friday night. I think she really hurt his feelings."

"How?"

"She said he's a lousy lover and too old to satisfy her."

"I can hear her saying that, but I would imagine he's not gonna let her go that easily."

Daisy bolted upright. "No! She said on the news that she will stay with—that other guy!"

I chuckled sarcastically and shook my head. "I don't think the boss is done with her yet, darlin'."

"He told me that he loves her."

"How does that make *you* feel?"

She turned indignant. "*I don't care.* He says that about lots of girls. I'm the one he comes home to."

"Fair enough."

"Sherry was a spy, telling all the—you know—things that were being said during the weekly business meetings. Did you know that I was banned from those meetings because of her? She said I made her uncomfortable."

"I can see that, too." I groaned softly. "You're her competition. You'll speak up when someone gets out of line. You're an obstacle in her path. And let's be fucking honest. He spoiled her rotten. That's a good description of her character: rotten to the core. She stinks like lunch meat left out in the sun."

"You don't think she's attractive?"

"Hardly," I said, pausing to choose my words. "I think she's one of the least attractive women we've ever had in this office. How many times do I have to tell you that?"

"Oh, did you know—?"

I put my hand up to stop her progress. "I *don't* know. I don't *want* to know. The only thing I know is what Felix tells me I know, and until then, all further questioning is suspended."

Daisy was disappointed but not ready to give up on it. "But the boss said—"

"Don't give me any of this 'the boss said' bullshit. If the boss wants me to know, he'll tell me. Otherwise, this whole situation has nothing to do with me. I am not a part of it. This is for people who lead extraordinary lives, and I am not one of them."

"But—but—*you!*" she sputtered. "You live like, like, like, there's no tomorrow!"

"Look, honey, there are two ways you can travel in this life." I paused to use body language. "Life is a weird kind of highway. It's a road with two lanes, but it only travels in one direction: forward. There's the fast lane, and there's the turtle lane. All these people—you and Felix—live life in the fast lane. Do you understand? Me—I'm in the turtle lane. I'm just moving at my own pace. I don't want to make any trouble in either lane. If I decided to step over into the fast lane, do you know what happens to turtles who make that mistake? They get flattened. They get crushed. No turtle should ever aspire to live in the fast lane. There's no reason for a turtle to be in the fast lane."

"I'm a turtle, too!" Daisy chirped.

"No. No, you're not. And I'm appalled that you would even say that. It's an insult to turtles everywhere."

"But don't you want to be famous? Have people talk about you?"

"Why would I want that? You can talk about me when I'm dead. I don't want to be the center of attention. It's bad for my business."

"What is your business?"

"Good question. And I'd like to keep it that way."

If you were rich and famous, you'd be eager to keep it that way, too. As the scandal wore on, Captain Felix was, first and foremost, trying to protect his reputation and that of the school. Therefore, he couldn't speak the truth. That the only reason he hired and spoiled Sherry was because he wanted to fuck her and/or fucked her, as everybody with eyeballs had assumed, and not, as he professed, for her teaching skills. *Nuh-uh.* That would have made him look like he didn't care about educating the students. With millions of dollars invested in Sherry's ability to draw students, Felix had to go on TV and *compliment* her. It was obvious to *everybody.*

From the beginning, Felix was angry and hurt, but he remained supportive of Sherry's "teaching talent," even though she just made him look like a total fool. And he knew this affair was going on. Daisy once let slip that they—Daisy, Felix, Sherry, and Kevin Kao—had dined together not more than a month before the scandal broke. Compare and contrast that to the gossip magazine photo spread. I hypothesized that somehow Felix got a hold of those cell phone shots of the enemy's dick in Sherry's mouth, and he tipped off the media himself, hoping to rack up some damage points on the enemy, but the whole thing backfired on him, and he lost his Golden Goose.

During her tear-jerking resignation speech broadcast live from enemy headquarters, Sherry renounced Captain Felix as an evil man who didn't care about students or teaching English, which wasn't even remotely true even if you're going for a pill-sized dose of this bullshit. Felix *loved* being an English teacher. He *loved* speaking English. But, of course, Sherry said she loved Kevin Kao and wanted to marry him, etc., which is how a minor league scandal turns into a bloodbath.

And so, Felix went beyond overdrive into hyperdrive. My man was fucking *possessed*. He went on the nightly news holding a check for one million dollars made out to Kevin Kao if he could prove that he was already divorced. *And wouldn't you fucking know it*, Kevin Kao had to admit that he couldn't accept the check because he was legally separated but still married to his 30-year-old, smoking hot, but ice-cold second wife, Candy Tsai. Kao said he would divorce her as soon as possible. Their divorce only added to the tabloid fire.

One night, I was working late on a last-minute deadline for Deborah. I had just finished the work when Felix breezed into the office *sans* Daisy, who was off at badminton.

"There you are!" he beamed, removing his hat. "So good to see you!"

"What's up?"

"Can I ask you a question?"

"Of course."

He stood behind the chair at his desk. "A fault confessed is a fault half-redressed."

"Yeah? That's not a question."

"Do you say this?"

"No, I don't."

Felix moved to sit on the edge of my desk. "People don't say this? A fault confessed is only half-redressed."

"Maybe they say it *somewhere*, but I don't know that I've heard it in conversation. *I* wouldn't say that. It sounds outdated. The question is, what do you *want* it to mean?"

Felix walked to the window and parted the blinds. "A fault confessed is only half-redressed."

"It means that confession is the beginning of forgiveness. But as soon as you throw the 'only' in there, it means that confessing doesn't right the wrong—you're only halfway to redressing—fixing—the fault."

"You don't say this?"

"Some people *might* say it, but—it's Shakespeare or something, right? It's gotta be a sixteenth-century idiom."

Felix turned away from the window to face me. "How about 'You have nothing but beauty'?"

"Why would you want to say *that?*"

Captain Felix put on his hat and bolted out the door. I wouldn't see him in person for several days. He went on TV and offered another one-million-dollar reward if Kevin Kao could prove that he wasn't wearing a toupee. That check wasn't cashed, either. *I fuckin' loved that move, Felix!*

As Sherry was spit-roasted in the media, Daisy's posture straightened a bit. She stood more upright. Her eyes seemed more hawkish. One day she scolded Felix for several minutes straight. She might still be screaming at him if I hadn't interrupted and said, "Hey, could you take it down a notch? I'm trying to work here." With her Queen Robot status unchallenged, Daisy was so much more demanding of other robots that I wished I hadn't corrected Captain Felix for his misuse of the term.

And of course, now that Sherry was the enemy, she was going to use every trick in *her* book. The first trick was accusing Felix of adultery with Daisy—because Felix was still technically married to another woman you'll hear about shortly, Barbara Wen.

Felix and Daisy had been "secret lovers" for a long time. Their relationship was closer to master and servant. After all, Felix "saved" Daisy from an ugly situation with her ex-husband. They were living together at the Captain's place in Muzha, but Daisy complained that she rarely saw him anymore. He was always flying to China "on business," she said. I knew he was eager to crack into the Chinese ESL market, but Daisy called bullshit. "He'll *never* make it in China," she hissed. "I know him. It will *never* happen."

On one hand, the idea made me cringe. On the other hand, they made a perfect couple. Anyway, Sherry made this accusation (in response to the toupee thing) on the news, and shortly thereafter, Daisy was interviewed by reporters and denied any wrongdoing. As a devoted employee, she had the utmost respect for Captain Felix, and their relationship was strictly professional. And so on. All of it pure fiction. It was Daisy's time to share the spotlight, and she nailed it.

★✳★

A woman named Margo ran the coffee shop in the lobby of our building. She used to live in Vancouver and spoke near-perfect English. We had been friends since my first day on the job. She was very local but very foreigner-friendly, a rare combination.

"I saw your boss's assistant on TV last night," Margo said one morning.

"I know."

"You see that guy sitting in the black car over there?" She pointed across the street to a late-model, black Mercedes-Benz sedan with tinted windows. Felix had the same model, all the way down to the rims. A man sat on the driver's side, window down, smoking. "He came in and asked about you earlier."

"Really? *That guy?* He doesn't look like a reporter."

"He's the driver," Margo said. "The reporter is in the back seat of the car. There's a camera guy in there, too. The driver said they've been looking for you for five days.

"I'm surprised it took them so long to find me."

"What are you going to do?"

"Do?"

Margo stepped out from behind the counter. "Talk to them. Give a statement."

"I don't have anything to say."

"Do you want me to translate for you? The reporter's English isn't enough good for an interview. They know your Mandarin isn't good enough, either. That's why they've been waiting around. They want to find you with a local who can translate."

"I'm not going on camera."

"But I can translate for you!"

"But I don't *want* a translator. I'm not talking to them."

Margo was bummed. She was wearing make-up and had done something with her hair, too. I just squashed her only chance to be on the news.

After observing the Benz from the window, I skipped the ritual cigarette on the cafe's small patio and beat it back to the office. I worked until 3:00 p.m. when my blood sugar dipped, and I had to get something to eat. Considering the surveillance outside the building, the best option was McDonald's five blocks away.

As I walked out the front door of KPHQ, Daisy came off the elevator. "Hi, Charlie. Where are you going?"

"Just gonna grab a quick bite to eat. I'll be back in twenty minutes."

"No, I mean *where* are you going? Café 55?"

"No, McDonald's. Why?"

She started stammering, "Just, you know, in case Felix asks."

I lightly tapped her shoulder and said, "Twenty minutes."

I reckoned the news crew would be watching the front gate, so I devised a plan. The building had several unsecured and easily exploited exits that bypassed the CCTV cameras and security gate in front. I took the stairs to the B1 garage, cut across the parking area to the opposite corner, and slipped through the propped-open emergency door (which was not wired to an alarm in the first place). I cut through a hallway behind the real estate firm on the ground floor, which led to a courtyard *behind the building* where all those poor real estate fuckers gathered to smoke. I kept walking until I hit the alley and lit a cigarette. It was kind of cool for a few moments. I've seen a few spy movies, like, yeah, now I can put that knowledge of the building's floor plan to good use! At any rate, I had successfully used the flawed system to avoid detection by the news crew. Or so I thought.

At McDonald's, I ordered my food, paid, got the food, and left. As I hit the sidewalk, a woman rushed up to me, stuffed a microphone in my face, and said something in English about 'foreigner close knowing the knowledge to end the scandal.' I put my free hand over the microphone and said, "*Bu yao! Wo bu zhidao. Wo bu mingbai.*" (No! I don't know. I

170

don't understand). As I pushed past the cameraman, I flashed to this scene replayed on the nightly news. I panicked, saying, "*Qing bie darao wo*," (leave me alone) and ran-walked to the corner, where I crossed against the traffic signal and almost got flattened by a mail truck. I didn't run back to the dorm; I walked, very fast.

Felix and Daisy came into the office at 5:12 p.m. and Daisy said, "The boss wants to buy you some wine."

"Why?"

"What kind do you like? Red or white?"

"Why?"

Felix approached my desk. "I'm sorry. I haven't been paying attention to you."

"It's not necessary. But you can do something for me."

"What do you need? I can help you. We have friends in high and low places." The 'friends' line was another one of the Captain's greatest hits, and I kept it on the bingo card of his verbal tropes.

"From now on, no TV people. Leave me out of it. I don't know anything. I don't want to talk to anybody. Those assholes ambushed me outside of McDonald's!"

Daisy coughed and cleared her throat, looked at Felix for a second, and they split. That was it. An hour later, Jerry Mouse came into the office with a case of Bogle Cabernet Sauvignon. "Where do you want me to put this?"

The next morning Felix came in alone and said, "Sir, do you have any plans this morning?"

"No."

"We have visitors."

On cue, the TV reporter from yesterday outside McDonald's, the cameraman, and the driver of the Benz appeared in our office. They bowed when they greeted Felix and bowed again as I stood up.

"I've seen these people before."

"This is [so-n-so from such-and-such]."

"I'm sorry," the reporter said. "*Wo xiang women xia dao ni le.*" (I think we scared you.)

"Tell them what you told me," Felix said. "What you told me last night."

"I said leave me out of it. I don't know anything. *Wo bu zhidao.*"

Captain Felix beamed and came to my side, nodding toward the reporter. "See, I told you."

The reporter and cameraman again bowed and backed out of the office.

"Don't worry," Felix said. "They won't bother you anymore."

From that moment forward, I saw the scandal as a pre-meditated publicity stunt, and everybody involved was going out of their way to keep the soap opera on the air. Daisy undoubtedly tipped off the news crew about my trip to McDonald's. She was the only person who knew where I was going, and they weren't watching the alley when I snuck out. They were *all* in on it together. So, I began to refer to them as **The Fantod Five**—Felix, Daisy, Sherry, Kevin Kao, and his soon-to-be ex-wife, a former TV talk show hostess named Tsai Xi (Candy Tsai) who was putting on an Emmy Award-winning performance as "the victim." Every day, another dramatic scene. They volleyed gestures of one-upmanship. It was Taiwanese reality TV, and I'd already lost the plot.

Part of what made this situation such a head-scratcher was my perception that Kevin Kao's soon-to-be ex-wife may not have been the brightest lantern at the festival, but 25 years his junior, Candy was considerably, by large degrees, younger and more attractive than Sherry.

The way I saw it, Kevin Kao was in the autumn of his years, a two-time loser in marriage, father of several children, and toupee artist-in-denial. I didn't feel sorry for the guy, I didn't benefit from his troubles, either, but trading the nubile and fertile talk show host for Sherry was such a *bad deal.* To me, it looked like he was bungling a suicide attempt—and would live to deeply regret it. Sherry might be dynamite in the sack, but she's fucking kryptonite out of it, this was a fact. Now, sure, to play advocate, who knows what people are really like at home? Personally, Candy Tsai looked like a handful, too. But it was guys like Felix and Kevin Kao who wound up pursuing these women in the first place.

After Kao was forced to publicly admit his adultery with Sherry, he equivocated because Candy cut him off in the bedroom six months ago, an excuse that flies like an eagle in Taiwanese society. Now I got it. *A fault confessed is half-redressed.*

The bullshit went on for another month with no end in sight. Felix was consumed with the media exposure and spent all his time giving interviews and making statements. When he was in the office, I was an afterthought. At some point he said to one of the robots, "I don't have time to think about it—just ask him (Charlie) to do it." If I didn't know any better—but I did—I'd say things were looking bad. Did I care? *No.* Could it possibly affect my life? *Yes.* So, I cared—a little.

I was watching the news at Sam's Club when a familiar face appeared on the screen.

"Hey, it's your boss," Arthur said.

"Yeah, I know. What's he saying?"

"I don't know. Something about that stupid teacher. Your boss, he talks too much. He should stop talking."

The news segment switched to a screenshot of a middle-aged, bow-tied, college professor-type talking head I'd never seen before. By reading his lips I could see he was speaking English. "Hey, what's this guy saying?"

"He's saying something about your boss."

"Turn it up or read the fucking subtitles for me."

"I can't. We lost the remote."

"Do it manually."

By the time Arthur got up and pawed around at the TV like he'd never seen a flat screen before in his life, the camera had switched to a shot of Sherry making yet another tearful statement.

"She says she loves somebody," quipped Arthur.

"Change the fucking channel."

"You don't want to watch?"

"I don't."

The next morning, the Nothing but Beauty issue was born. Captain Felix came into the office and spent five minutes repeating the same phrase on a recursive loop.

"You have nothing but beauty. Do you say this? You have nothing but beauty."

"No, but wait," I replied. "Who said it? Who did they say it about?"

"It doesn't matter. 'You have nothing but beauty.' Is it an insult?"

"Yes, but no...but yes, if you want to—"

"So, it can be both. It can mean two different things. Look here." He handed me a piece of paper containing five numbered questions photocopied from a grammar book, the answers highlighted in fluorescent orange marker. The phrase in question was answer #4. He repeated, "You have nothing but beauty. Is this an insult?"

"It is and it isn't."

"It's both?"

I tried to sound sympathetic. "*Maybe.*"

"It's always an insult."

"Not really." I shook my head, pursed my lips and puffed my cheeks.

"You have nothing but beauty—that is an insult."

"I'm not trying to argue with you, Felix, but I am advising you not to say it, no matter what you want it to mean."

"But you don't say that?" It was and it wasn't a question; he was begging for me to agree with him. "Is there another way to say it?"

"If you want to pay a compliment, you could say, 'You are beautiful through and through.' But I suspect that's not the issue."

Captain Felix coughed and winced. I wracked my brain for a few moments.

"In the negative sense," I said, "your beauty is only skin-deep. You are beautiful on the outside, rotten on the inside. You are nothing but a pretty face. Um. Actually, that's the—idea—whoever said it. That's the way *I* would say it, if I ever—"

Felix put his feet up on the desk, an Asian power move meaning: *I'm not listening until I hear what I want to hear.* "Would you say this? You have nothing but beauty?" He leaned back in his chair and said it again, "You have nothing but beauty. You don't say this?"

I sat back in my chair, folded my arms behind my head, and established eye contact with him.

"No, I most definitely would *not* say that—there's nothing wrong with the grammar. The issue is semantic. There are connotations and—never mind. It could mean two things, OK? The first is that the person you're talking about has nothing *but* beauty, which means their entire persona is permeated with beauty. Beautiful through and through. As in, 'They were nothing but gracious hosts.'" I paused to return his slight smile of bemusement. "OK, the second and obvious meaning is the one *you* want. It means the person is nothing but a pretty face, which is the way *I* would say it, but I *wouldn't* because it's a tired cliché and I'd think of something a little more sarcastic or sublime. If you want to say what I *think* you want to say about her, you're infinitely better off sticking with 'nothing but a pretty face.'"

Felix had a superiority complex that powered his aura. He was a super-wealthy, famous teacher and cartoon character on this tiny island; therefore, I could *never* be 100% right, and when I was, he dropped the subject. So, I didn't give a fuck whether he thought I was right or wrong, I told him exactly what I thought. He liked that about me. I was not his Yes Man.

He took his feet off the desk, sat forward and scowled. He'd essentially stopped listening at the word 'semantic.'

Lloyd came shuffling into the office with something hot off the printer: an email from Polly, our proofreader in Korea and final arbiter of grammar issues I had neither the desire nor the patience to master.

Polly had a couple of graduate degrees in language-related disciplines, so I always deferred to her judgment. That doesn't mean I agreed with her all the time, I just never challenged her. We were the publishing company's *yin* and *yang* of language consultancy. Whenever there was a conundrum of prepositions, they consulted Polly first. After she weighed in, Felix would say, "Tell me, from your instinct, does this sound right?" And I'd answer yes or no. I played everything by ear. Polly could discuss anomalies of the language in terms of subjective, predicate, and progressive, which I'm sure I learned in school somewhere, but I *never* thought in terms of that nature. Her approach was cold, analytical, and almost mathematic. Polly could confirm that the word 'jack' can be used as an intransitive verb (e.g., "I got jacked by some hoodlums last night") but she had no idea how to put it in fair play. You wanted to talk about semantics and different usages of idiom and slang, I was your man.

"You have nothing but beauty," Felix repeated, and now I wanted to beat him over the head with something at least as flat and heavy as my computer monitor. "Polly says it's an insult." He handed me the email printout. I didn't bother to look at it.

"That's fine. It can be an insult *and* it can be a compliment."

"It can be both."

"Polly says..."

"I know what Polly says. I'm not saying she's wrong."

"Polly says it can *only* be an insult."

"That's *not* a common way to insult someone. Polly needs to pull her head out of her ass."

"That's the way the Chinese would say it and understand it."

"Then say it in Chinese, where it only means one specific thing."

"You have nothing...but beauty. How about if I say it like that?"

"With the pause? No dice. Wait, why do you want to say this? Did you—?"

"You...have nothing...but...beauty."

I shook my head in defeat. Yvonne came scampering in with the Captain's favorite dictionary, the *1982 Webster's New Twentieth Century Unabridged Dictionary Second Edition in Deluxe Color*, which contains more arcane references to Greek architecture than a lifetime of Dennis Miller monologues.

"Nothing but beauty. It should mean that she only has beauty."

"Right. But it could mean almost the opposite. Do you want me to explain the denotation and connotation of the word beauty? I will, if you want." He shook his head. I continued. "Consider this sentence: 'We've got nothing but clear skies today.' That means everywhere you look, there's clear skies. 'We had nothing but a great time.' Means, the entire experience from top to bottom was a whole lot of fucking fun; you know what I'm saying? On the other hand, if you wanted to say something sucked, you could say 'It was nothing but a pain in the ass,' or 'We had nothing but cockroaches to keep us company.'"

Felix was further annoyed. "You have nothing but beauty. It means you have nothing but beauty."

"If you're trying to say that in American or British English—you're trying to put a round peg in a square hole. The definition of beauty does not translate between Chinese and English. No matter how many times you say it or how you say it, it still means two different things. But if you want to go ahead and say it, don't let me stand in the way."

I knew the look on his face when Felix was finished talking to me. In the beginning, I used to fear that look, thinking I was going to get fired for not telling him what he wanted to hear. At that stage of the game, I just shut the fuck up and went on about my business. Felix got flustered and left before lunch.

I went down to the coffee shop in the lobby as per usual around 3:00 p.m., where I discovered the dark energy behind the Nothing but Beauty ordeal.

"Did you read the paper this morning?" Margo asked, holding up a copy of *China Daily News*.

"Of course not. I can barely read Chinese. I know about two hundred characters. Enough to find a bathroom in an airport."

"Your boss is on the front page again." She smiled in anticipation.

"Yeah, so? What did he say now?"

"There is some controversy about his statement. He tried to insult that teacher, but he actually complimented her. He's supposed to be an authority figure in English. This was a big mistake."

"Nothing but beauty?"

"How did you know?"

"I told him not to say it."

She flipped a page and pointed to a picture of the college professor I saw on TV last night. "Zhang Yi said it in English and this guy said it was wrong because it can mean two different things."

"He's right. Who is that?"

"Some professor at the national university."

"Not good."

"Your boss is in love with that teacher, isn't he?"

"Kind of looks like it, doesn't it?"

"I think there's something wrong with him."

"You have no idea, honey. You're not even scratching the surface."

14

A Not-So Secret Mission

Some people put sequins and Post-it Notes on facts. Others use facts as coasters for their drinks. Every so often, facts come around to haunt you. Sometimes, facts are hidden or obscured. Facts are frequently irrelevant.

Here's a fact: the scandal wasn't going away. If anything, it would get bigger, brighter, louder, and worse. While life at Knowledge Press was buzzing with chaos and uncertainty, I was more than content with fading into the background. My days could be parsed into syllables. Wake up. Office. Get high. Office. Sam's Club. Sleep. Repeat. Repeat. I tried to be a ghost; however, I couldn't disappear completely. I was there when Felix needed me for whatever trivial matter and invisible by default when he didn't.

In the meantime, I was commissioned to edit and explicate a talking dictionary of the (so-called) most commonly used words in the English language—words most likely to show up on standardized tests. Legitimate work. I didn't feel completely idle. Every so often, like twice a week, when Daisy was clearly out of earshot, Captain would fake-remember I was sitting there. Our eyes would meet across the desk, and he'd say, "Charlie, you need adventure. Where do you want to go next? I'll buy the ticket for you. Anywhere you want to go."

For a couple of weeks in a row, my response was, "Lemme think about it."

Even though Felix sponsored the airfare, I couldn't afford *another* week of hotels and whatnot in an exotic location. I needed at least a month to catch up and stockpile some cash. I suppose I *could* have done it—easily, on credit cards—but just because you *can* doesn't mean you *should*. Financially, I was still getting paid by the hour for being (physically) in the office—strictly pay-for-play.

Either way, after I'd stalled him with half a dozen excuses, Felix *really* started leaning on me. The paranoia crept in, mostly because of the high-potency weed I smoked five times a day.

There was no reason to worry that Captain Felix wanted to get rid of me for good, but *something* was going on. Then the questioning became daily. "Charlie, have you decided where you want to go?" He'd call from the road if he couldn't make it into the office.

One Saturday morning it was just the two of us at KPHQ. Gretchen and the others didn't arrive until noon-ish. Felix was killing time, waiting for Daisy to return from badminton. I was reviewing some audio files for the talking dictionary and wearing headphones. We vaguely acknowledged each other. Five minutes passed, and Felix motioned for me to remove the headphones so he could talk.

Before he could get the question out of his mouth, I said, "The Philippines."

"The Philippines," he echoed, smiling and leaning back in his chair. "Don't expect too much. The girls are short and dark. It's a filthy place." Yeah, well, that was similar to the line he fed me about Thailand. So far, his travel advice hadn't exactly been *Lonely Planet*-caliber stuff.

He went to the safe and returned to his desk with a small stack of bills. "Here. Go ahead. Buy your ticket. Maybe I can go with you. If I have time..."

*Uh-oh, I did **not** like the sound of that.*

"Maybe I can go. I have so many monkeys on my back. You are free. I envy you."

This is where my personal life gets a bit complicated. I'm going to put this as simply as possible. I met my wife, Janet, during this time—through an online dating site. You don't need the specifics (just yet), except after a month of wireless love, I knew two things. One, I wanted to meet this woman [Janet] in person, in the flesh. Two, she lived in the Philippines. And so, details aside, you know how it turned out. She's my wife.

I looked at the calendar and circled on a date about two weeks away. Then I booked a flight. A couple of days later, I got a phone call from Daisy.

"Felix wants to talk to you."

"Put him on."

"Did you buy your ticket for the Philippines?"

"Yes. I leave next Thursday."

"Good. Very good. Give the receipt to Susie [the accountant]."

A few days later, I was sitting at my desk, chatting with Daisy, when Captain Felix arrived.

"Charlie! There you are! Just the person I want to see."

"Good morning, Felix. What can I do for you?"

"I have a special job for you. A secret mission." Daisy got up and left, closing the door on her way out. "It's a tough job."

"Alright. I'm in. Let me have it."

★✳★

The Captain's concept of a 'secret mission' for me usually meant retrieving information above and beyond a basic web search. Earlier in the year, I tracked down some shady property deals his estranged wife had transacted in the U.K. through a shell corporation in Singapore. And her dummy corporation in Southern California. Before that, Felix had me hunt down some foreign guys who were appropriating KP materials on a Chinese website. Ran a couple of background checks on potential business partners and learned all sorts of interesting things. Several "tell me what you know" situations with a 24-hour turnaround. Every mission had a simple directive: find the intel and get out of the way. Whatever happened after that was none of my business.

Felix moved his chair closer to my desk and sat down. He was very stiff and serious.

"About ten years ago—maybe fifteen years ago. No, maybe twenty years ago. I don't remember. I went to the Philippines with a tour group."

"I'm following so far."

"They took us to the embassy and gave me a special visa."

"How special? The Special Resident Retiree Visa (SRRV)?"

"Yes. That's the one." His face and posture relaxed.

"And in order to get that visa you had to open a Philippine bank account."

"Wah! How did you know that?"

"I'm up on Philippine immigration policies and the visa you're talking about. The deposit amount is twenty-five thousand U.S. Something close to one million Philippine pesos, yes? Anyway... So, what happened next?"

"They took me to the bank."

"What bank?"

"The big one in Cebu. Right there. In Manila."

"Manila? Or Cebu?"

"Yes."

"Never mind. That's not important...yet."

"I gave them the money and they gave me a stamp in my passport." His face was resolute as he mimicked a stamping gesture.

"And that's it? Did they take you to a bank? Who did?"

"The people at the embassy."

"Are you sure you went to the embassy? I think they took you to the Philippine Retirement Authority."

"That's right." He leaned back in the chair and folded his hands across his lap. "It was a special office."

"How often have you been back to the Philippines since getting the visa?"

"Oh, I've been there many times."

"Let me see your passport."

"The girls there are so cheap. But they're very small and very dark."

I held out my left arm and hand, beckoning. "Passport, please."

"I don't have it. The Philippine visa was...it was in...in my old passport. I lost it."

"What do you mean 'lost it'? Did it get stolen...or you don't know where it is?"

"I'll have to ask Mr. Chu."

"Hold on. Don't get *that* guy involved yet. How about the ID card and the paperwork? They issue an ID card with the visa. Where is it?"

"They didn't give me anything except a stamp in my passport." Again, acting out the stamping of his passport. "That's it. They didn't give me anything else." In Felixspeak, this meant *they*—meaning immigration—may have given him all that stuff and more, but he had no idea where it might be.

"How much money did you give them?"

"Fifty thousand dollars. U.S. But it should be a lot more now—with interest."

I chuckled and exhaled at the same time. "Where are the bank statements?"

"No bank statements."

"Where's the certificate of deposit? Passbook? ATM card?"

"..."

"You said this was anywhere from ten to twenty years ago?"

"Fifteen."

"OK. No problem."

"They didn't give me anything. Just the stamp in my—"

"Passport. I know."

"We were on a—tour group. Two weeks. At the end of the tour, they brought us to the embassy and gave us the visa. [Again, he made the stamping gesture.] I thought—it's a nice place—maybe it would be a good place to retire. Maybe, maybe, if I needed someplace to hide."

"First of all, they didn't take you to the so-called embassy.

[Taiwan does not have official diplomatic ties with the Philippines. Therefore, 50% of all foreign affairs are handled by a quote-unquote Economic and Cultural Office, which most people refer to as the embassy or the consulate since it serves essentially the same purposes. Manila Economic and Cultural Office (MECO) is located in Taipei. It's counterpart, the Taipei Economic and Cultural Office (TECO), is located in Makati City. For the most part, whenever we're talking about "the embassy" or "the consulate", we're talking about MECO or TECO.]

They took you to the Philippine Retirement Authority. Then they took you to the bank—do you remember that?"

He shook his head.

"Right. The bank is another story altogether. The gist of it is: you want your money back, yes?"

He smiled and said, "No problem. Do what you can. See if you can find it. I don't need it. I just want to know where it is."

It took two web searches and three phone calls to get all the necessary details. On the first call, the lady at the Philippine Retirement Authority (PRA) gave me his old passport number and current bank balance. She explained the procedures for reclaiming his bank deposits. Then I called the bank. They said to close his account and wire the money elsewhere, (a) his original passport containing the visa would have to be presented to the bank and (b) sent to immigration to get authenticated, along with a bunch of other paperwork, and followed by (c) an in-person interview. They gave me the corresponding bank and Swift code on the third and final call. I held my breath when I told the boss the 'good' news.

"Alright, listen. I found your money."

He was impressed. "You did! You're a genius! You can do anything!"

"Don't get too excited yet."

"Ohhh. The money is gone?"

"No, it's still there. Getting it back…" Slowly nodding. "We may have to jump through a bunch of hoops, but you'll get it back. I promise."

"No problem. I don't need it. I just want to know where it is."

"OK, well, now you do. Let me know if you change your mind."

Later that evening, around 8:30 p.m., I was out on the balcony, getting high, when Felix called.

"Where are you?" he boomed into the phone.

"In the dorm."

"Can you come into the office now?"

"Sure." I brushed my teeth, washed my face, and padded down the one flight of stairs. The office was completely deserted and dark except for the light in our private office. I found him sitting there with his legs propped up on the desk. He shifted his position as I entered.

"Sorry to bother you. This won't take long."

"What's up?"

"How difficult will it be to get my money out of the Philippines?"

"It won't be impossible, but you have to go over there in person at least twice."

"No problem. I can go there. We can go together. Have some fun."

"Right, then. If you want me to start the process, step one is to *find that old passport*. We can't do anything until you do. The bank says they won't process the paperwork without it."

He looked pained. "I lost it. I don't know where it is." He started rustling through the drawers of his desk. He got on the phone, called Mr. Chu and told him to drop everything and find that old passport. Their conversation got pretty heated.

At any rate, Felix set that particular wheel in motion, so I tried to explain the rest of the process. It took about 15 minutes of repeating key phrases like *notarized request to terminate* and *exit interview* before he kind of got the idea what was involved.

"They make it hard to get your money back," he said. "They'll do anything to keep your money."

"Well, yes. That's the idea."

"It's easy to get the visa but impossible to cancel it. They try to cheat you."

"Not quite. The visa was terminated a long time ago. In case you didn't know, that visa is only good for one year at a time. You gotta renew it every year."

"Pay membership fees?"

"Yeah, essentially. Your retirement visa expired fourteen years ago. But since you [air quotes] *lost* the original visa, they haven't caught on. If you had tried to enter the country on that old visa *without* getting a separate tourist visa, they'd either confiscate your passport and/or you'd be denied entry. *Wait. You know all this already, don't you?*"

"..."

"Yeah, alright, boss. It sounds like you just want to get your money back, so let's concentrate on that."

He seemed ready to give up on the whole thing. "No problem. There's no rush. I don't need the money."

Whether Felix really needed the money was irrelevant. The Sherry and Kevin Kao scandal had generated a lot of free publicity, but his personal fortunes may have been waning. Both Felix and Daisy complained bitterly about his estranged wife trying to bleed him dry. In hindsight, I believe the desire to reclaim the money was triggered by a combination of two unrelated events, the first being the fact that I had already booked my flight to the Philippines. Felix was a big 'two birds with one stone' type of guy.

The second event was the political and social unrest in Manila which had been going on for months.

A month before these conversations, the Manila hostage crisis happened on August 23, 2010. A former Philippine National Police officer, Rolando del Rosario Mendoza, boarded a tourist bus in Rizal Park and took the passengers hostage. Nine people (including eight tourists from Hong Kong and Mendoza himself) were killed in the incident.

Felix got a snoutful of that and declared, "They're killing the Chinese over there!" That's just the way his mind worked. Even though the political protests had nothing to do with Taiwan, a couple of Asians got bumped off somewhere, and suddenly, it was automatically open season on the Chinese. Somewhere along the line, it occurred to him that he was never going to retire in the Philippines and he put it all together. Or it all came together, like clouds before a rainstorm.

✶✷✶

The next day, Mr. Chu came into the office and tossed the Captain's passport at me, which landed face down on my desk.

"*You stupid motherfucker,*" I muttered.

Felix snapped at Mr. Chu in Mandarin, and Mr. Chu barked back. It was a major imposition to have Mr. Chu come down from the cram school, where he was transferred a few months ago, and drive all the way out to Muzha (where Felix lived). He spent an hour going through what I can only imagine was a shitshow at the Captain's house. Old Chu had a legitimate gripe.

"Just tell him to leave," I interrupted. "Get him out of here." As I checked the passport against the immigration details, and it was **not** the passport that Felix used to get the visa.

"This isn't it. This isn't the passport with the visa. It *has to be* the original passport."

"So, I can't get my money back?" Felix cried.

"No, I mean, yes. We can. There's a way around it. We have to get an affidavit of loss. I know how to do it."

"What do I have to do?"

"You have to come with me down to the consulate and sign the affidavit. The lawyer will notarize it."

He made the stink-face. "Too much hassle."

"No, it will be easy. We can—"

"Why can't I just go to the Philippines and get my money back? Why do I have to go over there twice?"

"It doesn't work like that. You first have to—"

He cut me off again. "Forget it. I just wanted to know where the money is."

OK, look. I'm trying to make this as easy as possible. First, we submit the paperwork and documentation to the PRA. They send all the documents to immigration for authorization to release your deposit, which takes what they call ten business days but I'm telling you it'll be more like two to three months. [**Brief interruption.**] *Then* we go to the bank. [**Short question.**] You must close the account in person. Period. Unless you want to stay in the Philippines for a month while this thing gets pushed through, you gotta work with me, boss. The guy from the PRA said that if you sign this affidavit and we get it notarized at the Philippine consulate here in town, then I can submit all the documents when I go over there next week—as your representative. [**Brief interjection.**] No, I don't need Power of Attorney. We can do the exit interview over the phone. That eliminates one trip for you. [**Another quick question.**] When the paperwork is processed, and the deposit is officially released, then you have to go and sign the bank transfer documents in person.

The Captain waved me off, clearly losing patience. He was right about one thing—the $50,000 deposit was now, thanks to interest, a considerably larger sum of money—close to $70,000—but in the grand scheme of things, in the Captain's world, it wasn't all that much. Not enough to motivate him.

It went on like this for a few more days. I spent a lot of time on the phone with the bank, immigration, and so on.

Finally, I said, "I'm going over there next week. If you're *serious* about this, let me know. Otherwise, I've done all I can."

"No problem. I can do it later. I have too many monkeys on my back. It's not urgent. Go. Have fun. Maybe next time I can go with you."

Here again, it appeared I was "saved" or at least my burden alleviated by circumstances. There was a new (and easily foreseen) twist to the scandal now—Sherry opened her own school rather than working directly for Kevin Kao (but backed by Kao), and she was hell-bent on taking students from our school by offering free tuition—which consumed the Captain's attention.

In the meantime, Daisy continued asking about the Philippines deal, specifically the procedural bullshit, but once all her questions were answered, she forgot about it. I plugged along and looked forward to my trip. Pretty much end of story.

* ✱ *

Two days before my departure for Manila, Felix breezed into the office and announced, "I can go with you! We can go together. I can take you to the happening place!"

I can take you to the happening place!

The phrase echoed in my head. How many times had I heard this from him? Lord knows, sometimes he *did* take me to *the happening place*, but I got the distinct impression that I knew a hell of a lot more about the Philippines than he did.

There were binary flashes of hope and panic: *this is a good idea, no, this is bad idea, it could be a good idea but it's probably a bad idea...* Captain Felix changed his mind so often that I never believed anything he said until I saw, for instance, proof of a plane ticket. But I sensed the inevitable. Daisy got on the phone with the travel agent, turned to me and asked, "What's your flight number?" and that's when it sunk in. *Fuuucccck meeeee.*

The pros and cons to consider: On one hand, all expenses would be covered. "Money is no object," Felix said, retrieving another stack of crisp new bills from the safe. On the other hand, I'd be on the hook for 'entertaining' Felix during certain hours of the day—which essentially meant being his bodyguard-slash-personal assistant. It also meant that he would not want to spend eight days in Manila (as per my original plan). He didn't like to stay in one place for too long, due to paranoia that he could be "kidnapped."

✳✳✳

I hadn't yet revealed my true intention for going to Manila—to meet the woman who would become my wife—for two reasons. First, Felix and Daisy were oddly invested in my personal life but diametrically inconsistent with their opinions. Marriage was a hot topic with bi-weekly mentions. Some days Felix would say, "I'm going to find you a wife," and the next day, "Stay single. They (women) try to cheat you."

Daisy would say, "Charlie will never get married," and a week later, she'd try to fix me up with yet another of her divorced badminton friends.

About a year earlier, we were in the office and Felix said, apropos of nothing, "Charlie, it's my duty to find you a wife."

I took a deep breath, exhaled, and said, "Felix, it's not your 'duty' to find *anything* for me."

Felix launched into a familiar spiel about "being alone here" and needing "someone to take care of [me]."

Daisy jumped in, "You don't want to wind up alone in your old age!"

"Charlie, I'm going to find you a wife," Felix insisted.

I clasped my hands in front of my chest and said, "*Please* don't do that, Felix. *Please.* I'm begging you."

I couldn't argue with them anymore. Whenever the subject came up, I just sat there nodding and vaguely smiling.

The second reason was I didn't know how it would play out between me and Janet. There was a good sense that we would connect, but there was doubt, too. We were 1,000 km apart. A lot can happen from point A to point B. Love, especially the internet kind, is a gamble. But it was a risk I wanted to take on *my* dime. I wanted this to be something I did on my own. This was why I embraced decisiveness. Once you decide to do something, jump in feet first, as it were, that's when you have some degree of control over the situation(s)—right or wrong, for better or for worse.

Here's how it goes. You meet somebody on the internet, and you think, "Yeah, I like this person. I'm gonna go see her," and then you click on **Purchase This Fare**. Whatever happens after that is an *adjustment*. Like jumping off a cliff or a bridge, you can land on your feet or land on your ass. Maybe you meet, and everything will go great. Maybe you'll get married. Conversely, you meet, and it isn't a love connection. OK, great. What next? Compelled by self-preservation, I had Plans A, B, and C for delicate and/or otherwise life-changing situations. Once Felix jumped on the Philippines trip, his ticket booked, I immediately put Plan B into action.

It'd be funny if I said Plan B was to strangle Felix and dump his body in a river because he was insufferable for the next two days. He asked questions and didn't listen to the answers. He made statements and walked out of the office and didn't return for five hours. He was all bluster and distraction. Zero concentration, negative focus.

The mission was getting his money back, end of. But the subject of his accommodation became contentious. I booked three nights at a nice place in Makati before I knew he was coming, and since I'd scored a promo deal, that money was non-refundable, i.e., ***this part of the plan is non-negotiable***. Deal with it. Captain Felix gave me the stink-face again.

The Dusit Thani Makati was a five-star hotel in Asia, maybe four-star in the rest of the world. Not the type of place I normally stay but (a) accommodation in the Metro Manila is wildly inconsistent and (b) in a town like that, location is everything. Either way, I got it for $125 a night. The walk-in rate was almost double that.

The day before we left, hungover and irritated, I took one last stab at getting Felix to drop the whole idea. I said, "OK, Felix. Since you know Manila so well, tell me. Where *exactly* do you want to stay? Name the place. Name the area. Name a street. I'll book that fucking room right now."

"I'll find somewhere cheap."

"Let me book you at the Dusit Thani," I pleaded. "I can get it for one-hundred and twenty-five a night."

"Wah! That's too much!" *Of course*, it was too much.

"It's not China, boss."

15

They Try to Cheat You

We arrived in Manila (IATA code: MNL) around 7:30 p.m., and the front desk of the Dusit Thani Hotel in Makati City was buzzing with activity. Captain Felix was not pleased about the $125-a-night room rate and kept bitching about it throughout the trip from Taipei.

"Asian hotels are very cheap," he said. "Asians are very cheap people. We don't want to spend money on a place to sleep." He further rationalized that it was pointless to stay in nice hotels since you couldn't possibly use all the amenities you pay for, even if you stayed more than one night, which as a rule, he didn't like to do.

Felix vowed to "find a cheaper place in the morning," which meant *I* would find him a cheaper place in the morning.

★✷★

Try to imagine Metro Manila as an Asian version of Los Angeles, having dozens of sub-cities and proprietary neighborhoods within the metropolitan boundaries. For example, Santa Monica is a city nestled within the greater L.A. area (and, technically, Los Angeles County). Hollywood, on the other hand, is a neighborhood of L.A. with its own zip code. Metro Manila consists of 16 urbanized cities, and the city of Manila itself is but a tiny part of the metropolitan area. Makati City, where most of this episode takes place, is one of the larger cities in Metro Manila and considered one of three major "first world" regions with a rambunctious central business district.

⋆✱⋆

This was our first trip outside mainland China, where Felix walked around like he owned the joint. Consequentially, I was curious to see him out of his comfort zone.

We hadn't even left MNL in a taxi when it became obvious that he barely understood a word of English spoken by Filipinos. From the airport to the taxi to the hotel to the front desk, he repeated, "You're calling the shots."

"Give me your passport," I said. He had already misplaced it twice; once in the taxi on the way to the airport in Taipei and once on the flight. Sometimes Felix was so absent-minded and lazy, that I wondered facetiously how he had any money at all.

Check-in at the Dusit Thani took much longer than expected. We started fourth in line at the front desk. Amongst the Armani-suited international men of business, the gracious hotel staff, small packs of Arab guys in costume, and everybody speaking some form of English, Captain Felix became suddenly small—shorter and slighter. He kept his baseball cap pulled down low. I made small talk for a few minutes, but we stood and waited for 20 minutes in silence.

Since I booked a minimum three-night stay for myself, I was given an automatic upgrade to a junior suite, and they generously gave one to Felix—a major coup—which put me up on the 10th floor and Felix on 8. We never stayed on the same floor in the same hotel.

As the clerk was preparing the key cards, Captain Felix was standing behind me, facing the opposite direction, when a very loud and long fart tore through the bustle of the lobby. The clerks had eyebrows halfway up their foreheads. A couple of Armani-suited guys shot nasty looks in our direction while I did everything I could with my face and body language to appear innocent. *It wasn't me, man.* Spinning on my heels, I leaned toward Captain Felix and snapped, "*Hey!* We're not in China. Don't do that here."

"Don't do what?" He turned around to face me.

"It's not okay to pass gas in public," I said. He looked confused. "*No farting in public!*"

"Oh..." he said, with an embarrassed and open-mouthed smile.

In full disclosure, the farting issue was one of the things that brought me to the brink of leaving Felix and KPHQ, but not right there in the hotel lobby. No, I was used to it by then.

Maybe a month into the gig, the Captain appeared in the office during the mid-afternoon to sign some papers. He was sitting at his desk with two robots on the Hot Seat and some guy from a bank. Suddenly, a series of farts ripped through the air, *pfffffhhht, rffffffhhhht, ffffffffffffhhhht*, and it was obviously Captain Felix. No one blinked an eye. I was about to piss myself. *He better get his ass into the bathroom and check his shorts because that last one was greasy!*

Fair enough, that was funny. I got up from my desk and left the office without so much as an "excuse me."

A couple of days later, it was just me, him, and Daisy, and it happened again. I shot a look over at Daisy, but she remained stone-faced. Then it happened the next day. And a week later, more farting in the control center. The joke stopped being funny and got annoying fast, especially when the office was fogged up with his stench and/or he was standing next to my desk. I routinely walked out and paced the stairwell outside the office whenever he did it. One day he ripped a stream in my direction like he aimed for me. I walked out for the rest of the day.

The next morning, I said to Daisy, "Hey, this is just a question. Don't get mad at me for asking."

"What?"

"Hasn't anybody ever told Felix that it is incredibly rude to fart in public or professional settings?"

"Oh!" she said, slapping the desk with both hands. "He said his doctor told him it's bad to hold it, you know, the gas. It's not healthy."

"Right, I get that. But there's a polite fuckin' way to do it."

She nodded and creased her lips. "He said he's the boss and he can do whatever he wants."

"Would you please find a way to tell him it's extremely offensive to me?"

Daisy blinked several times in a row. "I'll try."

And that's where I left it, but I swore to God that if he ever did something like that again, I'd be out of there permanently. Felix didn't fart in the office anymore, at least when I was around.

Back in the lobby of the Dusit Thani, we headed for the elevators, and I handed over his key card. "Don't lose it. You need it to activate the elevator. You're in 808. I'm in 1010."

"You must have a bigger room than me. You're on a higher floor."

"I don't think so, boss. We both got the same upgrade. I asked them to put us on different floors. Eight is a lucky number in Chinese culture, right? I thought you'd be happy with that. Plus, you're two floors closer to the sauna house."

His laugh started slow, low, and deep, an audible note of approval. He didn't have to say it, but he did anyway. "You're playing the game. You know what you're doing. You're on the right track."

In the spirit of deference, I *should* have switched rooms with him for one night, i.e., given him the room on the higher floor. But I didn't even entertain the idea until a week after the fact. And fuck that. I was calling the shots. Felix said so himself.

Meanwhile, I was fucking *hoping*—fingers crossed. If history repeated itself, this would be the last I'd see of Felix until morning. He'd either go to the sauna house or order room service and a massage. On "bodyguard duty" since noon, I was ready to breathe a slight sigh of relief.

We were still in the elevator when Felix asked, "What's the plan for tonight?"

Goddammit. "Are you sure you want to go out with me?"

"I want to see what you are going to see. I want—"

"I know what *you* want."

My original plan was to meet Janet, but Felix didn't know that yet. Thus, Plan B was activated: cruising around the sleazy nightlife options, with intimate details about the scene, courtesy of Chuck Das.

Go hard on this fucker. Scare him. Make him think it's going to be a nightmare.

"I'm talking about go-go bars, loud music, naked women, coming home at three in the morning. Possibly some drugs and illegal activity involved. Remember Fuzhou? You won't last five minutes in the places I'm going."

"I want to go where you are going," Felix proclaimed. "I want to walk a mile in your shoes."

"*For chrissakes*," I said, under my breath. "Meet me back down in the lobby in twenty minutes."

★✱★

Captain Felix didn't approve of smoking or drinking, and he hated loud music, which, again, made our relationship such a personal scalp-scratcher, considering my low-rent Hunter S. Thompson imitation. For whatever reason, he made me "The Exception to the Rules." His idea of entertainment was going to the "sauna house," which is also called simply: sauna, spa, massage parlor, and way out in the backwoods, whorehouse—places where 20 bucks (or 1,000 Philippine pesos) will go a long way. Twenty bucks will go different distances depending on the location. In Hong Kong, US$20 is a fastidious sushi lunch for one person at Genkii; in Changping, it's a hand job in a sauna house on Flower Street; in a provincial Fujian village, that's full service with overnight privileges. It also depends on which level of sauna house you visit.

Captain Felix loved the sauna houses for a bunch of reasons. The Chinese are blase about it. You walk into certain sauna houses and order from the menu posted at the front desk. At the better joints, you get to see a selection of women before deciding on the level of service. Some places are little more cat-and-mouse about the degree of prostitution. Many places have a speakeasy sleepover policy for an additional (but nominal) fee. You're anonymous at the sauna house unless you pay by credit card, which (paying by credit card in a sauna house) is so rare it's almost cause for alarm. They don't take ID, they don't write down your name—they take cash, thank you very much. You're not obligated to indulge in sexual activity. You can simply take a sauna.

The mid-level sauna house is where you find women eager to please but not terribly engaged—it was a job, and they wanted to do a good job. For them, it wasn't a lifestyle, it was, "Well, it's either this or an iPhone factory in Shenzhen. Jerking dudes off for twice the pay seems like a fair deal."

Felix had bum knees and "required" massage at least twice a day. At 67 years old, his issue with arthritis was real. I'd seen him struggle to make it up a single flight of stairs. He preferred his *masseuse* to be female, on the shy side of 20 years old, chatty if not bubbly, from the "country." ["Country girls are the best. It doesn't take much to make them happy."] And he needed one on each leg.

I made it crystal clear to Felix that we did the sauna house routine on the mainland, and the same type of sauna house service was readily available in Manila, but it was not on the Philippine dance card belonging to yours truly.

Some hotels like the Dusit Thani in Makati have this impressive lobby that sells an illusion that you're staying in a palace. Staying in a nice hotel always made me feel like I deserved that type of luxury.

We met in the lobby, and I almost told Felix to go back to his room and change his clothes. He was wearing the ubiquitous Non-Stop English ball cap, Nautica T-shirt one size too big, khaki knee-length shorts, and brown loafers with gray sweat socks halfway up his calves. The only way he could have looked more like a Taiwanese tourist is if he had a camera around his neck. I took a deep breath, thought about it for a couple of seconds, and shrugged. *That's the look he's going for in the first place, dummy.*

For the most part, I didn't care what Captain Felix looked like or how he dressed. It made no difference to me if he walked around with his sweater on inside-out. Daisy was his caretaker. I was his "bodyguard." Until now, it never occurred to me to be embarrassed for him. I sort of liked his fashion eccentricities—his über-wealthy lack of pretense and style—it was amusing. People on the ephemeris of his life could say or think whatever they wanted about the Captain. He couldn't care less. So that was refreshing. It showed character.

Ironically, *character* is the last thing you want to be dragging around a place like Manila. If you're going out on the town, you want your wingman to have something on the ball. Felix said he wanted to see whatever I was going to see, and suddenly—like this entire trip—I wasn't so sure that was a good idea. Janet and I had plans to meet around midnight, Felix didn't know that. I had serious doubts he would have the moxie to keep up for one night, let alone five. Based on my research and Chuck's report, I quickly drew up a greasy nightlife program for Captain Felix.

The first stop was Café Havana, a restaurant-slash-bar in Greenbelt, and by all accounts, a legitimate establishment. Café Havana was also notorious for being a prime pick-up location for freelancers and semi-pro women, one of several such hotspots in town. You had to be careful in places like Café Havana not to assume that every woman you see had services on offer—which I deliberately mentioned on the 10-minute walk from the hotel. Knowing in advance that the outdoor patio would be packed, making Havana the first destination was simple reconnaissance. I led Felix across the patio and described how the system worked.

"Many of these girls are high-end prowlers," I said, referring to the dozens of attractive Asian women sitting at tables in pairs and groups of threes, chatting amiably but on visual alert for white faces and deep pockets. "The majority of guys who come here are white males, thirty-plus, looking for a 'classy' type of girlfriend. Big spenders appreciate high maintenance. I didn't invent the system, that's just how it is. Now, see the women hanging out on the edge of the patio? They're mid-level freelancers. Their lottery odds are way up there. If they end the night with an extra 5,000 pesos in their pockets, it's been a good fucking *week*. You're spoiled for choice here. What do you say? 'Paradise for men; hell on earth for women?' You get a table, order a drink, and wait. It doesn't take but a minute before they've spotted you. If the husband-hunters are interested, they'll smile at you. Get your attention quickly. The freelancers will be interested no matter what you look like."

"How much is a freelancer?"

"Depends on the girl. For a low-level hustler, short-time, usually two thousand pesos (US$45). Long-time, more like four thousand (US$90). You can negotiate—but I wouldn't."

"You know everything!" Felix cried. "How do you know all this?"

"I know how to use the internet, and, like you, I have friends in high and low places."

Felix smiled. "What about the go-go bars?"

Café Havana's Latin house band started their second set, and the samba music was pumping. I took Felix by the arm and led him out to the taxi line. Next stop: EDSA Entertainment Complex in Pasay City.

"This," I said as we climbed out of the taxi in front of EDSA, "is where Muslim martyrs should really go when they die. This is go-go bar heaven."

* ✳ *

If I'm right and all of Manila is a moveable feast of prostitution, then the two-story EDSA Entertainment Complex was the temple vortex of the sex industry. It was the Eye of the Storm if the eye was shaved and looking back at you with lust, opportunity, and diabolic intentions. It was the EPCOT Center of Sex Tourism. Most sex tourists didn't stay in town long enough to see and experience all of it. A few different types of bars populated the plaza, but it was the same shit with different shingles: go-go bars with dancing girls as the featured attraction (= on display and for sale); beer bars where the setting was more cordial and casual (= sit down and a girl will approach).

The overall aesthetic of EDSA Entertainment Complex was: if you want it, we got it. Of course, for professional perverts, there were complex systems, protocols, interviews, and negotiations that the average rubbernecking sex tourist didn't have the bandwidth to process. Comically, at least to me, the EDSA Entertainment Complex had venues with B-movie strip club names like Firehouse, The Pit Stop, and The Cotton Club, but the scene was incredibly high-definition. [Note: The complex closed in 2020.] From the top girl, all the way down to, and in many cases, the *mamasan*, the female staff were "on the clock," and most bars required a bar fine to take them back to your hotel room (or the short-time Sogo Hotel across the street, only 500 pesos for 2 hours).

The bars were laid out around a U-shaped atrium, providing the illusion of a central hall. There was also a coffee shop and a restaurant. Once inside, I brusquely guided Felix past the swarm of touts and into The Cotton Club. The *mamasan* put us in a booth in the back row. A dozen or so women were on stage, dancing halfheartedly to hip-hop music. I ordered a beer (for me) and an orange juice with no ice (for

Felix). The DJ acknowledged our arrival by bumping the volume. We were set upon by floor girls—those deemed not sexy enough to be up on stage, but charming or talented in other ways. I peeled off a few 100 pesos notes to keep them at bay. When I say 'set upon' I don't mean it like they tackled us or anything. They were just *there*. Present and accounted for. On display. Ready for anything.

The boss drank his juice while I pounded my beer and lit a cigarette. "See anything you like?"

He laughed. "So many to choose from."

"Let's try the bar next door."

There were few customers at Firehouse but an abundance of girls on stage and prowling around the bar. A *mamasan* was the first to get to us. I ordered a beer and an orange juice no ice. Before she could start asking questions I said, "No girls right now. We're just looking." She walked away but not before shooting me that *mamasan* look of contempt. Within a minute, which is pretty much record time in a go-go bar, she returned with our drinks and a chit for the bar tab.

"I'll pay now," I said, handing her 300 pesos. "The rest is for you." That made her happy.

Of course, the music was incredibly loud and it was hard for Captain Felix to concentrate on the dancing girls. I kept a close eye on him and leaned in to ask, again, "You see anything you like?" He shook his head but several girls were right up his alley. I had already explained the bar fine-slash-lady-drink-slash-tip system of the go-go bar, but I had to repeat things for Felix like five or six times before they registered in his head, so I gave him another rundown, half to keep him in the game, and the other half to distract him from staring at the girls like he couldn't see them—which he couldn't.

OK, here we go. Bar fine starts at fifteen hundred pesos. One-five. Non-negotiable. [**Coughing sound, brief interjection.**] Bar fine just means 'take the girl out of the bar.' That's thirty bucks, the industry standard in Manila. There's a way around the bar fine system, but it requires social and cellular technology skills you don't have, and I'm not in the mood to mess with it tonight, so forget it. [**Short question.**] At least seven hundred of the bar fine goes to the house and *mamasan*. The girl might get five hundred of the bar fine. Maybe not, but who cares? That's not our business. [**Another short question.**] I was just getting to that. Lady drinks usually cost twice a normal drink, and you buy one for the girl of your choice. There are exceptions—but not here. Buy lady drinks only if you're interested. They'll ask—every girl that approaches will ask because they get a cut. However, the lady drink is mandatory if you sit her down and have a get-to-know-you chat. Name, age, interests, etc. Otherwise, it's like buying a used car off the lot without giving it a test drive. If a girl tells you in the first two minutes that she's go-go dancing to pay for her mother's dialysis, send her away. Try again. The point is, don't be cheap. Buy lady drinks. **[Short interjection.]** Yes, I know. Stop staring back. They're hungry for cash. Next step is to decide how long you want her. Short-time versus long-time is the same as China. Here, short-time is generally a couple of hours and as many pops as you can squeeze out—'pops' is slang for, well, you know. A lot of these expat cretins are jacked up on Viagra and fucking the shit out of these girls. Sometimes the girls will set a limit on pops, to cut down on the wear and tear. Long-time equals girlfriend experience. She will stay overnight and give you at least another pop in the morning. Don't forget, you go long-time, you're on the hook for feeding and watering the flowers as well. You know this already, in fact, *you* told *me*. **[Brief interjection.]** You're right. It adds up. Fast. You know that. **[Brief interruption.]** These girls aren't country girls tonight. They might come from the provinces but they're in Manila now, and they *will* try to cheat you. Make the deal crystal clear. Make sure you ask about massage skills before paying the bar fine. **[Short question.]** No, that's a woman. This isn't a ladyboy bar. Stay focused. If you find a girl you want to bar fine, don't worry—I'll handle everything. Forget it. Back on the subject. You want to know how much. Short-time girl is going to ask for two thousand flat rate and a buck and a half [1,500 pesos] minimum, as a 'tip,' but as long as you're a nice guy and not a repulsive physical specimen, you can get her for two thousand. The tip, the *xiaofei* is the only part of the deal you have any sort of control over. **[Anxious interjection.]** No, I mean, you can negotiate—but again, I said, don't negotiate with a hooker. Ever. Pay the girl what she wants or don't take her. You try to get cheap with a go-go dancer, and she's not going to give her best performance. Overpay a floor girl, and you just might have a life-changing experience. Anyway, the girls on stage don't have to go with you if they don't like you. **[Brief interjection.]** Most will, but it depends on what time of the night you get 'em. We're pretty early tonight, so none of the dancers have had a chance to pull a short-time and get back on stage. **[Short question.]** Most of the dancers are going to want the flat rate plus a two grand non-negotiable tip, at least because they're considered more attractive, but the flat rate is up to four thousand, and the bar fine is the same. If you look like a rookie or they think you're a sucker, they'll tell you the bar fine is double, or they'll ask for five thousand, long-time. **[Extended interruption by approaching floor girl.]** '*You're super cute,* *honey, but not tonight. Thanks.'* See? Circling like sharks now. OK. Long-time anything is super fucking expensive. Now, the rest of the floor girls milling around the bar are either waiting for their turn to get up and dance or, as you can see, they are wearing a different uniform, in some cases what they would consider 'street clothes,' and are not considered attractive enough to be up on stage. Bottom line: to take one of these girls out of here, two thousand. That's bar fine, lady drink, a drink for you, and a little extra tip for the folks. Total price for a short-time girl, all-in, bar fine, lady drink, tip— four thousand pesos. **[Brief interjection.]** Sounds like a lot, but the more you agree to pay, the less likely they'll try to steal from you.

Felix nodded, small and sort of confused, like a child. There was zero chance he would ever take a go-go dancer, floor girl, or anything other than a hotel-based sauna house girl back to his room. This was "reconnaissance." *Just looking.* I finished my beer and took him across the plaza to Obsession. There were maybe three other guys in the joint. We were swarmed as soon as we sat down. The *mamasan* and two street-clothed girls got real cozy, real fast. I repeated the beer/orange juice no ice order and politely asked the girls to come back in a few minutes. There were some real cuties in this place, and they all had great attitudes.

Three girls came back and sat with us. I bought them each a lady drink, and they got to work on their routine, which involved a lot of suggestively intimate physical contact while asking questions like, "What hotel you stay?" Even the girls onstage were smiling, which was rare in go-go bars, to be quite honest. The *mamasan* came with the drinks and I again offered to pay on the spot. She was considerably more gracious about it and introduced herself as Carmen.

I put an extra 100 in her hand and said, "Listen, Carmen, we're just in for a quick drink tonight. We'll be back again, probably tomorrow, OK, sweetie?" I gently smiled and slipped her another 100-note. Her eyes flashed and she stroked my paw. Between the throbbing music and the girls' accents, the Captain's level of discomfort had reached its apogee, so I pounded my beer in one swallow, stood up, and escorted him outside.

We hit yet another must-see: The Pit Stop. Then to Samba. By now, the boss had gotten acclimated and familiar with the procedure and the women. Though he was unable to communicate with anybody except for me, he seemed to be enjoying himself. He always had a couple of women in his lap, but the noise and the smoke were getting to him. Everybody was very sad to see us go.

Once in the taxi, I said, "OK, are you ready to take it to the next level?"

"I'm ready for action."

We took a short taxi ride to Ermita and stopped at L.A. Café (formerly known as Manila Bay Café), which presented as a regular bar with dartboards and pool tables upstairs and a live band every night. In reality, it was a freelancer bar, which meant there was no bar fine to take the girls out, although I suspected there must have been some sort of kickback involved. The girls didn't "work" there, technically, but working girls outnumbered customers 4-to-1 and everybody knew exactly what was going on in this joint. Oh, I forgot to mention the bar also had its own short-time hotel on the third floor of the building.

It was around 10:30 p.m. when we arrived. Felix was in relatively high spirits, and the place was packed. "This is the happening place!" he cried. Miraculously, the hostess found two seats at the bar for us, sandwiched between two expat/Filipina couples. Once again, I took a few minutes to reiterate the freelancer system. He nodded and said he was happy it wasn't as loud as EDSA Entertainment Complex. Meanwhile, I encouraged him to have a discreet look-see around. The women were three-deep, in a surround-sound circle of the bar. As far as call-em-what-they-are-hookers go, there were a lot of nice girls, but no one exceptional. The boss sipped his orange juice, hunched over the bar, while several girls made approaches. I turned them away with a soft smile and a shake of my head. "No, not tonight, ladies, thanks."

Though I was conscious of the Captain's comfort or lack thereof, part of me was hoping he was miserable. *Fuck him. He was the one who decided to come at the last minute. He's the one who is screwing up my plans.* Then I got sensitive and didn't want to torture him too much. I ordered a second beer and said, "Let's go check out the scene upstairs."

His face lit up. "Upstairs, what's upstairs?"

"Another version of this, but the girls are better."

There was a 200-peso cover charge to get upstairs at King's Club, where the pool tables were located and what most considered the upper-mid-range of freelancers in Manila. I handed the woman at the top of the stairs a 500-peso note and she waved us in. There was nothing happening. Just a couple of bored working girls, texting and shooting pool. We made a quick circle of the second floor, and I suggested we leave the bar and take a walk. Felix was relieved but paradoxically energetic. "Let's go see the real Manila."

Ermita is a lousy neighborhood in a great location, no matter how you look at it. We walked up and down Mabini Street, which, although fairly safe, is not an entirely pleasant experience. The touts, beggars, and hookers were very pushy and rude, among the peskiest I've ever encountered. Keeping them from getting at Felix required ninja-type reflexes. We walked around for 20 minutes or so before his knees gave out, and I got us a taxi back to the hotel. During the walk, I fessed up and told Felix about my plans to meet Janet, how I only wanted to visit the Philippines to see her.

"She sounds like a good girl," he said. "You're sure she's not a hooker?"

"She works in a call center, and yes, I'm sure she's not a hooker."

"When are you going to meet her?"

"Tonight."

"If you marry her, will you bring her to Taiwan?"

"I don't know, man. That's getting way ahead of things."

"Does she know that you smoke and drink?"

"Yes."

I left Felix in good spirits, standing in the lobby of the Dusit Thani, and made a beeline back to Café Havana, where I waited for Janet to arrive.

Felix and I agreed to meet in the lobby of the hotel at 9:00 a.m., and he was already there, pacing, when I strolled out of the elevator at 8:52. We had breakfast at the hotel buffet and headed over to the bank.

Things started going downhill the minute we set foot in the lobby of the Citibank Tower on Valero Street, where the Philippine Retirement Authority was located on the 29th floor. To get a visitor's pass from the security desk, you gotta hand over a piece of ID. I had my California driver's license, passport, and Taiwan Resident Alien Card (ARC). Felix had only his passport and a credit card. I slapped myself on the forehead and implored the security guard that Felix couldn't possibly hand over his passport to get a visitor's pass because he needed it (the passport) at the PRA. The dead-eyed security guard shrugged. *Your problem.*

"Let me see your credit card," I said to Felix. He handed me his black American Express card.

I turned to the security guard. "How about if he shows you his passport but he leaves you *this*?" The guy took the card and showed it to his partner, and he had never seen anything like it, either.

"No, sir. Sorry, sir. But we can accept a copy of his passport."

"I've got one of those." I produced a copy of the Captain's second-to-last passport.

"And the credit card," the guard said, reluctantly tossing our visitor's passes on the counter, resuming his 1,000-yard stare.

The Philippine Retirement Authority, though related to the Bureau of Immigration, operates on a different astral plane than anything you'll see in the snake pit of the main office in Intramuros; it's a world away from the desperate and pathetic chaos, a place where the bureaucracy of immigration and tourism takes on a kinder, gentler, more human sensibility. The main offices are spacious and welcoming. Everybody calls you Sir and wishes you a Good Morning. There are comfortable chairs to sit on, magazines to read, water to sip, and TV to watch, and once you make it past the reception desk, you're led into a casual lounge with couches and even more flat-screen TVs.

The first guy we dealt with at the PRA—one of several guys I spoke with via telephone—was on the tall and chubby side of Filipino men with a meticulously groomed and symmetrically flawless mustache you couldn't help but stare at it. He made light of the formalities, and I indicated my role as an intermediary. I filled out all the paperwork, listing my contact information in the required fields. Felix signed whatever I put in front of him. The letter of intent and banking codes—were dealt with lickety-split. Then it came to the matter of the passport and the affidavit of loss.

"So, we need an affidavit of loss," I said. "Is there an approved notary on-premises?"

"They try to cheat you," Felix interjected.

"Stop, *just don't*," I pleaded with Felix.

The mustache said, "Yes. They're on the sixth floor."

"Of this building?"

The mustache paused a little too long. "Yes." For the record, there are thousands of public notaries scattered across Manila. There are almost as many public notaries as money changers and hookers.

The "approved notary" was an unaffiliated law firm indeed on the sixth-floor *annex* of the building. Getting there required four security checkpoints and three different columns of elevators. The young female lawyer who dealt with us didn't understand what we were asking her to do: write and notarize an affidavit of loss. She took the Captain's current passport along with a template of an affidavit of loss I downloaded from the internet, a copy of the original passport bio page, furnished by the mustache, and disappeared into her office. We plunked down on the plush leather sofa in the lobby.

My ass hadn't even hit the cushion before Felix started in. "They'll do anything to keep your money. They try to cheat you."

I had other things on my mind. "Where do you want to stay tonight?"

"Some place cheap. I don't need much. Maybe I can stay in a sauna house."

"I'm not comfortable with that idea. I'd much prefer it if you were in the same hotel or somewhere close."

"Wah! You're right. For safety. Safety in numbers."

"All right. I know just the place. There's a Holiday Inn around the corner from the Dusit."

"You're meeting that girl again tonight?"

"No, tomorrow night."

"I can disappear. Don't worry about me. I can take care of myself."

"Nonsense. You and I can hang out, have dinner, and do some reconnaissance."

"I like the go-go bars. The one place, the–"

"OK OK."

Half an hour later the lawyer returned with the affidavit. I did a cursory, once-over check of the documents. We paid and made a hasty exit.

Back at the PRA, the mustache eyeballed the affidavit, handed it back to me and said, "OK, now it has to be authenticated by immigration," his motion to hand me the documents insinuating that this would be our responsibility.

"But you said it gets sent to immigration with the other documents."

"I can't begin to process the deposit release until it is authenticated and certified by immigration. Then, yes, I will forward all documents for processing."

"So, you're telling me...it must get notarized and *authenticated* before it can be submitted to be *authenticated* and approved? What's the difference between certified, notarized, and authenticated?"

The mustache guy stared straight ahead. My head dropped and I sighed before standing up, grabbing Felix by the arm and escorting him out of the office. In the elevator, Felix asked, "What did he say?"

"He said the difference between certified, notarized, and authenticated is somewhere around fifteen hundred pesos."

"Where is that place?"

The Office of the Deputy Commissioner is located on the second floor of the Philippines Bureau of Immigration in Intramuros. We were met by a prim official who was convinced she had spoken to me previously on the phone, even though we had not. At any rate, she seemed all set to authenticate the affidavit when the phone rang, which she answered. She chatted amiably away for ten minutes. Eventually, she hung up and said, "I'm sorry. You'll have to come back at one-thirty. It's lunchtime."

An hour and a half later, the woman authenticated the document by simply pressing a green stamp across the bottom, ***IMMIGRATION CERTIFIED***, accepting the 1,500 pesos payment, and sending us on our way. Total time elapsed: 30 seconds.

Back at the PRA, we were steered into a room with a young-looking guy identified as 'the director.' He ignored me but enthusiastically greeted Captain Felix.

"Do you remember me?" the director asked Felix.

Felix said to me, "I've never seen this guy before."

"I remember *you!*" the director beamed. "I'm the one who opened your account. It was my first. You were my first."

I spoke up, "I'm afraid Mr. Wen doesn't have much recollection of..."

"What? What do you mean?" the director looked worried. "Is he not of sound mind?"

"No, he's totally of a sound mind. He just doesn't remember."

The director got up and called the mustache guy to the door. They conferred for a minute. When he returned, the director said, eyeing me suspiciously, "I have concerns about Mr. Zhang's state of mind. I don't know if I can release his deposit unless I know he is doing so of a sound mind and his own free will. For all I know, you could be forcing him to withdraw the money."

"Do you want me to get another affidavit?" I felt my blood begin to boil.

"Who are you?" the director asked. "What is your role here?"

Felix stood up and whelped, "This is—is—robbery! You're trying to cheat me. I just—just—want my money back."

"Sit down," I said, gently touching the Captain's shoulder. I made eye contact with the director and said, "Sir, if I may answer? I work for Mr. Zhang. He's a highly respected international businessman. He simply has a vague recollection of getting this visa and making this transaction over fifteen years ago. In other words, he knows exactly what he's doing. It's just that his English isn't very good, and I'm here to assist."

The director sat back down and looked over our documentation.

"You lost your passport, huh?"

"Yes, he lost it."

"That's not very common, you know, most people don't lose their passports."

I folded my arms across my chest. "Well, he did."

The mustache guy conducted the exit interview, which was given to me, and I repeated the questions to Felix, who was slumped in his chair, bouncing his leg, thoroughly disinterested, and visibly wincing when the mustache spoke.

Q. What's the reason for terminating the visa?

Turning to Felix. "Why do you want to terminate your visa?"

207

"They didn't give me anything. They do everything in their power to keep your money."

"He doesn't plan on retiring in the Philippines, and he wants his money back."

"When can I get the money back?" Felix picked up a magazine and started thumbing through the pages.

Q. Does Mr. Zhang have any intention of applying for another visa within the next five years?

"Hey, put the magazine down. Listen to me. Do you have any intention of applying for a retirement visa within the next five years?"

"..."

Turning back to the mustache, "No, he doesn't."

"They try to cheat you," Felix said. "What does any of this have to do with my money?"

"Be quiet. I'll deal with them."

"They..."

"This is serious. Just a few more questions and we'll pay the fee."

Q. Does Mr. Zhang plan to return to the Philippines when the termination process is complete?

"Yes, most definitely yes. To get the money. You said it has to be done in person."

"That's correct."

We signed the paperwork, paid the fees, the mustache shook my hand, and Felix was already at the elevator. From there we took a taxi back to Makati, stopped at the Holiday Inn, and booked Felix a room for the next two nights. When I left him at 3:30 p.m., he said he was going to get a massage and take a nap. We agreed to meet in the Holiday Inn lobby at 7:00 p.m.

16

Rookie Mistakes

The evening started at Chili's in Greenbelt for dinner, when Felix reiterated that he would enjoy returning to a go-go bar at EDSA Entertainment Complex—specifically, Firehouse. He said something about one of the girls "looked Chinese." Didn't matter. *Finish your cheeseburger, we're on our way.*

We were immediately back in the saddle at Firehouse, buying lady drinks for good attitudes and soft hands. Felix loved the girls rubbing up on him. This is where it gets unnecessarily graphic and seedy, so I'll leave most of it up to your imagination.

After 90 minutes the noise level was getting to Felix, so we left, dropping approximately 4,000 pesos (500 each to the four girls, plus lady drinks, and *mamasan* tip). I wanted to hit Burgos Street, yet another pervert hotspot in primetime.

At 10:15 p.m., Burgos Street was wall-to-wall hookers, touts, and sex tourists. I took him to Rogues, a bar at the corner of Burgos and Makati Avenue, the entrance to hell. Mixed groups of flexing college boys milled around while a few grizzled veteran mongers held court at one section of the bar with their ladies sitting idly by in packs of three. After passing the doorman, we were met by an employee who cleared out a couple of seats at the bar.

What Felix had going against him in terms of age, he made up for with balls and blind passion. Suggest a place to go, something to see, and he was ready, right then and there, no need for luggage, let's go, get on the bus, now. But he wasn't a youngster anymore and I was familiar with his signs of fatigue. When he stopped asking questions, it meant he was getting tired. Therefore, around 11:30 p.m., Felix ran out of gas, and I escorted him back to the Holiday Inn.

At some point in the day, Felix made the acquaintance of a Holiday Inn doorman who recognized us at the entrance and approached on the sidewalk with a wide smile and almost open arms.

"Hello, my friend!" the doorman said to Felix.

"Don't give me that 'my friend' bullshit," I replied, arm extended in polite Heisman Trophy form.

"This guy can send us to the happening place," Felix said.

"Wait one moment," the doorman said.

During their previous encounter, the doorman told Captain Felix that he had a connection at one of the only places to see "the hottest live nude women on stage in Manila," a club in Paranaque called Dynasty. This was complete bullshit. It was technically illegal in the Philippines but there were *plenty* of places to see nude girls in Manila.

A certain brand of tout (aka street hustler) works on the fringes of hotel entrances, preying on foreigners like white on rice. The frontman is a rail-thin but slightly taller than the average Filipino. He's shifty like a lizard but somehow charming like a Gypsy. The sweeper is a brother-in-law who works the opposite side of the street, smiling because he's already sized you up from a block away. They work as a team. They're amped to fuck you as hard as possible because they know that chances are (a) you're not going to be there tomorrow and (b) most foreigners don't have the stones to complain or confront or pursue a crooked tout. Yeah, so, *the frontman* came walking up.

"This is my cousin," the doorman said. "He will take you to Dynasty in Paranaque."

Right here is where I made an amateur error: *I let it happen.* Before we could even get the frontman's name, a taxi came screeching up. The driver got out and greeted us, wearing a uniform and jacket bearing the Dynasty logo.

"I'll take you to Dynasty."

As soon as I saw the taxi driver's jacket, I knew what was going on. *A family operation. That's just great.*

"You *really* want to go to Dynasty, Felix?" I asked.

"I do," he replied.

We piled into the taxi and headed southeast. The frontman was along for the ride, sitting in the front seat.

The driver asked where we were from. I did the talking.

"How far to Paranaque?"

"Ten minutes drive *lang*," the driver replied.

"What's the entrance fee at Dynasty?" I asked.

"Six hundred pesos," the frontman said.

"That's it?"

"Six hundred pesos, one hour. You sit and buy a drink. If you see a girl you like, two hundred pesos for lady drink. Two hundred to keep you company."

I quickly did the math, figuring to write off 2,500 pesos plus another 500 for the frontman and the driver. "How much for the taxi ride to Dynasty?"

"No charge," the frontman said. "Part of the service, my friend."

My confidence in our safety began to waver as we rolled into a shitball neighborhood.

"Are you sure we can trust these guys?" Felix asked.

"No, we can't. But don't worry. I'm calling the shots."

"Stay at home, nothing can happen."

"That's the idea."

✶✷✶

We finally rolled up to Dynasty and the frontman quickly ushered us past the security guards toward a cashier's window just inside the entrance—"like a movie theater cashbox," Felix cheerfully noted. I paid the entry fee of 600 pesos each. We entered a medium-sized, rundown club/dinner theater with a domed ceiling and a large stage taking up a third of the space; the walls lined with doors to private rooms. And a noxious, permeating reek of ammonia. The frontman and the *mamasan* parked us in a row of chairs and tables about halfway back. We sat a few seats apart, the only paying customers—a really bad sign. Immediately, the music kicked up and a couple of nude girls with numbers on wristbands took the stage.

You couldn't call the movements they made dancing or even posing. More like showing. Not at all choreographed but staring straight ahead into nothingness, rubbing a breast, legs shoulder-width apart, and leaning slightly forward, tilting a hip to one side, pirouetting and taking two steps back, sometimes swaying seductively to the music. If they moved at all to the music. The girls in the go-go bars are much more active. This was more of a true cattle call.

The *mamasan* came over and asked for our drink order. The frontman hovered over my shoulder. The drinks came and I signed the chit for 200 pesos. Slowly but surely, the stage began to get crowded with girls, all topless, about half completely nude except for pumps and jewelry. Some looked shy, some looked embarrassed, but most of all, they looked bored and unhappy. I quickly zoomed in on one of the top girls, Number 4: tall and thin with a distinctly Northern Chinese face: high cheekbones, severe epicanthic fold, snow-white complexion, and shoulder-length jet black hair.

Every so often I checked on Felix. He smiled and gave me an OK. The music *had* to be killing him. The stench of ammonia had to be bothering him. It was certainly bothering me. The frontman leaned in over my shoulder. "You see a girl you like? Two hundred pesos."

Number 4 came off stage and joined me. She sat close and gave me a weak kiss on the cheek. "What's your name?" I asked. I don't remember what she said.

"You buy me a lady drink?" As soon as she said it, the waitress appeared, and she ordered a Jack and Coke. I signed a chit for another 400 pesos. Our conversation continued.

"So, (Number 4), what are you doing in a place like this?"

"I'm working. I come to work. This is my job."

"Yes, of course, (Number 4), but... How old are you?"

"I'm twenty-two."

"How long have you been here?"

"Two months." She held up three fingers.

"Are you a student?"

"No, I don't like school."

"You don't like school? What do you like?"

She paused to think. "I like dancing and I like the boom-boom."

"You like sex?"

She nodded and arched her eyebrows. "Everybody likes the boom-boom."

"Do you have a boyfriend?"

"No boyfriend. I don't fuck for love."

How sad is that? You'd have to be a heartless cretin not to feel some sort of pity when you hear that. It's also boner kryptonite.

Felix seemed to be enjoying himself. Number 33 had her hands in his pants while he appeared to be asleep with his head cocked back about 45 degrees, so he didn't hear me calling his name. The waitress came over and presented another chit, this one for the company and lady drink of Number 33, total: 400 pesos, which I signed. I told Number 4 to stay there for a minute and got up to check on Felix, to make sure this girl was giving him a hand job and not taking the money from his pockets.

Fifteen minutes or so passed and I ordered another round for everyone, including Number 12, who had now joined Felix and was massaging the other side of his lap. The waitress returned with a chit for 800 pesos. Again, I signed.

I wanted to get rid of Number 4, who rubbed my thigh absently despite telling her it wasn't necessary. She put my hand on her perfect breast and said, "See? Real." Otherwise, she sat looking straight ahead, sipping her drink. It wasn't until I said, "You can go now," that she showed any sign of emotion or personality. At first, she couldn't believe her ears.

"*What?* You want me to go?"

"Yeah, like, no offense, but, my friend and I have to leave now."

"Where do you stay?"

"That's not important."

"You don't want me?"

"I..." She nuzzled my neck, slopping it with her tongue, while taking my hand and stuffing it between her legs. I shook her off and stood up, calling to Felix. "Come on, let's get out of here."

Felix waved off Numbers 12 and 33 and said, "I'm with you."

The frontman had been hovering at the entrance, saw us getting up, came over and said, "What's the problem?"

"No problem. We want to leave now. One hour. That's enough."

"But the girls."

"What about them?"

"You don't take them?"

"No. Take us back to the hotel. We're done here." He motioned for us to follow him to the cashier's window. There was a short delay while a random waitress compiled the chits. She left the cashbox and disappeared to the area behind the stage. Felix, the frontman, the driver, and I stood at the entrance, waiting for the girl to return with the bill. I had 2,000 pesos in my hand, ready to pay, since according to the chits I signed, the bill was 1,800 pesos. The rest was a tip for the waitress. A few minutes went by.

Felix got impatient. "They're trying to cheat us."

"Don't worry. I'll handle it."

Finally, a short kid in his late teens approached and handed me a bill for 5,400 pesos (US$115). I took it from him, read it out loud, laughed, and handed it back to him. "*No fucking way.* Our bill should be no more than 1,800 pesos." I pointed at the frontman, something that's frowned upon in the Philippines. "*You.* Come over here. Look at this."

The frontman came over, looked at the bill, and backed off. "I don't know."

"Let me see the chits I signed," I said to the kid.

"We don't have it. The girl threw them out."

"Search the fucking garbage then. I'm not paying five grand for this."

The kid again handed me the bill. I handed it back to him.

Felix pressed in and said, "Don't worry, just pay it. They'll kill us."

"*No fucking way.*" I turned to the *mamasan* and said, "Are you in charge or what?" She held up her hands in surrender and ignorance and I said, "I want to see my signature on those chits, or nobody is getting paid."

The kid scampered off with the bill. The frontman drifted in and out of the entrance like he was waiting for something to arrive any minute. Numbers 4, 12, and 33 had also come up to the front of the bar to witness the commotion. Felix repeatedly begged me to pay the bill and leave it be. "We got cheated. Let's go."

The kid returned with a pile of crumpled chits, and I took them to the cashbox window. In each case, all they'd done was multiplied by three and write that figure on top of the original, in a different color pen, to make it more obvious. A chit reading 200 pesos became 600 pesos. The 800-peso chit became 2,400. It was *more* than obvious, which only fueled my indignation.

"I'm not fucking paying for this. I'll give you two thousand. Take it or leave it."

The frontman intervened. "This bill is real, sir. You must pay."

"Fuck off. They obviously altered the bill. I'm not paying."

Felix started digging cash out of his pocket.

"No! Stop!" I grabbed Felix by the wrist. "Don't give these motherfuckers *anything*. OK. That's it. We're leaving." I left the 2,000 pesos on the ledge of the cashier's window and led Felix outside. The security guards stood stoic, eyes crossed. Approximately 30 people were milling around on the street. The sounds of traffic drowned out everything else. The frontman and the driver were hot on our heels.

"*What about us? You owe us!*" the frontman screamed at me. We were right in front of the taxi that brought us there. The frontman posted up on me with his skinny chest expanded—not a good idea. He should have pulled a gun. By nature, I'm non-violent unless severely threatened or provoked. Unchained by a night of drinking, my adrenaline level was critical. I had this cunt by at least 40 pounds, several inches in height, and half a dozen beers in my belly.

I nudged Felix to the side, met the frintman chest-to-chest, and said, "We don't owe you anything." I saw the driver stop, turn around, and retreat into the club. "Now, get the fuck away from me."

The frontman backed off and raised his hand as if to strike my face. For all I knew, he was a boxer in another life and about to knock me the fuck out. Violence was in the air, which I subconsciously feared and yet manifested at the same time. The frontman was light as a cardboard cut-out as I briefly lifted him by the shoulders and half shoved, half tossed him against the taxi. There was a loud "thud" as he slammed into the front quarter panel. He folded over in shock. I turned to Felix and barked, "Keep walking!"

I quickly backed away, fully expecting a beer bottle to come crashing down on my skull, but the driver was nowhere in sight. The frontman was still reeling from the impact and hadn't regained his feet. After a few tentative paces, I darted around the back of the taxi, took Felix by the arm, and froggered him across four lanes of traffic to the other side of the street. The bystanders were gathering but no one seemed anxious to get involved. Fortunately, a taxi pulled up, so we got in and headed back to Makati.

In the taxi, Felix was breathless. "You're crazy, man!" He laughed and coughed.

"I'm not crazy. I'm just not going to get fucked around by these people."

"I told them you were my bodyguard. That you are a killer! You kill people!"

"You didn't."

"They said you look like an assassin. They said you're a killer!"

"Who said that?"

"All of them!"

"The doorman? The *mamasan?* The taxi driver?"

He smiled, shook his head and said, "I don't know."

Back at the Holiday Inn, the doorman was nowhere to be found. I took Felix up to his room and said, "If you see that doorman, tell him I'll be back."

"I think he ran away! Quit his job!"

"Mmm, I don't know about that. At any rate, get some rest. It's almost four o'clock."

"OK, I'll see you tomorrow. I'll call you."

I started walking back toward the Dusit Thani. *Felix,* I thought, *you're something else, man. Something else.*

17

The Elusive Ms. Wen

I was dead to the world when the phone next to the bed started ringing around 9:53 a.m. At the sixth or seventh ring, I picked up, expecting to hear Felix announce plans for lunch or massage. But it was the mustache guy from the Philippine Retirement Authority, Mr. Pinatabo.

"When Mr. Zhang applied for the resident visa," Mr. Pinatabo explained, "he also applied for and was granted a visa for his wife. Ms. Barbara Wen. Therefore, he was required to deposit twice the amount required by law to secure a retirement visa. Even though Ms. Wen neither signed nor witnessed Mr. Zhang's bank deposit, she is listed as the beneficiary of the account should anything untoward happen to Mr. Zhang, and in fact, her retirement visa was inextricably tied to the deposit amount made by Mr. Zhang. So, in other words, we can't process the deposit clearance until we go through the exact same process, minus the exit interview and personal appearances, for Ms. Wen."

Oh, and suck it.

Aside from my two-minute freak-out, which included phrases such as 'outright deception' and 'failure to disclose,' the conversation went as poorly as the universe would allow. Of course, I felt like my head was going to explode.

Felix took it in stride. "No problem."

"You didn't mention anything about your wife!"

"They didn't mention anything about my wife!"

I knew Felix was still married to Barbara. Everybody knew. Barbara was the puppeteer behind the financial success of the Zhang Yi empire. Felix had godlike amounts of money only because Barbara knew what she was doing with the numbers and books. Felix adopted Barbara's daughter from a previous marriage. They separated after 20 years of marriage, but never divorced. Another 10 years later, they were still haggling over the terms of the divorce. We only heard whispers around KPHQ about the elusive Ms. Wen.

"What do you want to do now?" I asked. "Contact your wife?"

"No! It's not possible."

"Is she fucking dead? Is she physically or mentally incapacitated?"

"Forget about it. We're not calling her."

"OK, well, we've got two days to kill."

"Let's go to that place?"

"Laoag?"

"Yes!"

"Too far. Let's go somewhere closer."

"How about Puerto Galera?"

The trip to Puerto Galera, in comparison, was uneventful. It took half a day to get there. We stayed at Steps and Garden, a five-minute walk from the port at Sabang. We had dinner and prowled around the bars in central Sabang. Felix managed to score a couple of girls for his in-room massage. I drank alone at a random scuba-themed bar and went back to the room to call Janet. We stayed on the phone until 2:30 a.m.

In the morning, Felix and I took the ferry boat back to Batangas and hired a driver for the trip back to Makati. We stayed at the City State Hotel in Malate and had dinner with Janet and her friend Desi. Unlike the situation with Fang, I kept the Captain in the loop with Janet.

The next day, Felix decided to cut his stay short and rebooked the 9:00 a.m. flight back to Taipei. To get in the front door of Terminal 3 at MNL, you gotta present your passport and e-ticket. I presented my itinerary dated for later in the week, which the security guard didn't notice. Therefore, I was able to handle Felix's check-in and got his boarding pass before leaving him at the security checkpoint.

"See you next week," I said.

"That was fun."

"It was interesting."

He reached for my hand and pressed what felt like money in my palm. "Here, this is for you. OK. Good luck with your girlfriend. Maybe you will marry her. Maybe she is the one."

"Maybe you should just leave now and get on the fucking plane before you miss it."

I waited until I was in a taxi and headed back to the Dusit Thani to open my hand and see what or how much Felix had given me. It was enough to make my heart skip a beat.

* ✱ *

This world is hostile to justice. Most of our crimes go undetected and/or unpunished. Without the philosophy of good and bad, right and wrong—it's probably safe to say these civic "blind spots" are in the greater interest of humanity.

Karma is the greatest leveler of all playing fields, but karma is moody, unreliable, and tends to play favorites. Therefore, it's difficult to say anyone ever gets what they deserve. You get what you get.

* ✱ *

Back at Knowledge Press HQ, life returned to a brand of quasi-normal. The old Sherry scandal lingered and festered, but everyone had their fill. Meanwhile, Felix became evasive whenever I asked about his wife. Regarding the money, he said, "I'll get it some other time." Despite feeling guilty and inept for his part in bungling the Philippines affair so far, Felix blamed the system of bureaucracy. Of course, I owned a share of the blame, but it wasn't *my* money. I wanted to get it back for him, but I couldn't do anything unless we got in touch with his wife.

Another two weeks passed before Felix called on the office landline. I hadn't seen him for a week.

"Charlie, your phone is off. Something is wrong. I've been trying to reach you."

"I'm looking at it right now, Felix. The phone's working fine."

"Oh, maybe I have the wrong number."

"I'll call you right now, so you have it again."

"Don't worry about that now. Did you get the paperwork straightened out with my money in the Philippines?"

"No...we need an affidavit of loss from your wife." I was irritated whenever he approached me with this line of questioning. He knew full-fucking-well that the Philippines bank deal was stalled until we got a hold of his wife. *Did he think that affidavit was just going to drop out of the sky? Did he think I was just going to call his wife on my own?*

We were talking about this mythical creature, Barbara Wen, his estranged wife, who dragged him into court once a month to review his financial statements so she could get her chunk of it. But as far as I could tell, there wasn't a trace of this woman's existence in Felix's life, certainly not in the office or the company dorm, other than the fact that both properties were in *the wife's name.* This was a woman described by Felix as "a greedy thief" who "cleaned me out and tried to ruin my business." Common sense told me otherwise. She had no intention of killing her Golden Goose. She just wanted to make sure Felix was producing eggs, those eggs were accounted for, and she got her share.

"Right, right," Felix trailed off. "My wife..."

"Felix, listen. Why haven't you divorced her yet?"

"She won't sign the papers. She won't sign the papers until she's cleaned me out."

"Ugh."

"I want you to call her," he said sternly. "Schedule an appointment at the lawyer's office."

"*Call your wife?*"

"That guy can help you."

"*What guy? What lawyer? Are you kidding?*"

"No problem. OK? It's a tough job. You can do it. Talk to you later."

"Yeah, right," I said about two seconds after he hung up. "I'm not calling *anybody*."

Five minutes later, Lloyd staggered into the control center and said Felix told him to help me call Barbara Wen. *Great. What does that mean? Help me how?* He laughed and wobbled out of the room, returning to the marketing department. "I need the wife's name and number!" I called after him. *This is going to be a disaster.*

About half an hour later, Mr. Chu came charging into the office, slamming doors, and talking about "fucking foreigner this" and "fuck that." He disappeared into the marketing department, where I could hear him screaming at Lloyd. *Another body is now regrettably involved in this whole affair.* Ten minutes later, Mr. Chu came into my office looking humble and horrified, "Come with me. I will call Ms. Wen." [Mr. Chu was Barbara's nephew, her sister's oldest son.]

We decamped to the empty accounting office and stood in front of a desk, both staring down at the phone. Mr. Chu mumbled something and produced a number written on the corner of a supermarket sales flyer. Thirty seconds passed without a word. He sighed several times.

"Well, fucking *call the bitch*," I said in plain English. "You think I'm gonna do it?"

When Barbara answered, Mr. Chu immediately apologized for disturbing her and wanted to make it ***crystal motherfucking clear*** that he had ***no idea why*** Felix told him to get involved or to contact her, but again, sorry, **here's the foreigner**—and he thrust the phone at my face.

I began to speak in Chinese, "*Ni hao, Wen nushi. Wo jiao Cha*–" (Yes, um, hello boss's wife. My name is Ch—)

"Where's my husband?" she replied in impeccable English. "Put my husband on the phone."

"He's not here, ma'am."

"Who are you? What do you want?"

"My name is Charlie. I work for Felix. I'm an editor. And I'm calling because I'd like to make an appointment with you to sign an affidavit of loss, about the retirement visa you acquired in the Philippines."

There was a moment of dead silence, then, "Tell my husband to contact my lawyer." Click.

I stood with the earpiece held to the side of my head for a good 10-15 seconds. Finally, I made eye contact with Mr. Chu.

He asked, "*Ta shuo shenme liao?*" (What did she say?)

"*Ta shuo de dianhua lushi.*" (She said to call her lawyer.)

A sheet of horror passed Chu's face. I walked out and went back to my desk.

Another five minutes later, Felix called on the office landline.

"Charlie, did you speak with my wife?"

"Hello...Felix. Kind of. She said you should call her lawyer."

Felix laughed. "OK, no problem. All she wants is money."

"Do you want me to call the lawyer? Gimme the details. I'll call him."

"She's greedy. She will want half of the money."

"There's no other way around it."

"*Mei guanxi.* It doesn't matter."

It mattered enough that a week later, I found myself sitting in a back-office conference room of the Manila Commerce and Economic Office in Taipei (MECO) with Felix, his lawyer, Felix's wife (Barbara Wen), her lawyer, two consulate representatives, and one consulate attorney, trying to hammer out a deal. Both consulate reps were dumbfounded as I explained the situation.

"So, the retirement visa is long gone. We are not concerned with the visa itself. As you are aware, to get that retirement visa, you must open a Philippine bank account with a sizable deposit to secure the visa. For whatever reason, Mr. Zhang here, has decided not to retire in the Philippines and wants his deposit back. But the bank won't release the deposit unless he presents the original passports of both himself and his wife, Ms. Wen, in which the visas were acquired and issued, and/or the resident ID cards they were issued at the time of approval. Neither of these documents can be located. We need an affidavit of loss that can *only be notarized here*, at the consulate, by you, before Mr. Zhang can access his money."

"They didn't give us anything!" Felix cried. "Just a stamp in the passport!"

"You didn't receive a resident ID card when applying for the visa?" the consulate lawyer asked.

"Nothing!" Felix cried.

"You mean these?" the wife said, producing her expired passport and a Philippine resident ID card from her purse. "I have his old passport and ID card, too."

I shot a wicked look across the table to Felix. **You fucking cunt.** He bounced slightly and stared at the wife's lawyer's breasts.

"That's what I don't understand," said the consulate lawyer said. "Why do we need an affidavit of loss if Ms. Wen has these items?"

Her lawyer piped in, "Because she isn't willing to turn them over."

"Not exactly," I said. "When Mr. Zhang and I submitted the original paperwork to recover the money, the subject of Ms. Wen was never brought up. Neither by the PRA, nor Mr. Zhang. It's his money. Ms. Wen didn't sign any paperwork on the bank deposit. However, since they applied for the visa jointly, Mr. Zhang paid the deposit twice, once for himself and once for Ms. Wen, making her the beneficiary, and I think you can see where I'm going with this. It's *his* money. Mr. Zhang's official request to get his money back states that he lost all pertinent documents. Ms. Wen, here, doesn't want to give up her passport because—"

"You can have the ID cards," said the wife's lawyer. "But she won't surrender her passport," turning to me, "for how long?"

I said, "It could take anywhere up to three months before her *expired passport* is actually returned to her."

"Yeah, that's not going to happen," deadpanned the wife's lawyer.

"*The passport is expired!*" Felix cried. He was right. There was no reason for Ms. Wen to hold that passport hostage.

"The point is," I broke in. "We, meaning Mr. Zhang and I, have already submitted legal documents indicating that these documents cannot be located." I let the statement linger, drumming my fingertips on the tabletop. "As far as we are concerned, the documents remain missing."

"Then you should withdraw the petition," one of the consulate suits said, "and start over."

"*It doesn't work like that.*" I slowly tilted my head to the left. "It's too late. They accepted Mr. Zhang's paperwork, they reviewed his signature card, *and then* they came up with this story about having to recover Ms. Wen's passport. We've paid fees on top of fees to make this happen.

223

They're already set to make the wire transfer. As soon as they see an affidavit of loss from Ms. *Wen*, they send it to immigration, they give it a rubber stamp, and it's a done deal."

"So," the consulate lawyer said, "you want me to draft an affidavit of loss for Ms. Wen's passport and ID card, even though she has them in her possession?"

"What passport? What ID card?" Ms. Wen said, stuffing the items back into her purse.

Felix scowled. "She doesn't have anything! She just wants money!"

"Look," I said earnestly to the consulate lawyer, leaning in, gently reaching across to touch his arm. "*I'm* the one who did all the paperwork for this deal. It's *my* fault. If I had known Ms. Wen was involved, I would have done things a lot differently. *A lot differently.* But here we are. Ms. Wen is willing to sign an affidavit saying she cannot locate her expired passport or Philippine ID card, and I need you to notarize it. That's all we're asking you to do."

Both consulate suits got up and left the conference room. I watched them stand face-to-face in the atrium and discuss the situation. Felix leaned back and pretended to read a newspaper while the wife's lawyer, a plain-faced woman in her 40s, who I originally mistook to be a family member of some sort, leaned over to me and asked where I was from.

The Captain's lawyer, a well-dressed but tiny Taiwanese guy with a nasty combover who hadn't said a word thus far, was now trying to make conversation with Barbara Wen, who, despite being tightly composed, didn't look like a money-grubbing monster. She seemed like a nice person. I took a long look at the mysterious Ms. Wen, pleasantly surprised, half expecting her to be a vixen-type, gold-digging, mainland *tai-tai*. But she was a generically austere Taiwanese woman in her mid-60s, casually dressed and modest in demeanor, with no ostentatious displays of wealth. A couple of times I caught her glaring across the table at Felix, and I imagined her thoughts, "You stupid, pathetic piece of shit. Why did I marry you?"

The consulate lawyer sat there staring at me with that ugly piebald face. Finally, the taller of the consulate suits came in and summoned the consulate lawyer. When the lawyer returned, he spoke directly to me.

"Are you a lawyer?"

"No. Haha." It was funny.

"Do you have Power of Attorney from Mr. Zhang?"

"No."

"Will Mr. Zhang personally visit the bank to make the wire transfer?"

"Yes."

He turned to Felix's lawyer, and said, "*Nin de kehu liaojie zhengzai fasheng de shiqing?*" (You and your client understand what is going on here?)

"Yes," the lawyer replied. "The foreigner is our representative."

"OK," the consulate lawyer said to me. "I'll need to see the affidavit of loss Mr. Wen submitted to the bank."

I produced a copy of the affidavit.

Felix couldn't restrain himself. "How much is this going to cost?"

A week later, I flew to Manila and delivered the secondary, Ms. Wen's affidavit of loss to the mustache at the PRA in Makati. He was—how you say? *Not entirely pleased to see me.* After grilling him over redundant details and protocol, I put the affidavit on his desk and slid it toward him with both hands. "Look, Mr. Pinatabo, I appreciate everything you've done for me—*for Mr. Zhang.* But I want you to do me a favor."

He froze. "A personal favor? I am not in a position to—"

"To grant personal favors, I know," clearing my throat. "Please check the envelope to make sure everything is...in...there."

The mustache examined the documents and said everything seemed to be in place. Ms. Wen's affidavit looked good-to go.

A week after *that*, I was back at KPHQ, sitting in the office, minding my own business when my cell phone rang. I immediately recognized the Philippine country code.

"Sir Charlie, yes, it's Mr. Pinatabo from the Philippine Retirement Authority."

"..."

"As I was processing Mr. Zhang's paperwork, I noticed an error in *his* affidavit of loss which would surely draw the attention of immigration."

"OK, Mr. Pinatabo. Please, continue."

"It seems that the passport number stated, listed, included on *his* affidavit of loss, does not correspond to his original passport."

" . . ."

"Yes, in fact, the passport which Mr. Zhang claims to have lost, according to this affidavit, is his current passport."

I didn't respond because I was frantically rifling through my files for a copy of that affidavit. I found it, did a quick eyeball scan, and noticed M983625 as the current passport number, and *the passport indicated by the affidavit as being lost.*

"Sir," the mustache said. "Mr. Zhang's original passport number is H873487, which is not included in the affidavit."

I couldn't fucking believe it! **The mustache was right.** The affidavit clearly stated that Mr. Zhang had lost his current passport M983625, not the original H873487. I was about to go interstellar on the mustache when I took a deep breath and said, "Thank you for pointing that out." I replayed the scene with the young lawyer on the sixth-floor annex of Citibank Tower. The affidavit template listed the original lost passport number, but I handed her his current passport. Either way, it was a costly fuck-up. Meanwhile, the mustache rambled on, and I discovered another potentially damaging error on the affidavit: the passport expiration date was wrong, too. I later told Janet that I felt like I had shot myself in both feet and then set the house on fire.

"Sir, what do you want to do next?" asked the mustache.

"Do?" *I want to fucking choke the life out of you and your children.*

"You can either have our law offices amend the affidavit or you can..."

"Stop."

"Sir?"

"What does this mean? Is his refund denied?"

"No, sir. I haven't sent it to immigration yet for final approval."

"So, we need an accurate affidavit?"

"Yes, of course."

"I'll be in touch."

Later that evening Felix came in the office and did his usual feet-up on the desk routine while the robots scurried around to meet his needs. As he was getting ready to leave, I said, "We have a problem."

"What problem? I can help you. Whatever you need. I am your family now."

"It's not my problem *per se*. It's your money in the Philippines."

"They cheat you. They…"

"Remember that lawyer in Manila who drew up your affidavit of loss? She bungled it."

"Bungle?"

"Fucked it up. It wasn't *entirely* her fault."

He smiled broadly. "No problem. I understand. We can talk about it tomorrow."

"*No!*" The sharp tone surprised both of us. "We will *not* talk about it tomorrow. This needs to be taken care of *immediately!*"

"What can I do? How can I help you? I'm here to help."

"You can meet me tomorrow morning at ten o'clock sharp in front of MECO (the Philippine consulate) with your current passport."

"Again?" he scoffed. "Too much trouble."

"Fuck that. *Be there.*"

The next morning, Felix was discombobulated and irritable, which I tempered by being short and sweet.

"Passport?" I said curtly. "This will take ten minutes. Fifteen if the lawyer has other clients."

"They will do anything to keep your money."

It was more like an hour, but I finally managed to get the consulate lawyer to notarize a second affidavit of loss. The lawyer put up a good fight, though. Once he signed and sealed the document, I sent Felix on his way.

18

Finishing the Job

Two weeks later, back in Makati again—my third trip since October—I hand-delivered the new affidavit—pre-certified by the Bureau of Immigration—to the mustache (Mr. Pinatabo) at the Philippine Retirement Authority. He promised to call when the clearance came from immigration, roughly ten business days or two weeks from that moment.

After spending a few days with Janet, I returned to Taipei and KPHQ. Everything was back to business. Felix and Daisy were still squabbling over the Sherry scandal, but nobody cared about it anymore.

Janet and I spent at least three hours per night on Skype. During the last of the three previous visits, we got "engaged" for lack of a better term. Saying goodbye to each other was brutal every time I left. She didn't trust what I was doing in Taiwan, so I asked her one day, "Would you feel better about things if we were married?" She said yes.

It was almost Christmas, and I still hadn't heard from the mustache or anyone at the PRA. I called a few times and got put on infinite hold. I sent several mild-mannered but inquiring emails.

I left Taipei on Christmas Eve to spend the holidays with Janet in Metro Manila. We had plans to celebrate New Year's Eve at a resort in Zambales. I couldn't have been more excited about it. On December 28, I had nothing better to do, so I paid a visit to Mr. Pinatabo at the PRA. When he saw me turn the corner, he let out a girlish whelp, and I swear to God, he looked like he wanted to dive under the nearest desk.

"Yes, yes, of course, immigration has authorized the documents," he said. "We are just waiting on the director's approval and signature."

"Bring me the director."

"He's not here. The director is not here."

"When will he be back?"

"Tomorrow."

The next day, I returned to the PRA and asked for the director. The receptionist told me to wait: the director was in a meeting. I waited patiently for 20 minutes, and after pacing the aisle for another 20 minutes, I caught sight of the director entering a conference room off the lobby. Looked like he was getting ready to treat himself to a pastry. I walked past the front desk—the receptionist was busy texting on her cell phone and didn't notice—and stood at the threshold of the conference room door.

"Hey, chief, 'member me?"

The director was startled but maintained his grin on the coy side of smug. "You're the friend of the Taiwanese guy who wants his money back."

"That's right! You really *do* have a good memory."

The director leaned back in his chair. "How can I help you?"

I took a few steps into the office and put my hands on the backrest of the nearest chair. "You could help me by signing Mr. Zhang's deposit clearance."

"Give me ten minutes," the director said and left the room. He returned with the mustache and the deposit release was signed right then and there.

"Nice," I said. "Good work, wise decision."

Later that night I called Felix and told him the news: His money was free and clear. All he needed to do was come to the Philippines and make the withdrawal in person. He was happy and said all the usual stuff about getting the job done and monkeys on his back.

"Do you have any idea when you want to come back and get the money?" I asked.

"Let's talk about it when you return to Taipei."

He wished me a Merry Christmas and a Happy New Year. *Likewise, Felix. Give my regards to Daisy.*

229

About the Author

Christian Adams, author of *The Lazy Bastard Guide to Mandarin* and *Year of the Rat*, lives in the Philippines with his family. He is also an independent musician and the sole proprietor of Black Sunshine Media.